Historical Problems:
Studies and Documents

Edited by
PROFESSOR G. R. ELTON
University of Cambridge

2
GERMANY IN THE
AGE OF BISMARCK

In the same series

1. ANTI-CATHOLICISM IN VICTORIAN ENGLAND
by E. R. Norman

3. PROBLEMS OF EMPIRE: BRITAIN AND INDIA, 1757–1813
by P. J. Marshall

by the same author

GERMANY: A BRIEF HISTORY
    (*Batsford*)

THE FAILURE OF THE PRUSSIAN REFORM MOVEMENT, 1807–1819

EUROPEAN POSITIVISM IN THE NINETEENTH CENTURY
    (*Cornell and Oxford*)

GERMANY
IN THE
AGE OF BISMARCK

W. M. Simon

University of Keele
Professor and Head of the Department of History

LONDON: GEORGE ALLEN AND UNWIN LTD
NEW YORK: BARNES AND NOBLE INC

FIRST PUBLISHED IN 1968

PRINTED IN GREAT BRITAIN
in 10 on 11 point Plantin type
BY WILLMER BROTHERS LIMITED
BIRKENHEAD

GENERAL INTRODUCTION

The reader and the teacher of history might be forgiven for thinking that there are now too many series of historical documents in existence, all claiming to offer light on particular problems and all able to fulfil their claims. At any rate, the general editor of yet another series feels obliged to explain why he is helping one more collection of such volumes into existence.

One purpose of this series is to put at the disposal of the student original materials illustrating historical problems, but this is no longer anything out of the way. A little less usual is the decision to admit every sort of historical question: there are no barriers of time or place or theme. However, what really distinguishes this enterprise is the fact that it combines generous collections of documents with introductory essays long enough to explore the theme widely and deeply. In the doctrine of educationalists, it is the original documents that should be given to the student; in the experience of teachers, documents thrown naked before the untrained mind turn from pearls to paste. The study of history cannot be confined either to the learning up of results without a consideration of the foundations, or to a review of those foundations without the assistance of the expert mind. The task of teaching involves explanation and instruction, and these volumes recognize this possibly unfashionable fact. Beyond that, they enable the writers to say new and important things about their subject matter: to write history of an exploratory kind, which is the only important historical writing there is.

As a result, each volume will be a historical monograph worth the attention which all such monographs deserve, and each volume will stand on its own. While the format of the series is uniform, the contents will vary according to need. Some problems require the reconsideration which makes the known enlighteningly new; others need the attention of original research; yet others will have to enter controversy because the prevailing notions on many historical questions are demonstrably wrong. The authors of this series are free to treat their subject in whatever manner it seems to them to require. They will present some of their evidence for inspection and help the learner to see how history is written, but they will themselves also write history.

G.R.E.

PREFACE

The documents in the second half of this book have been selected
to provide students and other readers with some of the primary
materials on which professional historians base their judgments.
The editor's own account in Part I should not deter the reader from
forming his own assessment of the many problems presented by
Bismarck's Germany.

Cross-references to the numbered documents are inserted at the
appropriate places in Part I, in the form of numbers in parentheses
to distinguish them from footnote numbers in superscript. The
sources from which the selections are taken are identified in a note
to each document. Where these are in German the selected passages
have been translated by the editor.

University of Keele   W.M.S.
November 1967

CONTENTS

PART 1: THE AGE OF BISMARCK

I

Introductory:
Prussia and Germany in 1862

OTTO VON BISMARCK, who became Prime Minister of Prussia in September 1862, had been born in 1815, the year in which Europe at the Congress of Vienna settled its affairs as best it could after the storms and turmoil aroused by the French Revolution and the régime and military campaigns of Napoleon I. To understand the nature and the problems of Prussia and Germany when Bismarck assumed control —for that matter to understand Bismarck himself—some attention must unavoidably be paid, first of all, to the years between his birth and his elevation to power.[1]

A considerable number of German problems did not, in fact, confront the Congress of Vienna save that it ratified or tacitly accepted situations and solutions already existing, found, or imposed. Napoleon had finally given the *coup de grâce* to the long tottering Holy Roman Empire, whose endemic weakness since the Middle Ages had contributed so much to the historic disunity of Germany. By nearly common consent the Empire and its institutions were not restored, though the Congress of Vienna was faced with the problem of replacing it. Napoleon had also decreed the abolition of all the ecclesiastical states of Germany and of most of the small secular territories too, and their absorption into the larger kingdoms and duchies; again, the disappearance of this legacy of German disunity was regretted by few except the deposed rulers, and the vanished sovereignties were not restored. Still, over thirty states remained; but of these, two had in the course of the eighteenth century emerged as definitely superior in power and influence to the rest, Austria and Prussia. This was a position that inevitably implied some degree of rivalry, latent or overt,

[1] I cannot avoid referring here to my *Germany: a Brief History,* New York, 1966, London, 1967, which is inevitably reflected in this background sketch. The main body of the present essay, on the other hand, is not only considerably more detailed than the pages there devoted to the age of Bismarck but also completely rewritten and brought up to date.

for leadership in Germany, and in 1815 the Austrian statesman Count Metternich, in whose capital the Congress of Vienna met, had just stolen a march on Prussia by winning the friendship of the states of south Germany, particularly Bavaria.

In these south German states, the beneficiaries of Napoleon's reorganization, and in some other states as well, the preceding decade had seen a good deal of domestic reform in the direction of 'enlightened absolutism' and Napoleonic centralized government. In Prussia also there had been a movement in this direction, but it had proved so far largely abortive in the areas of politics and administration, and Prussia remained in practice an absolute state, in which the monarchy ruled by means of a strong and interlocking army and civil service, and with the support of a very large element of the petty nobility (*Junker*). These were in reality nothing more than (often impoverished) squires or country gentry, and their prominence reflected the overwhelmingly agrarian nature of the Prussian economy.

The unsuccessful reform movement in Prussia, as well as the successful ones elsewhere, bore witness to a new intellectual ferment stimulated in Germany by the French Revolution and by Napoleon's conquests. Where even intellectuals had in the eighteenth century mostly acquiesced in, if not indeed supported, the social and political *status quo*, there was now, within the still small middle class and among the higher civil servants, widespread dissatisfaction with the traditional, semi-absolutist, semi-feudal pattern of public life in Germany. This dissatisfaction, usually based on an awareness of the various alternatives recently evolved in France, could be associated either (especially in Napoleon's client states in south Germany) with pro-French sentiments or (especially in Prussia) with violent anti-French nationalism. The latter combination was particularly antipathetic to Metternich, who was indeed opposed to nationalism in any form because the Austrian Empire was a multi-national state which, as Metternich saw it, was in danger of disintegrating if nationalist agitation were allowed. Since in Austria's great rival, Prussia, nationalism seemed to be allied with reform, Metternich concluded that Austria could not afford to have reform agitation either. Above all, he was concerned that Prussia must not be allowed to place herself at the head of any movement toward political integration or unification in Germany, since that would attract the loyalty of German-speaking elements in Austria away from the Habsburg dynasty and from the historic Danubian state.

Since Metternich had succeeded in allying himself with the south German states, who also feared Prussian domination of Germany, and since the non-German states represented at Vienna also disliked the idea of an effectively united Germany, there could be only one answer to the question of what to put in the place of the defunct Holy Roman Empire: another loose organization. This was the nature of the German Confederation (*Bund*) that emerged from the Congress largely to Metternich's specifications. But from almost any point of view it was a distinct improvement on the old Empire, and it forms, indeed, part of the evidence that, whatever his limitations, Metternich was by far the most intelligent and even the most imaginative German statesman of his day. Any attempt at imposing on Germany a degree of structural unity much tighter than that of the *Bund* would have brought the rivalry between Austria and Prussia to a head instead of allowing them to co-exist, in Metternich's phrase, in 'peaceful dualism'.

This is not to say that all was sweetness and light in Germany after 1815. Metternich was reviled by all those who, under the stimulus of a rapidly growing nationalism, longed for German political unity, and also in many reforming and progressive circles, particularly in Prussia. In the larger states of south Germany—Bavaria, Württemberg, Baden—the energies of both conservatives and liberals (this word was just coming into use) tended to be concentrated on affairs within their borders. Within four years of the end of the war, all these states had been furnished with new constitutions, issued from above by the grace of the prince. In this respect as well as in their contents, these constitutions resembled the famous Charter granted in 1814 by Louis XVIII: as in France, monarchy voluntarily limited itself by creating representative assemblies elected on a narrowly restricted franchise and equipped with circumscribed powers. Sovereignty remained with the monarch, and the ministers remained responsible to him. This was not parliamentary government, but at least there were parliaments in which deputies could freely talk politics, which had been the original purpose even of the English parliament—admittedly a long time ago. Here the South German liberals could, if they wished, urge policies on the government and press for greater powers for themselves. Here the ministers could expound their own and their sovereign's intentions and actions. Almost all could agree, at least, to reject Metternich's view that elected assemblies were ruled out by the terms of the Act setting up the Confederation. Metternich would have preferred a return to the more traditional type of assembly on feudal lines. Not even these appeared in the states of northwest Germany. Liberated from Napoleonic rule, their populations were immediately subjected to the full weight of *ancien-régime* absolutism at its worst.

In Prussia, as we saw, absolutism had suffered only slight inroads at the hands of the reform movement. Encouraged by a promise of a constitution extracted from the king in 1815, the reformers renewed their efforts, but within four years it was clear that they had failed again to effect any significant changes. The reasons for their failure were many and complex; the result is easier to assess. Just at the time when constitutionalism was advancing in south Germany, Prussia reverted to unreconstructed bureaucratic and militaristic absolutism. The institutions and the political and social climate of Prussia for the next hundred years were determined in 1819. The failure of the reform movement disappointed all those liberals, not only in Prussia but throughout Germany, who were looking to a politically rejuvenated Prussia to provide leadership in Germany.

To Metternich, on the other hand, the fall of the reformers was welcome; indeed he had connived at it. He had far more to fear, on all counts, from a liberal Prussia than from a liberal Baden. Needless to say, the Habsburg Empire itself experienced no resurgence of a reform movement after 1815. The career of Joseph II operated as a permanent cautionary tale against attempts to centralize, let alone to Germanize, the machinery of government. Indeed, among the changes which Metternich vainly urged on his emperor was a measure of administrative decentralization to the provinces. If Metternich here again demonstrated his perspicacity by seeing that such a move might assuage some of the nationalist discontent, it remains true, on the other hand, that his political acumen, though more sensitive than anyone else's, was in the long run not quite far-sighted enough. His anticipation that liberalism would involve nationalism, with the corollary that therefore liberalism must be suppressed, was an unfortunate brand of self-fulfilling prophecy. It caused liberals to react strongly against Metternich and all his works, including the *Bund*, and to adopt the cause of a unitary and constitutional national state. It therefore tended to call to life the very alliance between liberalism and nationalism that Metternich above all feared.

The danger, however, did not immediately seem very great, since the liberal movement spent most of the 1820s licking its wounds and concentrating on the development and consolidation of territorial constitutionalism. But after 1830 and the revolutions in France and Belgium the German liberals took new heart, and the movement increased both in size and in activity. Here a caution is in order, for the word 'liberal', then as now, covered a multitude of sins or virtues, depending on the point of view. What liberals had in common was, roughly speaking, an interest in limiting the powers of the executive by means of representative assemblies with a view, in part, to protecting the freedom of the individual against arbitrary interference. Within this general framework there was room for much variety. Liberalism could take its stand, as for the most part it did in south Germany and in the Prussian Rhineland province (which had been a part of France for twenty years), on the Enlightenment, Natural Law, the doctrine of human rationality, and French models; or (more usually in north and east Germany) it could adopt the more historically conditioned perspective of J. G. Herder, or even of Edmund Burke, and prefer the English precedent. Liberalism could be cautious and conservative, or it could be radical and even republican. In Germany it was weighted heavily toward the former. Neither Montesquieu's doctrine of the separation of powers nor Rousseau's doctrine of popular sovereignty made much headway. German liberals were respectful toward princes and not very active even on behalf of the introduction of responsible government. They aimed not so much to participate in government as to restrict the scope of government.

It is, nevertheless, true to say that after 1830 and especially after 1840 liberalism gradually developed more momentum. This was particularly evident in the revival of interest in German unity, in what was coming to be called the 'German question'. For the first time the idea was mooted that Austro-Prussian rivalry might be overcome and unity achieved by excluding Austria altogether and giving Prussia the unchallenged leadership of Germany. But this notion remained academic in both senses: it was discussed at all mainly by small groups of intellectuals; and its realization was in any event still dependent on Prussia first making herself over into a constitutional state. Of this there was little enough sign, despite the hopes centred on Frederick William IV on his accession in 1840. What did take place especially after 1840 and especially in the Rhineland, was a significant economic resurgence after the depression of the early post-war years. This development was due to such factors as the lifting of legal restrictions on the sale of land which had been one of the few positive achievements of the reform movement in Prussia, the building of the first railways, and above all the customs union (*Zollverein*) which, on Prussian initiative, removed many obstacles to trade within Germany. This economic revival, while changing agricultural life too, had its most important social and political effects in the numerically small commercial and industrial sectors. For the first time in Germany the middle class, formerly made up almost entirely of professional men, contained a considerable proportion of businessmen. The conviction held by many of them that the bourgeoisie ought to have political rights commensurate with their economic status was, indeed, a principal source of strength for the growing liberal movement.

The *Zollverein* was probably as important in its psychological effects as in its immediate economic ones, if not more so. It broke down not only traditional barriers against commercial activity but also many traditional habits of thought on many subjects. Rapid

B

change began to seem to many people a natural rather than an un-natural state of affairs. Novelty revealed its attractions to weigh against its dangers. The year 1840 is therefore often taken as a land-mark in the cultural as well as in the political and social history of Germany. Of course, dates in this field can only be convenient sym-bols, indicating no more than general tendencies. Thus the great philosopher G. W. F. Hegel, who had dominated not merely the universities but intellectual life in Germany generally until his death in 1831, remained the towering influence on German thought even after 1840 and into the age of Bismarck, where we shall concern our-selves with him again. The principal challenges to Hegel had come from historians (especially the young Leopold Ranke) and theologians (above all Friedrich Schleiermacher). These were two of the liveliest disciplines at German universities. History was enjoying a consider-able boom, encouraged by the Romantic movement; theological and ecclesiastical issues had by no means lost their interest or importance. The natural sciences, however, were also coming into prominence again, supported by as well as supporting the new industry and tech-nology.

Unfortunately, novelty and change usually leave some groups in society behind, often through no fault of their own. This was the situation in Germany in the 1840s of the artisans and other inde-pendent workers who on the one hand were affected by the decline of the traditional guild system (hastened in many states by government intervention) and on the other hand were not part of the new in-dustrial system. Since such men still outnumbered factory workers by perhaps two to one, their feeling of discontent and insecurity was by no means negligible. But the entire urban population of Germany in 1848 was in turn still outnumbered in about the same ratio by the country dwellers; and among certain groups of peasants, though mainly among the relatively more prosperous ones, there were also some rumblings of dissatisfaction. The revolutions of 1848 in Germany can therefore not be attributed to economic misery or ex-plained in terms of a 'class struggle'. It would be at any rate closer to the truth to see them as the coming of age of German liberalism. It was the liberals, nourished by the opportunities for political activity in some of the states since 1815, and fortified by the economic revival, who led the revolutions and espoused the cause of the less fortu-nate. But their solution to social problems was political; only very few of them really came to grips with the details of the economic situation. Moreover, their political solution stopped short of giving the classes below them any political power or influence of their own; like bourgeois liberals everywhere, they saw themselves as the political representatives of the whole Third Estate. The radicals who went beyond liberal constitutionalism to press for republican democracy were very few.

When, therefore, in March 1948, the liberals to their great surprise found themselves, owing to the sudden weakness of rulers intimidated by the February Revolution in France, in charge of all the governments of Germany, nothing was more natural than that they should graft bourgeois constitutionalism on to the existing monarchical structure. Nothing was more natural, either, than that, most conspicuously in Austria and Prussia, they should before long counsel moderation and even align themselves with the forces of counter-revolution in order to guard against the danger, more imagined than real, of power passing to the masses. This tactic, however, played into the hands of the princes, who had never done more than pay lip-service to the liberal cause anyway. Frederick William IV of Prussia in particular had never understood such notions as responsible government, let alone been willing to put them into practice. Moreover, even at the height of liberal power, in the spring and summer of 1848, the king had retained control of the army; and when at the end of the year he made up his mind to put an end to all the liberal nonsense and sent a detachment of troops to evict the elected National Assembly from its meeting-place there was nothing the liberals could do about it. There had always been something unreal about their ascendancy, just as there had been something unreal about the March revolutions themselves.

The same air of shadow-boxing can, in the light of hindsight at any rate, be seen to have hung over the German liberals' deliberations on the question of German unity. The fault lay not so much with the liberals who dominated the Frankfurt parliament, elected to frame a constitution for a united Germany, who were entirely determined to proceed in a practical and realistic manner, but rather with the nature of the problem, which was no easier to solve in 1848 than it had been before. The liberals took it quite for granted that a united Germany must be a monarchy; but where were they to find a monarch? The Habsburg emperor, who was still the natural choice, and his ministers would have nothing to do with any project for a united Germany which would include the German-speaking parts of Austria without the rest. When the Frankfurt liberals reluctantly fell back upon the expedient of excluding Austria and offering the hereditary crown of the resulting 'Little Germany' (*Kleindeutschland*) to Frederick William IV, he declined, as much because he considered that the Frankfurt parliament did not have the crown of Germany in its gift as because, good conservative that he was, he would not do anything to offend the Habsburgs.

At that point the liberal attempt to unite Germany collapsed. By this time, in any event, the Frankfurt parliament was entirely isolated (and soon dissolved itself); counter-revolution was in full swing throughout the German states. Just as Metternich had been the first minister obliged to flee in March 1848, so Austria was the first state where the forces of order resumed full control. Not even here, however, did the pendulum swing all the way back to conditions prevailing before the revolution. If anything, the energetic leadership of Prince Schwarzenberg tended, rather, toward some of the policies of Joseph II. The administration of the empire was centralized under a system of ministerial absolutism which effectively concentrated power in the hands of the German Austrians. It was as a corollary to this policy that Schwarzenberg refused, even more firmly than Metternich had done, to countenance the creation of a united Germany which would set up a conflict of loyalties among German-speaking Austrians and therefore threaten the integrity of the Habsburg empire and even the dynasty itself.

In Prussia, also, the summary dismissal of the liberal ministry and of the elected assembly did not betoken a literal restoration. Indeed, Frederick William IV went so far as to grant a constitution without, as happened in Austria, revoking it again. He did, to be sure, revise it twice, but in this revised form it remained the constitution of Prussia until the end of the monarchy. Since it became the principal source of tension and object of conflict between the monarchy and liberal forces throughout the age of Bismarck and beyond, its main features are worth stressing. It resembled the south German constitutions of thirty years earlier in preserving monarchical sovereignty and in providing for a bicameral legislature with limited powers, one chamber of which was wholly elective. It was unique in the system of suffrage governing this election. The male adult population was divided into three groups according to the amount of taxes they paid. The result was that those in the higher tax brackets had on average about four votes to each one available to the mass of the population. This plutocratic suffrage at first favoured, as it was intended to, the wealthy landowners who for the most part voted Conservative; but as with more rapid industrialization wealth tended to spread more widely to the middle class, the three-class suffrage became an article in the liberal creed. But this apparent access of strength weakened the liberals morally and was in fact to play into the hands of Bismarck.

Bismarck had had experience in the Prussian civil service as well as in various political assemblies and had disliked both. He was a dedicated advocate of the *ancien-régime* system in which the king and the nobility governed in harmony and to their mutual benefit and resisted all political incursions from outsiders. In foreign policy, like Frederick William IV and most other conservatives, he accepted

Habsburg supremacy in Germany and the Metternich system of 'peaceful dualism' between Austria and Prussia. These views, as well as the energy with which he expressed them, commended themselves to the king when, after the dissolution of the Frankfurt parliament and the abortion of further attempts at a tighter federal structure for Germany, the old *Bund* was revived in 1851, and he appointed Bismarck as chief Prussian delegate to the Diet of the Confederation (which also met in Frankfurt). In this capacity Bismarck was not long in discovering that the Metternich system had been replaced by Schwarzenberg's policy of actively challenging Prussia for leadership in Germany. Bismarck thereupon radically changed his tune, took up the Austrian challenge at the Diet, and urged upon his government a policy of Prussian aggrandizement in Germany. At first he was successful in this last respect only in the economic field, where the *Zollverein*, under Prussian leadership, was expanded despite Austrian hostility. Later the clumsiness of Austrian foreign policy during the Crimean War caused the Habsburg empire to lose face in Germany. But still Bismarck could not persuade the king to lift a finger against the Habsburgs.

Nor did Bismarck fare any better when Frederick William IV in 1858 was officially declared insane and his brother, Prince William, became regent. William removed Bismarck from Frankfurt and sent him as ambassador to St Petersburg to cool his ardour. In fact, William went even farther: he dismissed the entire cabinet (as well as the group of unofficial advisers behind the throne). The ministers appointed in their place, although by temperament conservative enough, mostly designated themselves as liberals, which was enough to cause most of the country to jump to the quite unjustified conclusion that William was himself a liberal. At any rate, partly to please him, the electorate returned a majority of Liberals to the Lower House of the Diet in 1859. Thus the stage was set for the so-called 'New Era' which William's advent was thought to have begun. But only three years later the majority in the Lower House were openly hostile to William, and Bismarck had been called to office as the king's man[2] to crush them.

---

[2] William ceased to be regent and became King William I on the death of Frederick William IV early in 1861.

2

Bismarck and the
Constitutional Conflict in Prussia

In fact, the phrase 'New Era' had been a misnomer all along. It reflected not merely the excessive hopes that public opinion in Prussia habitually placed in almost any new occupant of the throne, but also a genuine confusion of issues. To put it, to begin with, very roughly, the Liberals agreed with the general tenor of William's foreign policy; they disagreed with his real view of the constitution and disagreed among themselves on what to do about it; and they found that military affairs were compounded of elements of both foreign and domestic policy. The confusion was not due to any deception practised on them by William, who for his part found all the issues perfectly clear. He was moderately in favour of Prussia taking the lead in Germany; he had found, when the army was mobilized (though not used) in 1859 during the war between Austria and France in Italy, that it was a defective instrument in support of any active foreign policy; and he was not willing to tolerate interference with the steps he proposed to take to strengthen it. As early as 1859 he had no hesitation in dismissing his minister of war for reluctance to comply; it was not likely that he would brook resistance from elected deputies. Not that the Liberals had the slightest desire to resist an increase in the army as such, which was objectively entirely justified by the growth in population; but they distrusted the intention of some members of the military leadership and were confirmed in their distrust by the details of the regent's proposals, which seemed pretty clearly to indicate a desire to use the expanded army as an instrument of internal policy against the middle class. The principal exponent of such a policy was known to be the chief military adviser to the Crown, Edwin von Manteuffel. He and generals like him were still living in a feudal world of their own in which the Prussian officer was a loyal paladin of the Crown and in return expected the monarch to keep faith with him and to maintain his status in society. Manteuffel exerted considerable influence not only directly on William but also on the new minister of war, Albrecht von Roon. Roon was not a feudal reactionary like Manteuffel, but a conservative upholder of the monarchy determined to keep control of the army vested in the Crown and to interpret the constitution in every case in the monarchy's favour.

Roon's appointment in itself therefore was of political as well as military importance, since it introduced a strong note of dissension into the ministry. The majority of the right-wing Liberals in the New Era ministry advocated ministerial responsibility to the Lower House of the Diet. William, Roon, and conservatives in general feared that such a system would prove to be the first step toward full parliamentary government. On Roon's urging William at first declined altogether to have anything to do with the ministry's proposal, and then yielded to the extent of allowing the formulation of a version so weakened as almost to negate the purpose.[1] The Liberal ministers regarded this as reasonably satisfactory progress. 'They were liberals of the older generation, many of them men of the highest aristocratic standing, who disliked speedy action. They appreciated the wide scope of the power of the King and were more concerned with the problem of leading the monarch slowly and gently along the road to constitutional government than they were with that of satisfying immediately the public demand for action in that direction. Accustomed to positions of dignified prestige in the local community as in the state, they preferred to act as individuals and disliked party organization, party control or discipline, campaigning for votes, or anything associated with popular politics.'[2] The Liberals in the Lower House, however, by the very fact of meeting together as elected representatives, had some incipient feeling, at least, for party politics. They regarded it as self-evident that ministers should be responsible to them. This, indeed, was but one part of their program. They wanted reform of the Upper House, reform of local government, removal of various privileges still remaining with the *Junker* class, abolition or reduction of mercantilist restrictions on free trade and economic expansion. But above all they were interested in their own powers as a majority of an elected assembly. They tended to cast the Lower House in the role of a genuine parliament with full legislative powers.

---

[1] This version (which, significantly, was actually passed by the heavily conservative and partly nominated Upper House of the Diet in the spring of 1862, but never laid before the Lower House because of the events about to be related) provided: (1) that both Houses of the Diet must agree on any complaint to be made against a minister, (2) that such complaints must be confined to alleged violations of the constitution, (3) that the Crown would retain the power to pardon a minister thus impeached.

[2] Eugene N. Anderson, *The Social and Political Conflict in Prussia, 1858–1864*, Lincoln, Nebraska, 1954, pp. 278–9.

They were reconciled, to be sure, after the disappointments of 1848, to the necessity of being realistic and to the impossibility of attaining all these aims quickly. Still, it did begin to seem to some of them that, making all allowances, they were not getting much benefit from a ministry of self-styled Liberals. This group therefore proposed to abandon the passive tactics recommended to them by the ministers and to press actively for a modest program of constitutional and fiscal reform. The numbers of this left wing had been increased by recent by-elections, and by 1861 they felt themselves a strong enough minority to break away and form an independent Progressive Party. In terms of votes, at least, they were very soon justified: at the next elections they were returned as the largest single party, able to command a majority in combination with sympathizers (the Centre Left) who did not formally join them; and after fresh elections in 1862 this trend continued, with right-wing Liberals suffering badly and the Conservatives nearly eliminated. These repeated elections were held because every time that the Lower House, with its anti-government majority, rejected the military budget to pay for the controversial measures to increase the army, it was dissolved.

It was the House elected in 1862 that first confronted Bismarck, called, at Roon's suggestion, to take office as prime minister for the express purpose of defending the monarchy. To Roon, Bismarck, and the king the attitude and actions of the majority of the Lower House amounted to a presumptuous attempt at usurping power. The Progressives and their allies saw things quite differently.[3] They did not regard themselves as in revolt against the Crown or even the constitution. On the contrary, they took their stand explicitly on the constitution and, in the manner of reformers in absolute states over the centuries, looked to the Crown for relief. The Crown must be induced to abandon its subservience to the *Junkers*, who were being allowed to use the state for their own benefit, and instead conclude an alliance with themselves, the Third Estate, the representatives of the people. The liberals' conscious antagonism to the *Junkers*, their conscious awareness of themselves as middle-class, derived to a considerable extent from their growing economic prosperity brought about by rapidly accelerating industrialization. They regarded it as only right and proper that their political power and social status should catch up with the realities of their economic position and achievements.

[3] We now have detailed and discriminating analyses of this 'parliament that resisted Bismarck'. See, in addition to Anderson (cited above, n.2), Adalbert Hess, *Das Parlament, das Bismarck widerstrebte: zur Politik und sozialen Zusammensetzung des preussischen Abgeordnetenhauses der Konfliktszeit (1862–1866)*, Cologne and Opladen, 1964 and Heinrich August Winkler, *Preussischer Liberalismus und deutscher Nationalstaat: Studien zur Geschichte der Deutschen Fortschrittspartei, 1861–1866*, Tübingen, 1964.

Yet at the same time their newly found self-confidence was under-mined by a nagging awareness of elements of weakness which their election victories concealed but did not remove. The *ancien régime* over which, as the Third Estate, they would have to prevail—the very alliance between the Crown and the *Junkers* which they aimed to dissolve—was far more firmly entrenched than that of Louis XVI. In addition, their appeal to realism was itself more than a little hollow. The bourgeois liberal majority of the Lower House were not entitled to regard themselves as the Third Estate, in the sense of representing all non-feudal elements, in a society in which the workers were begin-ning to organize themselves and to express independent views. This was, indeed, one of the principal problems at issue among the liberals, continually threatening their solidarity *vis-à-vis* the government in the constitutional conflict.

On the face of it, their numerical superiority was crushing. In a House containing 352 deputies, the government could count on the regular support of only eleven Conservatives. The Catholic Centre Party and the Polish deputies, totalling fifty-six, were not committed to either side. The liberal forces therefore usually disposed of a majority of more than four to one at the worst. But the Progressives, the spearhead of the opposition, made up only rather less than half (135) of this majority, the rest being contributed by 103 moderate Centre-Left liberals and forty-seven centre and right-wing ('consti-tutionalist' or 'whig') liberals. The Progressives themselves were in turn divided into two groups of unequal size. The acknowledged leaders of the party were Baron von Hoverbeck and Max von Forcken-beck, both members of the minor East Prussian nobility, motivated by classical liberal principles, including free trade. A more radical minority of democrats included men of the stamp of Franz Waldeck, who had sat in the elected Prussian National Assembly in 1848 and had drawn up the constitution adopted by that body.[4] This group urged the early adoption of equal suffrage and had to be repeatedly persuaded to remove this bone of contention in order to preserve unity within the party and within the larger liberal coalition. Not that most liberals were entirely happy with the existing three-class suffrage, even though it gave them their electoral majority. They saw that this system was bound to produce class-based parties, which would be consonant neither with liberal ideology nor in the long run with liberal self-interest. The image of the Third Estate depended upon the acceptance of the theory of virtual representation, whereby the liberal deputies represented the interests of the whole people

[4] It is significant, however, that only one quarter of the Progressive deputies had served in any political assembly before 1859; fully 64% were newcomers to the Lower House in 1862.

politically while not reflecting their composition socially. But no alternative suffrage could be devised that was acceptable to most liberals —an alternative, that is, that would not be likely to reverse the liberal majority and crush the middle-class between the hammer of the *Junkers* and the anvil of peasants and urban workers. Thus the liberals could take no convincing stand against the existing system, while their dilemma tended to tighten into a vicious circle and their solidarity was weakened.

Another of the great issues of the day promised, on the other hand, to provide cement for the liberal movement. This was the question of German unity, or quite simply the 'German question', as it was often called. The Italian war between France and Austria and Austria's defeat had made plain at least two things: that foreign policy was conducted in Germany over the heads of the people, and that Prussia was unquestionably the leading German power. The direct consequence was the formation in 1859 of the *Deutsche Nationalverein* dedicated to the propagation of the idea of German unity under Prussian leadership. This body contained liberals of all shades of opinion who desired German unity at all; most of them were Prussian, though some of the most influential were not, including the Hanoverian Rudolf von Bennigsen, its head. It was particularly significant that almost all the radicals, who in 1848 had advocated *grossdeutsch* unification, i.e. including German-speaking Austria, now abandoned this position and accepted that unity would have to be *kleindeutsch*. Nevertheless, the *Nationalverein* contained the same tension between the radical democratic minority and the orthodox liberal majority as the Prussian Lower House. The democrats, being republicans, pursued national unification in the first place as a stick with which to beat the dynasties and the institution of monarchy. For the liberals, on the other hand, national unity was desirable as an essential step toward economic and cultural progress and as a means of overcoming the military nature of the Prussian monarchy, partly by spreading the defence burden more evenly over Germany. This conflict of aims not only presaged a possible divergence of priorities but also exposed among the liberals the same kind of potential vicious circle as the position of the Prussian liberals on the suffrage: a more liberal Prussian government was required in the first place if the aims of the *Nationalverein* were to be attained (Docs. 3–6, 11).

The liberals in the Prussian Lower House, in their struggle against Bismarck, suffered from a further handicap not felt in the *Nationalverein*, one which followed from the compatibility in Prussia (and in Germany generally) of office-holding and parliamentary membership. Fully half of the members of the Lower House were civil servants

THE AGE OF BISMARCK

on leave.[5] It was serious enough that, in a period of open conflct between the Crown and the elected assembly, such persons were liable to a division of loyalties; it was worse still that the government retained the right to discipline, transfer, or demote many such officials, a fate which befell ten of them within a year of the outbreak of the conflict. Judges and other judicial officials could be punished only by a court judgment, but even this was not beyond the power of the government to achieve: one such deputy was sentenced to prison as a direct consequence of a speech made in the House, despite parliamentary immunity.

Such ruthlessness was typical of the way in which Bismarck, for his part, waged the struggle against the liberals' attempt to assert their parliamentary rights in the context of the disputed military budget. Bismarck was determined not to give an inch in his defence of monarchical sovereignty in general and of the Crown's control of the army in particular. From his very first speech as prime minister he adopted a militant posture and refused to entertain any proposals of compromise with the liberals. On the contrary, he increased the government's censorship and police powers. The constitutional issue itself he dealt with by means of the theory of a gap in the constitution which only the Crown could fill; and it is noticeable that in the same speech in which he put this forward he went out of his way to point out that the conflict was ultimately a question of power (Doc. 1).

Against such tactics the liberal majority were ill equipped, inexperienced, and badly organized, the more so when Bismarck began to exploit the divisions in their ranks on the suffrage and on the priorities between liberal reform and national unification. Bismarck held a conception of foreign policy which for a conservative was revolutionary in both ends and means: he was dedicated to the idea of Prussia as a Great Power, was prepared to pursue this aim boldly if opportunity offered, and appreciated the possibilities of *kleindeutsch* unification under Prussian leadership as a way of attaining it (Doc. 2). This policy alienated the orthodox, narrowly Prussian conservatives with whom he had many other natural affinities, but ultimately won him the support, though not the affection, of liberals throughout Germany. The Prussian liberals' uncertainty whenever questions

[5] See the book by Hess cited above, n.3. Other interesting statistics include the following: of close to 100 large landowners among the 352 deputies, more than half were members of the Progressive or Left-Centre parties. Only a third as many made a living from industry or trade, and only 10% of Progressives belonged in this category. While only 5% of the House were practising lawyers, at least half of the members had studied law at a university. This information is very illuminating for the composition of the House as a whole and of the Progressive Party in particular, and throws light on the relative fluidity making itself felt in Prussian society.

touching national unity or national prestige were raised had already been demonstrated during the revolution of 1848 with respect to both Poland and Schleswig-Holstein. The same two issues reappeared in the first two years of Bismarck's tenure of office. Liberals traditionally supported the cause of Polish independence, both on general grounds of national autonomy and specifically because the bulk of Polish territory had been incorporated into Russia since the Congress of Vienna ('Congress Poland'), and the Russian Tsarist autocracy was particularly repugnant to liberal principles. But when a revolt broke out in Poland against just this autocracy most Prussian liberals, in urging Prussian support of the revolt, emphasized foreign-policy considerations—the value of an independent Poland as a buffer against Russia—at the expense of ideological or nationalist grounds. Their difficulty arose from the fact that large numbers of Poles lived in Prussia too, and an independent 'Congress Poland' might stimulate an irredentist movement among them. Only the democrats, for the most part, remained true to the liberal principle of national independence as such. These divisions remained for the moment of little practical importance because liberals of all shades could unite in condemning Bismarck's pro-Russian policy as a revival of the Holy Alliance; nonetheless they were a straw in the wind.

The Schleswig-Holstein problem was a notoriously more complicated one, which it is unnecessary to try to unravel completely here. Suffice it to say that the two duchies had for centuries been jointly in personal union with the Danish crown, a situation confirmed in international law as recently as 1852 in the London Protocol; that Holstein was wholly German-speaking while in parts of Schleswig there was a Danish majority; that Holstein but not Schleswig was a member of the German Confederation; and that in 1863 the king of Denmark decreed the incorporation of Schleswig into Denmark. The Prussian liberals' first reaction was to urge the Prussian government to espouse the cause of the Duke of Augustenburg, a German prince who was the son of one of the pretenders to the succession in Schleswig and Holstein, with the implication that they would vote money in support of such a policy and its military execution. The Diet of the Confederation also adopted the Augustenburg cause. Some Prussian democrats, on the other hand, took the line that an authoritarian Prussia could do nothing for the cause of freedom or German unity anywhere, and moreover rejected the Augustenburg claim as being founded on the obsolete principle of legitimacy. Bismarck, for his part, also dissociated himself from Augustenburg, thereby simultaneously rebuffing the Confederation, which he wished to undermine, by declaring its resolution incompatible with the London Protocol, and rejected the liberals' implied offer. Instead he concluded an agree-

THE AGE OF BISMARCK 29

ment with Austria to settle the Schleswig-Holstein problem between themselves. Against this policy, also, all Prussian liberals could unite. But once Austro-Prussian military operations were under way, some democrats again broke away from the majority line, which now advocated the incorporation of Schleswig into the German Confederation, and argued that liberal principles required an opportunity for self-determination for the Danish population. After the successful end of the military campaign the liberal majority veered round to advocating the annexation of both duchies to Prussia, partly as a means of liberalizing the kingdom; again some democrats dissented. Even some of the more radical spokesmen of the Lower House in the constitutional conflict, however, began to praise Bismarck for his success; that is to say, to place value on actions favourable to German unity even if carried out by a reactionary government without that end in view.

For it can now be regarded as established that Bismarck had no idea of gaining the duchies for Germany, still less of ensnaring Austria by involving her in the joint action against Denmark. It did turn out that the Danish war of 1864 was, as it were, the first instalment of a process which culminated in the Austrian war of 1866 and thence in *kleindeutsch* unification; but Bismarck did not intend it as such. He was above all an opportunist, whether that be regarded as praise or as blame. Perhaps the most astonishing example of this quality was displayed not long before the war of 1866, when Austria made another of her periodic proposals to strengthen the Confederation. Bismarck countered with a proposal for a German parliament elected by universal suffrage—an 1848 parliament! The majority of Prussian liberals had no hesitation in not only rejecting but ridiculing this gambit. 'Few Germans', as A. J. P. Taylor says, 'would take Bismarck seriously as a radical'.[6] But by their rejection the liberals once more publicly weakened their position in the Prussian constitutional conflict. Bismarck had, of course, appreciated their vulnerability on this flank. Yet his move had not been merely a tactical one, still less bluff; for only a year later he put the proposal into operation. He could see just as well as the liberals that he might be able to out-manoeuvre them by attracting the votes of the peasants and conservatively-minded members of the lower middle class.

Then Bismarck reverted to his attack on the liberals' other flank, their nationalism, their devotion to German unity. He took his policy of undermining the Confederation to its logical conclusion by withdrawing from it. This move in turn led directly to the war against Austria which Prussia won in a brilliant six weeks' campaign. At its end Bismarck had succeeded in excluding Austria from Germany and in making Prussia completely dominant in north Germany. These

[6] *Bismarck: the Man and the Statesman*, London, 1955, p. 82.

results fulfilled the liberals' dearest wishes; but what were they now to do about the constitutional conflict? An indication of the answer was to be found in new elections which had taken place before the news of the decisive victory over Austria had arrived. The Progressives, who were not alone in the belief that Bismarck had launched the war as a means of escape from his domestic difficulties, campaigned under the slogan 'No war for Bismarck's purposes'. The electorate, valuing Prussia's position in Germany more highly than parliamentary government, answered by depriving the party of half its seats, and the Conservatives found themselves once more the largest party in a parliament for which fundamentally they had no use. It was not to the Conservatives, however, but to the liberals, including many Progressives, that Bismarck could look for support of his successful but revolutionary foreign policy. He therefore for the first time gave the liberals a chance to end the constitutional conflict without humiliation by means of an indemnity bill in which he offered an admission that he had governed and collected taxes illegally for four years if in return they would vote him the taxes retrospectively. The Lower House passed the bill by 230 votes to seventy-five. The minority consisted of the pro-Austrian Catholics, the left wing of the Progressives, and the right wing of the Conservatives. Both liberals and Conservatives were therefore divided amongst themselves—divided, one might say, over whether or not they should remain true to their ideology: in the case of the liberals, whether they would accept the realization of their German dreams by the reactionary minister who for four years had treated the Prussian constitution with contempt and by the methods of 'blood and iron' rather than of 'moral conquests'; the Conservatives, whether they could forgive Bismarck his use against Austria of revolutionary instruments—universal suffrage and an alliance with Italy—and his violation of the legitimate rights of sovereign princes in his reorganization of north Germany. Justifications of the various points of view were abundant in the Prussian parliament, in the press, and elsewhere (Docs. 6–13).

By way of comment and summary on this much-debated problem, two suggestions may be made. First, that the reactions called forth by the events of the year 1866 were extremely complex. There is no doubt whatever that there was a genuine swing to Bismarck. The documents speak eloquently of the conversions wrought by the military victories against Austria, and the minority of the unconverted could with justice refer wryly to the worship of success. Even some of Bismarck's friends pointed out to him that if he had not won the war he would have been reviled instead of exalted, and indeed it is important to remember that it was by no means a foregone conclusion that Prussia would win; pessimism was widespread in the Prussian camp, and the Austrian government was confident of victory. But if surprise at the triumph of Prussian arms was matched by an even more rapid change of mood, symbolized in the vote on the indemnity bill, at the same time we must not lose sight of the fact that in a wider perspective the change had been in preparation for some time. We have seen its symptoms and some of its underlying causes at any rate among the liberals. The swing to Bismarck should be seen in the context, perhaps as a culmination, of the swing toward realism, the weakening of ideology, the strength of economic considerations, that had been developing since 1848 (and not only in Germany).

The second general comment is that the minority who did not swing, those who adhered to their previous convictions, were right. The minority among the Conservatives were right in that Bismarck never returned to party orthodoxy; the minority among the liberals were right in that the tactical calculation of the majority that the unification of Germany would promote the parliamentarization of Prussia proved completely mistaken.[7]

---

[7] Political scientists may be left to judge, on the other hand, whether alliances of extreme Right and extreme Left are likely to be fruitful. This as well as other interesting problems are raised by one of the best contributions to the centennial reflections on the events of 1866: Karl-Georg Faber, 'Realpolitik als Ideologie: die Bedeutung des Jahres 1866 für das politische Denken in Deutschland,' *Historische Zeitschrift*, Vol. 203 (1966), pp. 1–45, which, however, does not always quote its sources accurately.

3

Bismarck and the
Unification of Germany

IF the liberals of north Germany gravitated toward Bismarck before 1866 and flocked to him in that year, this was less conspicuously true in south Germany. Although supporters of *kleindeutsch* unification were not lacking there, they were not so numerous. For one thing, political radicalism was traditionally strongest in the southwest; for another, Bavarian Catholics tended to stand by Austria against Prussia; moreover, south German hostility toward the sort of Prussia that Bismarck represented was never far below the surface. It is significant, for instance, that south German membership in the *Nationalverein* had declined relatively even before 1866. Thus Bismarck never seriously considered including the states of south Germany in the federation set up in the wake of the defeat of Austria.

In Austria itself, needless to say, the defeat, the demise of the old Confederation, and the consequent extrusion from Germany were bitterly resented. The Habsburg empire had fallen on evil days since the proud era of Schwarzenberg only fifteen years earlier. Even before 1866, the monarchy had tried various constitutional experiments designed to attract greater popular support than the centralized absolutism of the early 1850s. After the defeat, this need became more pressing than ever, and the monarchy's response to it was the Compromise (*Ausgleich*) that went into effect the following year. The compromise referred to was with the Magyars (Hungarians), and the empire was known henceforth as the Dual Monarchy of Austria-Hungary. The Emperor Francis Joseph allowed himself to be crowned king in Hungary, he accepted most of the reforms carried out in Hungary during the 1848 revolution, and in general recognized Hungary as a separate state united with Austria only through the Habsburg dynasty. There were only three ministers common to both countries, with restricted powers, and there was a common legislature composed of delegates from the two halves of the monarchy. The Magyars were granted the same kind of dominant position (in both national and social senses) over other ethnic groups in their half of the empire that the Germans enjoyed in Austria (except for considerable autonomy allowed to the Poles of Galicia). In practice the Magyars had achieved more than mere equality with the Germans: they had attained a position from which they could exert irresistible pressure on the emperor.

This was a situation that was very acceptable to Bismarck, who wished to divert the attention of the Habsburgs and of the Austrian Germans away from Germany, particularly while he was busy reorganizing Germany north of the river Main. The whole area was included in a new North German Confederation in which Prussia, apart from having annexed outright the kingdom of Hanover and certain other territories, enjoyed overwhelming political superiority deriving from the constitution devised for it at Bismarck's direction and accepted by a constituent assembly under Bismarck's guidance. This assembly was dominated by the new National Liberal Party, composed of those Prussian liberals (the majority) who had come over to Bismarck with the indemnity bill together with the pro-Prussian liberals from the non-Prussian (annexed) lands. Much to their discomfiture they were obliged to accept direct and equal manhood suffrage for the *Reichstag* of the Confederation. Bismarck proposed this not, of course, to bolster parliamentary institutions but to weaken them. The new *Reichstag* was to be strong enough to weigh in the balance against the princes and legislatures of the states making up the federation (including even the Prussian legislature). Bismarck's whole constitutional structure, in fact, including the concessions that he allowed the National Liberals to wring from him, was designed as a delicate system of interlocking balances, with himself, as prime minister of Prussia and federal chancellor, at the fulcrum. Even the two houses of the federal legislature were in potential counterpoise. The upper house, the *Bundesrat* or Federal Council, preserved certain links with the Diet of the old Confederation in that member states sent delegations. But since Prussia acquired the votes of the annexed states, giving her a veto over legislation requiring a two-thirds majority, and since Austria was excluded, Bismarck could afford to give this body much greater power. It was, in fact, in constitutional law the *locus* of sovereignty of the federation. With Prussia presiding, the princes or their delegates debated here behind closed doors and came to anonymous decisions. The king of Prussia, besides being president of the federation, was also commander-in-chief of the army, whose affairs were not to to be within the competence of the *Reichstag* or—one of Bismarck's neatest strokes, in view of the causes of the Prussian constitutional conflict—of the Prussian Diet either. This was, however, one of the points on

c

which Bismarck made a concession to the National Liberals as he saw that the *Reichstag* could be more useful to him if it were not a mere debating society, and it was provided that after the first four years the military budget should be submitted to the *Reichstag*. Bismarck trusted himself to deal with any difficulties that this step might raise. On points of the constitution that he considered essential to the Prussian Crown, and hence to himself as the king's trusted servant, Bismarck stood firm. It is significant that the Prussian crown prince was his intermediary in negotiations with the National Liberals: the North German Confederation was little more than an extension of Prussia and Prussian power. Bismarck never thought of 'Germany' in the nationalist terms of the liberals, but always above all of Prussia;[1] to this extent he was a conservative and disappointed even the liberals' nationalist aspirations, not to mention their political ones.

It was, on the other hand, inevitable that the mere creation of the North German Confederation should provoke nationalist sensibilities abroad. Not only, obviously, was Austria-Hungary distressed by the turn of events in Germany, but France, in particular, was sensitive to changes in the balance of power and especially to the evident possibility that the states of south Germany too, traditionally to some extent a French sphere of influence, might fall into Prussia's orbit instead. Bismarck for several years did all he could to heal the wounds of the recent enemy as well as to allay the fears of a potential one. But by 1870 the situation had changed. Where Bismarck had previously been well content to leave the southern states out of his federation, an election victory of the Catholic, anti-Prussian party in Bavaria threatened Prussia's friendly relations with the independent southern states (Docs. 17–18). Partly, at any rate, for this reason, Bismarck began to think seriously of mastering the new danger by taking those states into the Confederation after all. To what extent he thereupon engineered the Hohenzollern candidacy to the Spanish throne as a deliberate device to provoke the French into a war which would deliver the south German states into his grasp is still debated among historians (Docs. 19–22). What is certain is that Bismarck himself afterwards assiduously cultivated the idea that the Franco-Prussian War of 1870–71 was a part of his grand design for German unification, just as he afterwards put forward his own version of his clash with the military in the course of that war which may be compared with the contemporary diary of the Chief of Operations at army headquarters (Doc. 23).

However that may be, the successful outcome of the war against France enabled Bismarck to incorporate the south German states into his federation, now renamed the German Empire with the king of

[1] See, in this connection as well, Doc. 2 below.

Prussia as emperor instead of president, but in its essentials un-changed from the Prussian-dominated edifice constructed in 1867, tailor-made to Bismarck's general conception of Prussia's place in Germany and in the world as well as for his personal and political convenience (Doc. 24). Nevertheless, the absorption of the south German states, particularly Bavaria, did present some problems and did bring about some important though not fundamental changes, and it is only in the constitution of 1871 that the ingenuity of Bismarck's political balancing act is fully on display.

As in 1866–67, the crown prince was involved in the negotiations in 1870–71, this time with the princes of south Germany. He saw himself as emperor in the near future and wished to establish his superiority to the other princes, whom he despised as insufficiently inspired with German nationalism. He was all for forcing the princes' hand, but such a plan ran counter to Bismarck's political instincts. To antagonize the princes, who had after all been Prussia's allies in the war with France, by the use of Prussian armed might against them would deprive him of one of his counters in the political game and would make him far too dependent on the German people and their representatives in the *Reichstag*. He much preferred to use the carrot, though he was not above flourishing the big stick at times to show who held it. Since the south German princes were disunited among themselves, the task of persuasion was scarcely even a serious test for Bismarck's skill. Only the eccentric king of Bavaria, Ludwig II, was really recalcitrant; the princes of Baden and Württemberg were so eager to forestall any special privileges for Bavaria that they did not join in a united front against Bismarck and so allowed him to maintain the special privileges for Prussia in the new as in the old federation. Bismarck was quite willing to make a number of nominal concessions so long as he retained the substance of power for the Prussian Crown and hence for himself. In dealing with Bavaria, more-over, Bismarck supplemented the normal channels of communication with clandestine financial inducements (if bribes is considered too strong a word), which have only recently been fully documented, for joining the new empire. The Bavarian state treasury as well as various individuals had transferred to them some of the Prussian windfall from the indemnity paid by the French, while Ludwig II himself was compensated for his loss of full sovereignty by more pseudo-Gothic castles financed from monies seized by Prussia from the dethroned king of Hanover in 1866 and administered by Bismarck as a secret fund (the *Welfenfonds*). The public concessions to Bavaria in the constitution concerned such matters as railways, membership and chairmanship of committees of the Federal Council, taxes on beer and brandy, and postal affairs; some of these were extended to Baden and Württemberg as well. The most important privilege reserved for Bavaria alone was retention of a theoretically separate army. It was Prussia, however, that benefited most substantially from the federal nature of the empire. The king of Prussia as emperor was president of the empire, a position which involved substantial executive rights and responsibilities, and Bismarck as imperial chancellor was of course the emperor's principal adviser. Moreover, Bismarck as Prussian foreign minister instructed the Prussian delegation to the Federal Council, which under the constitution had veto power over any proposed changes affecting the army, the navy, customs and consumption taxes, and administration, as well as over constitutional amendments. All federal states controlled their own police, judiciary, and education, many kinds of taxation, as well as railways and mining; but since Prussia was far and away the largest and most populous state of the empire such provisions enhanced rather than limited the scope of the Prussian government, of which Bismarck under his third hat as prime minister was the head. Prussia and Bismarck stood to gain from almost every provision of the constitution, those that favoured the states as much as those that favoured the empire.

Meanwhile the theoretical problems posed by German federalism provided a fascinating subject of discussion for a whole generation of constitutional lawyers, political scientists, and historians. Not since the creation of the United States, where the relationship between the states and the central government had recently attracted world attention again with the Civil War and its aftermath, had the phenomenon of federalism appeared so prominently. In the most general terms, the principal question for debate concerned the location of sovereignty in a federation. One answer, which followed the *Federalist* doctrine in America but which attracted little support in Germany, was simply that sovereignty was divided between the federation and the states. If, then, sovereignty was not divided because indivisible, where did it rest? On one side it was argued, for instance by Max von Seydel, who significantly enough was a Bavarian and a follower of that other Southerner John Calhoun, that the empire was a confederation constituted by treaties among sovereign states (like the old Metternich *Bund*). The preponderant view, however, was that sovereignty belonged exclusively to the empire. In that case, however, what species of animal were the member states? Here again there were various theories, but the prevalent answer, first given prominence by Paul Laband and taken up by a whole school that came to be known as 'legal positivists', was that while the empire possessed absolute sovereignty because it could potentially acquire for itself competence in all fields, nevertheless the member states were genuinely autonomous political entities with their own underived right to rule except where the empire intervened: 'the member State is master, looking down; subject, looking up.'[2] This was an especially ingenious compromise in view of Laband's assertion that the Federal Council was the sovereign of the empire, and the Federal Council was, of course, composed of delegations representing the governments of the states. The whole effect of legal positivist jurisprudence was to provide theoretical support for Bismarck's de facto constitutional creation and to ratify in advance all actions taken by it so long as they were formally correct. Some theories went even farther in the direction of giving Prussia and Bismarck carte blanche in Germany. The historian Heinrich von Treitschke, for instance, one of the many German liberals who had come over to Bismarck in 1866 and, though a Saxon, thereafter one of the most ardent advocates of Prussia's mission in Germany, maintained that in practice the empire was not a federal state at all but a developing unitary state under Prussia's aegis, and that therefore the question of sovereignty in a federal state was idle. The same realistic view was taken by Hugo Preuss, one of the future architects of the Weimar Republic, but with regret rather than with applause, as in Treitschke's case.

Realism is also advisable for the historian a hundred years later. Whatever the correct answers to problems of constitutional law, realism dictates above all a constant awareness of the far-reaching political power of Prussia in the Germany that Bismarck made, and the consequent importance for all of Germany of the facts of power within Prussia. These include not only the maintenance, under the constitution of 1850, of three-class suffrage and the continuing effect of the government's victory in the conflict of the 1860s, but such extra-constitutional facts as the unassailable prestige of old King William I which inevitably transferred itself to him in his capacity as emperor as well, although in strict constitutional law he was only president of the empire and not a monarch at all, let alone a monarch by divine right. This prestige in practice almost invariably further increased the authority of Bismarck as federal chancellor, since William only very rarely interfered with Bismarck's activities. The federal army was in a sense even more independent than the Prussian army had ever been, since it was not only inevitably dominated by its Prussian officers and contingents but also controlled by the emperor through the agency of the Prussian minister of war, who in turn was not responsible for it to the Prussian Diet since it was a federal and not a Prussian army. The Reichstag could in theory exercise control over the federal army by means of the budget, but Bismarck as chancellor was the only federal minister and he had considerable

---

[2] Cited by Rupert Emerson, State and Sovereignty in Modern Germany, New Haven, London, and Oxford, 1928, p. 103.

experience of dealing with obstreperous assemblies on military matters.

The full realities and implications of the Bismarckian constitution are in many respects clearer today than they were at the time. King William himself was most reluctant to accept the imperial crown, believing that it diminished his power as king of Prussia. Had it not been for Bismarck's gifts of persuasion and for his trust in Bismarck, William might well have repeated, in rather different circumstances, his brother's refusal of an imperial title in 1849. In fact, it has been said with justice that Bismarck's solution of the 'German question' was not *kleindeutsch* or 'little German' at all, which in the minds of the liberals who pursued it was a solution involving a liberal Prussia leading Germany by merging in it, but *grosspreussisch* or 'great Prussian', involving an extension of Prussian conservative institutions and customs to the rest of Germany.

4

Political Problems and Developments in Bismarck's Germany

IF it is true that the real nature of the Bismarckian constitution is more easily appreciated in the light of hindsight, it is also true that Bismarck's Germany is not to be understood by a mere study of the constitution of 1871. That constitution provided, as it were, the framework of politics; but political life usually develops a dynamic of its own, and not even Bismarck could command it to stand still. He did not even particularly wish to do so. If it is perhaps going too far to suggest that Bismarck deliberately created problems in order to save himself from boredom by solving them, it is certainly true that in his domestic politics as much as in foreign affairs (including the process of German unification) what Bismarck prided himself on was his ability to overcome tensions as they arose, not a capacity to stop them appearing. Neither temperamentally nor even intellectually was Bismarck a man for the long run. Even such religious convictions as he had tended to confirm his belief that the best one could do was to prevent disorder from gaining ground, that not all problems could be anticipated, and that settlements seldom if ever proved permanent.[1] Indeed, if political development after 1871 had not brought the delicate balances in the constitution into play we should hardly be able to appreciate them. Pragmatic as always, Bismarck made no attempt to interfere with unexpected developments so long as they did not threaten what he regarded as essential.

Thus, for example, Bismarck had no fear of the *Reichstag* and was right not to have any, because even though after 1871 the *Reichstag* developed a certain momentum of its own which he had not anticipated, this was at worst inconvenient and served as a safety valve. In the last resort, if all else failed, Bismarck relied on the electorate to support him if he had to dissolve a recalcitrant *Reichstag*. It was not

[1] See, in this connection also, Bismarck's reference to the clause *rebus sic stantibus* (Doc. 62).

the *Reichstag* that persuaded him to abandon one of his most settled determinations, that of being the only federal official empowered to appear before the *Reichstag*. (It is necessary to use the vague phrase 'appear before' because Bismarck was not answerable to the *Reichstag* in the sense of being obliged to reply to questions directed to him, still less responsible to it in the sense of being liable to dismissal if he did not have its confidence—indeed a vote of no confidence was itself an unheard of practice in Bismarck's time.) It was administrative necessity, not the desire of the *Reichstag* (which he had ignored in 1867), that compelled him in 1878 to provide for a number of secretaries of state who, in addition to their executive duties, could deputize for him in the *Reichstag*. (So elastic was the Bismarckian constitution that this change was made by a simple decree, not by constitutional amendment.) But, unlike even the Prussian ministers among whom, strictly speaking, Bismarck was only *primus inter pares,* the federal secretaries of state were his subordinates. They were prohibited from independent correspondence with the emperor or with the Prussian ministers, from making proposals to the *Reichstag* or to the Federal Council, and from consulting together in Bismarck's absence to settle differences of opinion. It is small wonder that no men of exceptional talents are to be found among the secretaries of state down the years, with the rather lamentable exception of Count Bülow at the end of the century.

But if Bismarck thus retained control of his immediate subordinates at the policy-making level, he was no more able to supervise, still less to direct, the multifarious and rapidly multiplying bureaucratic legions throughout the country than absolute monarchs had been in the simpler days of the eighteenth century. The mere existence of a federal civil service created momentum tending toward centralization and a unitary state at the expense of the member states of the empire. The federal government and civil service, moreover, exercised direct and untrammelled sovereignty over Alsace-Lorraine, which as annexed territory had not been a sovereign state before 1871 and was not represented in the Federal Council.[2] There was, on the whole, some tendency over the years for the federal principle and the Federal Council to diminish in prestige, some tendency toward the sort of unitary state that the liberal movement had always wanted, some tendency even in Prussia for the idea of 'Germany' and of a German mission in the world to gain the upper hand over loyalty to Prussian traditions and Prussian cultural and other values—a tendency, in other words, for the sort of nationalism that liberals not only in Germany but throughout Europe stood for to assert itself, even though

[2] In 1911 a constitutional amendment was to give Alsace-Lorraine representation in the Federal Council subject to certain restrictions.

Germany had been unified not by them but by Bismarck. The conception of a homogeneous national state was replacing the older Prussian idea of the state above nationalities and indeed above the people. This development was not altogether welcome to Bismarck, who wanted to keep all the pillars of the Prussian monarchy intact and wanted to preserve the federal element in the constitution as one of the instruments of Prussian hegemony in Germany. On the other hand, it is again an aspect of the favourable terms on which he had 'compromised' with the liberals that it was the intolerant sides of nationalism, intensifying the tough and authoritarian streak that Bismarck's Germany inherited from the Prussian tradition, that became conspicuous.

There was certainly never any danger that Prussia would be submerged in Germany in practice. Nine tenths of government is administration, and most federal civil servants were inevitably Prussians; in any event the Prussian civil service continued to have greater scope than the federal. Of even more fundamental importance for the character of Prussian and German politics and society was the fact that authoritarian administration from the centre had unquestionably prevailed over the idea of local and regional administrative autonomy. This idea had been part of the heritage of classical German liberalism since the beginning of the century. Local government was regarded as the logical area to begin the education of the people in democracy: 'self-government' in Germany was almost synonymous with local control of local government. It was almost the only political reform that the National Liberals still demanded with much vigour. Even here they were by now motivated as much by bourgeois self-interest and sheer partisan animus against the *Junkers*, whom they conceived to be in control of the central government, as by liberal principles. They now tended to conceive of local self-government not as a corollary of, or even as a preparation for, constitutional government at the centre, but as a substitute for it. Their leading spokesman on this topic was Rudolf Gneist, originally a student of comparative law who had become especially interested in the English jury system. From lay justice it was a natural step to lay government, and Gneist came to see in the justices of the peace the essence of English liberal government. But Gneist was in fact out of touch with English conditions in his own day. He thought the Reform Bill of 1832 a mistake and played down the role of parliament throughout. He was much more in sympathy with the English Tories than with the Liberals. He depicted the justices of the peace as animated by a Kantian categorical imperative which he contrasted sharply with the 'materialism' that he attributed to the English middle class and to John Stuart Mill specifically. At one time he suggested to Queen Victoria a *coup d'état* against parliament and a return to government through the Privy Council. 'To recommend monarchical reaction as a political step forward to the only major European state that possessed a vigorous free constitution rooted in tradition was surely the acme of professional dogmatism.'[3] It was surely also a remarkably clear indication of the true place in the political spectrum of the German National Liberals. In any event, from his distorted view of English political life Gneist derived an ideal for Germany of local government in the hands of an unpaid élite.

Gneist's purpose was to benefit the middle class; but it is interesting that his specific proposals were taken up with particular vigour by the Free Conservative Party (those conservatives who had come over to Bismarck and Germany unity in and since 1866). As the nearest German equivalent to the English gentry the Free Conservatives applied the analogy of the justices of the peace to themselves. They were also very keen on autonomy for the Prussian provinces, partly because they were especially strong in Silesia, partly as a means of furthering German unity. This latter was a revival of an idea that had formerly been popular with the liberals, that Prussia could best help German unification by dissolving herself into her constituent provinces. After 1866 the Prussian liberals (except those in the newly annexed provinces) emphasized representative self-government at district rather than provincial level, to break the power of the *Junkers* in rural affairs.

In fact, except in Hanover, Schleswig-Holstein, and the other territories annexed to Prussia, where local and regional institutions were left alone as much as possible to avoid unnecessary friction, not very much in the way of either provincial autonomy or local self-government was achieved in Prussia. Bismarck was not willing to sacrifice any substantial powers of the civil service to provincial autonomy; the liberals were not clear amongst themselves what exactly they wanted at local level; and the Upper House of the Diet was an actual or potential stumbling-block for any proposal for thoroughgoing reform. Even the modest bill on local government of 1872 was passed only by virtue of the appointment of twenty-five new members to the Upper House. This law, which applied only to Prussia's eastern provinces, removed the legal basis for sheer unadulterated manorial administration in the countryside, but the fears of the Conservatives proved unfounded: the aristocratic character of rural government remained in practice much as before. The administrative separation

---

[3] Heinrich Heffter, *Die deutsche Selbstverwaltung im 19. Jahrhundert*, Stuttgart, 1950, p. 389. Gneist's denunciation of Mill is especially remarkable in view of Mill's acknowledged debt to Wilhelm von Humboldt, the founder of German liberalism.

of town and country was not touched; the *Junker* estates remained separate administrative units; local elections were arranged so as to put the towns at a permanent disadvantage and usually produced safe Conservative majorities. Nevertheless the law was regarded as enough of a step forward for the National Liberals to press for its application to the western provinces, but without success. It was, however, imitated in a number of other German states; in Baden, paradoxically enough, adoption of its principles meant repeal of a much more far-reaching reform of local government effected in 1870. At the other end of the political spectrum, Mecklenburg, the most backward and unashamedly feudal of all the German states, was characteristically among those where nothing happened at all. The effort of some National Liberal *Reichstag* deputies from Mecklenburg to write into the federal constitution a requirement for representative government in all states was, equally characteristically, rejected by Bismarck in the Federal Council.

Provincial, as distinct from local, self-government was for practical purposes a problem confined to Prussia. The reform achieved in this field in 1875 was even less far-reaching than the local government law of 1872 and was supported even by the Conservatives in the Upper House, who saw that the 1872 law was not working out so badly. In essence the law provided for election of deputies to provincial Diets by the districts. Since the districts were mostly Conservative, so were the provincial Diets; anyway the latter were not given much to do. In no important sense could they be regarded as an education in self-government according to the classical liberal recipe. The only place where such an education might be regarded as taking place was within the towns. To be sure, a bill to extend urban self-government in the older Prussian provinces was rejected by the Upper House in 1876, but even so the towns, under reforms going back to the beginning of the century, enjoyed more autonomy than either the provinces or the districts. Conditions were better still in some of the annexed Prussian territories and in some of the other states. Since with the progress of industrialization towns and cities played an increasingly important political and social role, their institutions occupied an increasingly important place in the general administrative structure. Some observers maintained that the mayoralty of a large city carried the greatest power and independence of any administrative post in Prussia, and such a man as Johannes Miquel, later a leading National Liberal politician and Prussian minister, had come into prominence as mayor of Frankfurt.[4] On the other hand, the same social

[4] It is probably better known that Konrad Adenauer, the first chancellor of West Germany after World War II, had been at one time mayor of Cologne; the Social Democratic leader Willy Brandt was mayor of West Berlin.

forces which made for increased urban influence also made for increasingly plutocratic and sometimes grotesque effects of the three-class suffrage, which applied to elections at all levels in Prussia. In Essen the head of the firm of Krupp, by virtue of paying a third of the taxes in the city, comprised a third of the electorate and so elected a third of the deputies to the city council.

Taking one thing with another, it is fair to say that the historic alliance of Prussian conservatism with the monarchical-bureaucratic state remained unshaken by the unification of Germany and by the administrative reforms of the 1870s.[5] The liberal majority in the Lower House of the Diet were condemned to impotence by their original defeat in the constitutional conflict: 'In view of the strong connections between constitution and administration, when the liberals resigned themselves to doing without parliamentary government' they also made vigorous local self-government impossible.'[6] This strong connection was very noticeable even in the theories of Gneist himself. He held that the rule of law required in the first place government according to the letter of the constitution, coupled with the classical liberal claim to judicial protection against arbitrary administrative decisions. The very fact of Gneist's concentration on the reform of local administration meant, however, that in practice he accepted Prussian 'monarchical constitutionalism' at the centre and supported the whole Bismarckian system of government. Here he was making common cause with his legal brethren the positivists and with such famous National Liberal historians as Heinrich von Sybel and Treitschke, who celebrated Bismarck's achievement in their books. Treitschke, however, interestingly enough, had a much more realistic appreciation of English political life than Gneist, who had made a study of it. The most realistic appreciation of all was that of Bismarck himself, who had no inhibitions about acknowledging the relevance of English constitutional practice and convention since 1832. It is an aspect of the tragedy of German liberalism that those who understood the English political system best were hostile to it.

Treitschke and the other National Liberal historians prided themselves on Germany's separate and different political development. After the early years of the Empire, their function as intellectual defenders of Bismarck's state was more and more taken over by the legal positivists, who largely ignored history altogether. For them the law

[5] In the 1880's, with a Conservative majority in the Lower House and a reactionary minister of the interior, even the modest achievements in the field of self-government of the previous decade were once more reduced (see below, chap. 6). By 1890 there was again less self-government in Prussia than anywhere else in Germany except perhaps Mecklenburg.

[6] Heffter, *Deutsche Selbstverwaltung*, p. 649.

was to be found in the statute books, not in the history books: history was arbitrary and changeable, the law was fixed and certain. This anti-historical attitude was the more remarkable in that Laband's juristic method was derived from a legal doctrine essentially historical in outlook, that of C. F. von Savigny. So, in part, was the political teaching of Otto Gierke, but he also did more justice to the theory of Natural Law, which the legal positivists, of course, totally excluded (Doc. 27). Gierke's theories were more complex, more profound, and also less influential than Gneist's. In his search for a reconcilation of the facts and effects of the German past with political morality and the social needs of the present, one of Gierke's key ideas was that of the community (*Genossenschaft*) as a counterweight to authority (*Obrigkeit*) and the state. But the traditional institutions which had formerly given political expression to this notion had become bastions of privilege, and the task was to clothe it in new forms appropriate to the nineteenth century. In addition to a popular representative assembly, Gierke suggested administration of justice by laymen and, above all, local autonomy and freedom of private association. Gierke therefore arrived, though by a different road, at conclusions in some respects similar to Gneist's. Also like Gneist, Gierke in his striving after political expression for the people stopped short of the essentials of the Bismarckian constitutional system, especially the strong monarchy. Though much younger than Gneist, Gierke still spoke for the fundamental willingness of the German National Liberals to compromise, to content themselves with a parliament that might check but could not govern, with the conception of a community of citizens, and with the rule of law, narrowly interpreted, and to accept the state as an arbiter above the parties and above the people.

Gierke, born in 1844, was still not free, as Gneist and Treitschke in their different ways were not free, from the influence of the philosophy of Hegel, who died in 1831, or from the political theory of F. J. Stahl, the conservative exponent of the principle of 'monarchical constitutionalism'.[7] Not only Hegel's dialectical method, which could easily be adapted to make any contradiction capable of resolution and to make compromise appear as a virtue in itself, but Hegel's view of the state as a moral entity, a view susceptible of metamorphosis into adulation of the state, thus served to produce political theories even from liberals which in practice served as intellectual underpinnings for Bismarck's illiberal conceptions and actions. Not that Bismarck would have been desolated by the absence of such theories. His need for intellectual defence of his system was limited. Despite the German liberal intellectuals' characteristic denunciation of

[7] For treatments of Hegel and Stahl, see my *Germany: a Brief History*, pp. 135-8, 141-2, 188-9, 238-9, 241-2.

materialism (which itself derived not so much specifically from Hegel as from the Idealistic tradition of philosophy of which Hegel was a leading exponent), it was precisely the material interests of the liberal bourgeoisie that Bismarck manipulated to keep his system in equilibrium.

Even before his concentration on this task,[8] Bismarck gave signs of using the tactic of splitting off the left wing of the National Liberals, and thus weakening the party as a whole, on another matter—or rather on the same matter on which he had already won his great triumph in the Prussian constitutional conflict in 1866. In 1871, amid the euphoria of victory, the National Liberals in the new *Reichstag* had joined in voting money for the army for a period of four years. But this was not enough for the government, who wished to evade parliamentary control of the army altogether. To this end they brought a once-and-for-all military budget to the *Reichstag* in 1874. The National Liberals, though quite willing to grant all that was asked for the army, wanted to maintain the principle of legislative control. This was the constitutional conflict of the 1860s in the making all over again, and like it the new deadlock was broken by a so-called compromise which worked heavily in favour of the executive. The determination of most of the National Liberals collapsed at the first threat of a dissolution, Eduard Lasker and a small band on the left wing of the party were isolated, and not even all the Progressives voted against the compromise, which provided for a military budget seven years at a time. This was perhaps the strongest case in the strongest position that the National Liberals ever had to assert the principle of legislative superiority over the executive.

Within the executive, not even the principle of civilian political control over the army, enunciated by Clausewitz and vigorously asserted by Bismarck before 1871, was maintained thereafter. As soon as the generals gave up notions of a military conspiracy Bismarck was willing to give them all kinds of extra-legal political power, deriving from and therefore strengthening the Crown and correspondingly weakening the *Reichstag*. The scope of the Military Cabinet (the king's personal advisers) and the General Staff were enlarged at the expense of the minister of war. The chief of the Military Cabinet, Albedyll, though a disciple of his predecessor Edwin von Manteuffel, the chief exponent of the idea of a military *coup d'état* in the 1860s, was quite prepared to work through these more devious channels; so was the deputy chief of the General Staff, Waldersee, another politically ambitious general. Between them they achieved, first, the appointment as minister of war of one of the apostles of military autonomy in

[8] See below, chap. 6.

1870, Bronsart von Schellendorff (Doc. 23); second, direct access for the chief of the General Staff to the king in peacetime as well as wartime. In this as well as a number of other ways, the army, the mainstay of the Prussian state in the days of absolutism, was deliberately augmented to bolster the authoritarian nature of Bismarck's Germany.

It scarcely needs repeating that this reinforced militarism was only one of the many devices tolerated or employed by Bismarck as counterweights to the *Reichstag* and the political parties which were supposed to represent the German people. Bismarck had created a popular assembly elected by equal suffrage not in order to institute parliamentary government but, as he said himself, to overcome parliamentarianism. The political parties he held in contempt and regarded at best as objects of manipulation. In practice, the *Reichstag* and therefore the parties participated in legislation but had no control over the government (still less over the Crown and the army). They were not part of the government, as in a Cabinet system, but rather hostile to it. They tended, therefore, to fall into a negative, cavilling, and frustrated frame of mind. Nevertheless, handicapped as it was by its limited powers, by its own inadequate procedure, by the abscence of any inducement, financial or otherwise, for outstanding personalities to seek election to it, the *Reichstag* managed to develop some momentum of its own. The parties were at least objects of promises, threats, and concessions. They also acquired their own internal organization and dynamics, particularly those of them that became mass parties. The multi-party system became a fact of political life, even though the parties had no constitutional existence at all. Moreover, committees of the *Reichstag* offered some solid political nourishment even if the plenary sessions did not. Civil servants were sometimes more forthcoming in a less formal confrontation. Especially on economic questions the committees and sometimes even the *Reichstag* as a whole were able to do useful work.

No doubt this was as much because economic questions, in the early years at least, interested Bismarck very little as because they interested the political parties particularly. Most of the parties, in fact, in response to equal suffrage and in consequence of their development as organized mass parties, turned increasingly into economic and social pressure-groups. Bismarck's growing interest in economic matters and his attempts to take advantage of the parties' conversion into economic pressure-groups in order to destroy them will be considered later. First, however, his confrontation with the one major party that was not an economic pressure-group deserves a chapter to itself.

5

Religious and cultural aspects of Bismarck's Germany

THE Centre Party in Germany, like most other parties, consisted of an expanded and modified version of a pre-1870 Prussian party. A Prussian party by that name had existed only since 1859, but it was the same organization as the Catholic Party founded in 1852 for the explicit purpose of defending the Catholic Church and population in Prussia against a state that was felt to be too secular when it was not too Protestant. The change of name in 1859, after the retirement of Frederick William IV, indicated an abatement of hostility to the state and a willingness to adopt a neutral attitude toward the government which was maintained for a decade. The party was, however, opposed to Bismarck's *kleindeutsch* unification, and its Bavarian wing continued after 1870 to emphasize Bavarian particularism at the expense of German unity. Moreover, the Centre identified itself with the party representating the Polish population in eastern districts of Prussia which was in its turn instinctively hostile to the state and therefore a thorn in Bismarck's side. But the Centre Party drew wide electoral support from various sections of the population throughout the country, making it (with its Polish allies) the second-largest party in the *Reichstag,* and it possessed a very valuable asset in Ludwig Windthorst, one of the best party leaders and parliamentarians that Germany has seen. It was a political force to be reckoned with.

Such a force was not one that Bismarck would lightly take on as a foe. Indeed, there is little substance in the view that Bismarck 'declared war' on the party, a view which is based on the untenable assumption that Bismarck initiated everything that happened around him and ignores anything that happened that does not fit this assumption. In this instance as in many others, Bismarck became active only at a time when the conflict was already relatively far advanced. It was initially, moreover, a conflict on a question which not only Bismarck but the government as a whole had tried to avoid. The dogma of papal infallibility accepted by a majority of the Vatican Council in 1870 did not at first disturb the friendly relations subsisting between Prussia and the papacy. It was the rejection of the dogma by a considerable minority of German Catholics (the so-called Old Catholics, drawn mainly from the more educated sections of the population) that gave the state grounds for intervention. Various minor incidents lent colour to the view that the Old Catholics were being deprived by the Church of civil rights which it was the function of the state to guarantee to them (Doc. 31). Even so, Bismarck for the time being remained sceptical about the Old Catholics and wished the state to preserve neutrality in what he regarded as an internal quarrel of the Church, while resisting any invasion of its own jurisdiction. For this defensive purpose, Bismarck agreed with his minister for public worship and education, Heinrich von Mühler, legislation already on the statute books was adequate.

It was only toward the end of the year 1871 that he swung over to a policy of active intervention, and then not mainly on religious but on political grounds. These were partly general and partly specific. The most general ground was Bismarck's growing disillusionment with the attitude of the Centre Party which he began to stigmatize as hostile to the state (*reichsfeindlich*). The very first debate of the new imperial *Reichstag*, in March, had revealed the gap between the Centre and the majority parties. The latter supported Bismarck's historic declaration that Germany was now 'satiated' and in her own self-interest would henceforth pursue a policy of non-intervention in the affairs of Europe, whereas the Centre wished to leave open the possibility of intervention on behalf of the papacy, which had just been deprived of its temporal power in Italy. On another important issue, the Centre wanted the Bill of Rights in the Prussian constitution incorporated into the imperial constitution, while the liberals preferred to include the Fundamental Rights produced by the Frankfurt parliament of 1848, which were less explicit about Roman Catholics. This was the sort of issue, Bismarck feared, that might not only cement the alliance between the Centre and the Poles but also attract some Progressives to the Centre's cause. Catholic clerical support for nationalist agitation among the Poles of the eastern provinces was in any event already causing the government increasing concern. Fuel was added to the flames of Bismarck's growing displeasure from two other sources. The pro-Prussian government of Bavaria, facing elections, desired federal legislation to prevent 'abuse of the pulpit' for political purposes; and the question of religious instruction in the schools, already an issue in the Polish provinces, was raised in an acute form by the acquisition of the new federal territory of Alsace-Lorraine.

Once he had decided to act, Bismarck moved with characteristic

D

energy and ruthlessness. In full session of the Prussian Council of Ministers he accused Mühler of pursuing too timid a policy with respect to Catholic support of nationalist agitation in the schools of Polish Prussia, and forced through not only the state's exclusive right of inspection of all schools but also its right of inspection of religious instruction (Doc. 34). Mühler could not accommodate himself to what he regarded as an aggressive policy toward the Church (Docs. 28–30, 32–33) and was dismissed early in 1872, to be replaced by the anti-clerical Adalbert Falk. Bismarck himself, however, although the dogma of infallibility—and for the matter the whole institutional as well as doctrinal tendency of the Roman Catholic Church—offended his personal religious outlook,[1] was even yet not moved by religious considerations properly speaking. His targets were still, not the Catholic Church either in Germany or in Rome, but the Centre Party and Polish nationalism as forces hostile to the state he had just established, which must be subdued and prevented from reciprocally strengthening each other. He did not hesitate even to seek the support of the papacy, which he regarded as a conservative force, against German political Catholicism—but in vain while Pius IX was pope. The leadership of the Centre Party, for its part, was not decisively guided by religious motives in its political actions either; Windthorst personally rejected the dogma of infallibility.

It was therefore no more than appropriate that the confrontation should have had general political repercussions. The dismissed minister, Mühler, was strongly Protestant and had close links with the Conservatives and with the king and court (William I had been persuaded to part with him only by dint of an intrigue). Bismarck's abandonment of him and of his defensive policy, and the appointment of Falk, were the signal for a sharp cooling of relations between the government and the Conservative Party. This party was traditionally a stronghold of orthodox Protestantism, and on this score had common ground with the Centre in opposing the secular and Erastian principles which Bismarck and Falk seemed to be adopting. Moreover, a large group within the party, never reconciled to Bismarck's unification, sympathized with the Centre's federalism; Ludwig von Gerlach, a leading figure in the Conservative Party and a devout Lutheran, joined the Centre Party in 1871. Conversely, the most

---

[1] 'As a Protestant Christian for whom man's individual responsibility to God is the highest good he rejected the pope's claim to infallible authority in matters of faith. . . . As a Protestant politician he could not swallow the totalitarian claims of the Roman hierarchy or the encroachments of the hierarchy on the state's sphere. At the core of his being Bismarck was a great religious individualist.' Erich Schmidt-Volkmar, *Der Kulturkampf in Deutschland, 1871–1890*, Göttingen, 1962, pp. 30–1.

THE AGE OF BISMARCK 51

ardent support for Bismarck's new policy came from the liberals—and not only from the National Liberals: it was a prominent member of the Progressive Party, a leading figure in the constitutional conflict of the preceding decade, Rudolf Virchow, who coined the word *Kulturkampf* to describe the struggle in which the government was involved, depicting it as an episode in the age-long struggle between clerical obscurantism and enlightened secular liberalism. The very fact that he now relied more heavily on the liberals for political support tended to make Bismarck shift his policy towards theirs. Later on, when he determined to shake off this dependence, he was able to make use of the weakness of their position: a policy of religious discrimination and persecution (however mild) was fundamentally incompatible with liberal principles, and the German liberals' espousal of it derived from adherence to a vaguely conceived heritage of the Enlightenment rather than from strong contemporary currents of German opinion and revealed the shallowness of their roots in German society (Doc. 39). But even at the height of the struggle Bismarck never shared the characteristic liberal *Kulturkampf* mentality.

The same could not be said of the new minister, Falk, a lawyer by profession who regarded it as his mission to inscribe liberal and secular principles in the statute book. For all his admiration of Bismarck, and the latter's respect for Falk's integrity and dedication, there was therefore from the beginning a certain tension between the two men (Doc. 37). 'Even in his waging of the *Kulturkampf* Bismarck remained the resourceful improviser, whereas Falk placed the greatest emphasis on a systematic conduct of the struggle.'[2]

On his appointment Falk was instructed by Bismarck 'to restore the rights of the state *vis-à-vis* the Church with as little commotion as possible'.[3] The most immediate and urgent means to this end was the school inspection law over which Bismarck had fallen out with Mühler. But it was not a law which could be passed without commotion. The Upper House of the Prussian Diet, dominated by Conservatives, rejected it, and it took threats of a creation of peers or, alternatively, of his resignation on Bismarck's part to persuade the king and the Conservatives to let him have his way. The law thus passed, removing all Prussian schools from ecclesiastical influence and determining that the state was to have the chief influence on young people, 'was the real *Kulturkampf* law'.[4]

Bismarck had insisted on making it applicable to all parts of the

[2] Schmidt-Volkmar, *Kulturkampf*, p. 79.
[3] *Ibid.*
[4] *Ibid.*, p. 82.

kingdom, but it was in fact enforced only in the eastern provinces. This apparent anomaly is to be explained not only by the lack of enough school inspectors immediately available, but also by reference to the original occasion for the bill, namely the widespread use of the Polish language and agitation of the Polish nationalist cause in the schools of the Polish-populated districts of which Catholic clerics were reported to be the mainstay (see Doc. 35). Quite apart from issues involving the Church, the government's persistent preoccupation with Polish nationalism as a potentially disruptive force was demonstrated by laws passed in 1873 and 1876 requiring the use of the German language in schools and in official exchanges. (Similar, though less harsh, measures were taken against the Danes in Schleswig.) The climax of Bismarck's anti-Polonism was not reached until 1886, at a time when the *Kulturkampf* itself was almost at an end. All Poles of Russian or Austrian citizenship were evicted, a measure which Bismarck defended by saying: 'We want to get rid of the foreign Poles because we have enough of our own'; he followed it up by the establishment of a Colonization Commission with a view to 'strengthening the German element in the provinces of West Prussia and Posnania against attempted polonization'. Through this commission the state would purchase any Polish-owned farms offered for sale and lease them to Germans. Although economic considerations were involved here, it is clear that Bismarck was chiefly motivated throughout by concern for the security of the Prussian state (Doc. 38). In seeking to protect it, however, Bismarck by appealing to nationalist sentiments not only by implication abandoned the supra-national image of the Prussian state that he had sincerely cultivated but also 'conjured up spirits that he was then unable to exorcise'.[5] In their support of Bismarck's measures, moreover, the Prussian liberals contributed to the strongly authoritarian, intolerant, and right-wing overtones that nationalism was acquiring in Germany. The failure of liberalism and nationalism to mesh, foreshadowed, for that matter, in the liberals' attitude to Polish nationalism in 1848, was nowhere so complete or so fraught with danger as in Germany. In their Polish policy the liberals were as untrue to their principles as in their *Kulturkampft* mentality.

After the passage of the school inspection law, Bismarck became involved in a long and unedifying squabble with one of the Polish bishops which in the end not only drove the entire Catholic episcopate in Prussia into united opposition but also convinced the papacy that Bismarck had embarked on a policy of hostility. Prussian-Vatican relations deteriorated accordingly, whereas Bismarck would have pre-

[5] Oswald Hauser, 'Zum Problem der Nationalisierung Preussens,' *Historische Zeitschrift*, Vol. 202, 1966, p. 537.

ferred to keep the confrontation domestic. The conflict within Prussia, meanwhile, was intensified by the passage of a law in July 1872, prohibiting the Jesuit Order from functioning in Prussia. This, again, arose out of increasing concern in the government (including even Mühler) over the Jesuits' support for Polish nationalism. By March 1872 the preliminary step was taken of expelling all foreign Jesuits from the Polish provinces. In May a full-dress debate took place in the *Reichstag* on petitions for and against a total ban on the Order. A resolution was adopted which fell short of advocating action so drastic, but Bismarck nevertheless caused a law imposing a total ban to be framed. The resulting draft was widely criticized within the government, and another draft was submitted to the *Reichstag* corresponding more nearly to its original resolution. But now the liberals in the *Reichstag* succeeded in restoring the total ban. Bismarck was not above accepting the help of parliamentary parties against his own ministers when it suited him.

The law banning the Jesuits concluded the first phase of the *Kulturkampf*, comprising, in addition, the school inspection law and the elimination of the special Catholic section in the ministry of public worship accomplished before Mühler's resignation and over his protests. The second phase consisted of a series of laws passed chiefly in May of 1873 (the so-called 'May Laws') and in 1874. They had their origin in the failure of Bismarck's attempt to confine the conflict to the political sphere. By the end of 1872 he found ranged against him not only the Centre Party but the united Catholic episcopate supported by the Vatican. He therefore abandoned the view that existing legislation was adequate to deal with clerical opposition and decided on measures which would revoke certain rights conceded to the Church in the Prussian constitution and would have the effect, so far as the Church was concerned, of restoring the conditions of absolute monarchy before 1848 when it was confined to spiritual matters.

But Bismarck was ill during much of 1873, and the laws of that year consequently bore the predominant stamp of Falk. 'Whereas Bismarck was concerned with the power of the Prussian state, Falk concentrated on Prussia as a cultural nation.'[6] The most important of these laws gave the state exclusive control over the training and appointment of priests. The one in which Bismarck was most interested restricted the disciplinary powers of the Catholic hierarchy (see Doc. 36). He still wished, if possible, to avoid antagonizing the Conservatives and the Protestant Church further, and in particular soft-pedalled the issue of compulsory civil marriage. A law imposing this

6 Schmidt-Volkmar, *Kulturkampf*, p. 114.

was not passed until the following year. Even so, the body of laws of 1873 went beyond the limits of what would be required for a separation of Church and state and represented an unequivocal subordination of the Church to the state. This was, indeed, explicitly asserted by one of their chief drafters, Emil Friedberg, one of a group of self-styled 'historical positivists' who set out to vindicate the untrammelled sovereignty of the state which, they said, had been invaded by the papacy and the German Catholics. They claimed that the measures were not inspired by any animus but were the inescapable result of a scientific historical analysis of the situation. Heinrich von Treitschke also defended the May Laws as historically justified.

The laws were enforced with particular harshness in the Polish provinces. On the other hand, the courts reversed many administrative actions purported to be taken under them, and as weapons of battle against a clergy united behind their bishops they were inadequate. The government was therefore driven to ever harsher measures: to the arrest of the archbishop of Posen and to a law removing recalcitrant bishops from their sees. The highest point of the *Kulturkampf* was reached in 1875. In response to a papal encyclical declaring the previous laws invalid the Prussian government passed a bill denying state funds to any Catholic activities, and then introduced another (partly designed to nullify judicial intervention) repealing sections of the constitution guaranteeing the independence of the Protestant as well as the Catholic Church. To this latter bill Falk and the majority of ministers, as well as William I, were opposed, and Bismarck had to produce one of his periodic threats of resignation in order to get it before the Diet. There, however, the majority had no scruples about altering the fundamental law of the country to gain particular ends. 'It may surely be doubted whether even a titan such as Bismarck could put the clock back two generations and go unpunished.'[7] It was Falk, on the other hand, who fathered the last of the *Kulturkampf* laws, which perhaps went farthest in the direction of invading the Catholic Church's internal life. This was a law extending the ban on the Jesuits to all other Orders and Congregations, regarded as under foreign direction and hostile to the state (Doc. 35). Significantly, Falk did not provide adequate state funds with which to replace the educational work that had been carried out by the Orders. The whole tenor of the state's actions had become vindictive, not constructive.

Having sown the wind, the Prussian government reaped the whirlwind. The Church and the Poles each united in adversity more firmly

[7] *Ibid.*, p. 141.

than ever, and also drew closer than ever to one another. German Catholics voted for Polish candidates in elections, and the Polish Party gained seats. The Centre Party likewise flourished in martyrdom and in its turn cemented its alliances with the Church and the Poles and other minorities. The party doubled its seats in the Prussian Diet in 1873 and in the *Reichstag* in 1874. The number of Roman Catholic newspapers, similarly, almost doubled between 1870 and 1880. Short of totalitarian methods which were unknown at the time, the still evolving Prussian and German political machines were not capable of dealing with interlocking movements with deep intellectual, emotional, and social roots (the Polish population, in particular, was maturing fast socially). On the contrary, it was the tradition of the Prussian state on the one hand, and the liberal tradition on the other, that were in jeopardy. The liberals had once more been put in a position where they disavowed their principles. Because of the *Kulturkampf*, the National Liberals in 1873 opposed a Centre motion for the abolition of the three-class suffrage in Prussia, and even the Progressives prevaricated, attitudes scarcely calculated to increase their credit among the population. So far as the Prussian state was concerned, this was the first time in its history that a large mass of citizens had been badly shaken in their loyalty to the monarchy. Moreover, although within Germany the Prussian pattern of behaviour toward the Catholic Church and Catholic political parties was, generally speaking, followed by the other governments, in the realm of foreign policy properly speaking the *Kulturkampf* was a heavy liability for Bismarck. In addition to his other preoccupations in this field, he had to concern himself with maintaining existing tensions between other states and the Vatican, and conversely with preventing a coalition of Catholic states against Germany promoted by the Vatican.

As always a realist, Bismarck began to see that the *Kulturkampf* did not pay, and to cast about for ways and means of putting an end to it without, as he put it, 'going to Canossa'—that is, without losing face in Germany, without a humiliating surrender to the papacy, without further strengthening the *Reichsfeinde* at home, and without giving up what he considered the essential part of the *Kulturkampf* legislation. The distinction between what was essential and what was not tended to be congruent with the distinction between what had corresponded with his own intentions and what could be represented as corresponding with those of Falk and the liberals. On the other hand, the continued opposition to the *Kulturkampf* of the emperor, the Conservatives, and the Protestant Church could be turned to account in any deceleration or partial abandonment of it. Other factors, also, were turning Bismarck's thoughts towards exchanging

Parliamentary dependence on the liberals for a policy in line with
Conservative desires: considerations of an economic nature and the
growing threat (as he saw it) of socialism both pointed in that direction.[8] Two attempts on the aged emperor's life in 1878, which Bismarck represented as manifestations of a socialist conspiracy, enabled
him to set a firmly conservative course.

Nevertheless, the political situation was still too complex and unstable, in Bismarck's judgment, to permit a settlement of the *Kulturkampf* as a purely domestic matter. Here again, a golden opportunity
offered itself in the same year, and Bismarck took it. The death of
Pius IX brought to the papal throne the less intractable Leo XIII,
and Bismarck launched a long and complicated diplomatic initiative
to settle the conflict direct with the Vatican. This was no easy task.
It was not so much the liberals who were obstreperous: they accommodated themselves yet again to following Bismarck's lead, even
swallowing the dismissal of Falk in 1879. It was Windthorst and the
Centre Party, rather, who declined to accept the pope's advice to compromise, so that Bismarck was heard to say that the papacy had
German interests at heart more than the *Reichstag* majority. It therefore took all of eight years before the *Kulturkampf* was officially pro-
nounced at an end. Although administrative leniency was introduced
earlier, it was not until 1885 that any of the May Laws began to be
repealed. One of them was never repealed, and another only in part.
Of the total *Kulturkampf* legislation, twice as much was retained as
was taken off the books.

It is, however, not in quantitative terms, of course, that the settlement of the *Kulturkampf* should be appraised. Some of the laws
which were repealed were regarded by Bismarck as tactical moves
against the Church and as having little intrinsic significance. Conversely, that part of the law on the training of clergy which was retained was unobjectionable to the Church, though very important to
the state. Equally if not more important was the school inspection
law, also retained. The foreign Jesuits, though not the Orders in
general, remained banned. Compulsory civil marriage, by which
Bismarck had originally set little store, proved in the long run a
sensible and non-controversial measure.

On the other hand, it is undeniable that the *Kulturkampf* as a whole
had been a divisive episode in German life whose weakening effects
could not be entirely obliterated by any settlement. Bismarck had
conjured up a quarrel between Church and state in one of the few
states where it had hardly existed before, and his undoubted diplomatic skill and perseverance in settling it on terms which are generally

8 See chap. 6, below.

regarded as a compromise on balance favourable to the state should not be allowed to conceal the original miscalculation that made this large-scale diplomatic effort necessary. We should, of course, avoid the trap, paradoxically prepared by the cult of Bismarck-worship, of adjudging as a complete failure anything in which he became involved in which he fell short of complete victory. But it remains true that the goal at which he had aimed at the outset, destruction of the Centre Party and of its political allies, had not been attained. It smacks of special pleading to reply[9] that as a result of the *Kulturkampf* that party became more positively integrated into the state; that conversely the struggle had made the state conscious of the limitations within which it must work; that the real victor in the conflict was none of the parties to it, but the idea of the *Reich*; and that the *volteface* and suppression of his own prejudices required of Bismarck in breaking off the struggle proved the rare strength of his character. Morally as well as tactically, the honours must surely go to the Centre Party and above all to Windthorst, subjected for a decade and a half to all the pressure of which the ingenuity and ruthlessness of Bismarck, and the machinery of the Prussian state, were capable.

Nor was it only as a political force, through the Centre Party, that Roman Catholicism in Germany was rejuvenated. Internally, the dissident Old Catholic movement, which had been the original occasion for the first moves against the Church by the state, sharply diminished in numbers after a few years. In its perennial struggle against the forces of secularism on the one hand and Protestantism on the other, which did not end with the end of the *Kulturkampf*, the Church derived new spiritual strength from its ordeal. Nor was it diverted from its concern with social questions in an age of rapid industrialization. In this field, in particular, it could compete on very favourable terms for the continued allegiance of its working-class membership with the Protestant Churches, which continued to display hardly any understanding of or interest in social problems.[10]

This attitude was intimately bound up with the long Protestant tradition, in Prussia and Germany, of affirmation of the state's authority and of the quasi-divine right of the Prussian monarchy which was easily (though in constitutional law incorrectly) transferred to the Hohenzollern emperorship. Many believing Protestants rejoiced in the contrast between themselves and the Catholics who rejected the Bismarckian unification. Many, also, in the beginning rejoiced at the *Kulturkampf* in the name of slogans such as opposition to Ultramontanism and 'political priests', 'freedom of conscience',

[9] Schmidt-Volkmar, *Kulturkampf*, pp. 358–62.

[10] For a discussion of these problems, and further details of various plans for dealing with them, see below, chap. 6.

and so on. With its increasing severity large numbers of Protestants, as we saw, recognized the *Kulturkampf* as a liberal and secular attack on Christianity and ecclesiastical institutions in general. Such an original Protestant opponent of the *kleindeutsch* unification as Constantin Frantz seized the opportunity to reiterate his warnings that in their veneration of the monarchy the National Liberals were selling out not only their liberalism but also their Protestantism, and to foster opposition to Prussia among non-Prussian Lutherans. In matters of Church organization this latter movement enjoyed some success, but not much in the realm of politics. As the *Kulturkampf* cooled off, Protestant theological students once more paraded under such banners as 'throne, bayonet, and catechism'. Even such a self-styled theological Modernist as Albrecht Ritschl defended the idea of a state Church with an amalgam of Lutheran and Calvinist arguments. His 'Modernism' consisted in no more than a curious attack on the political theory of the social contact and Natural Law which he stigmatized as 'medieval' and Catholic and with which he contrasted the 'modern' theory of the organic society and organic law. It is, no doubt, one of the stranger by-products of the *Kulturkampf* that this conservative-historical theory, originally popularized in Germany in the aftermath of the French Revolution by the Romantics often in alliance with Catholicism, should now have been turned against Catholicism.

'History' and 'Natural Law' can notoriously be invoked on behalf of almost any cause, not least against any theistic religion whatsoever. The Social Darwinist Ernst Haeckel's *Natural History of Creation* (1868) preached a monistic, materialistic 'religion of nature' as 'the true religion of the future'. Other Social Darwinists invoked both nature and history to justify Bismarck's unification. The socialist movement appropriated Darwinism in a Marxist guise according to which inequality, privilege, and exploitation were 'against Nature'. Marxists, of course, had to be careful, as Engels was in his *Anti-Dühring* (1877), to avoid equating the Darwinian struggle for survival with capitalist competition: man was to be distinguished from the animals, and human progress from animal evolution, by elimination of the struggle for survival. Capitalists and the spokesmen for heavy industry, on the other hand, could also find in Darwin and the Social Darwinists support for their view of society. There is no originality in pointing out that capitalists and socialists had in common a devotion to popularized materialism as a philosophy of life and to technology as the means to progress, and German society was not the only one where these articles of faith proved insufficient.

6

Economic and social problems in Bismarck's Germany

THE waning of idealism, Hegelian or not, and the waxing of materialism in Germany undoubtedly possessed a philosophical momentum of their own. But there can equally be no doubt that Bismarck also made his distinctive contribution here, as he did to almost every aspect of national life. His point of departure in this field was his feeling of discomfort at the extent, in his judgment excessive, to which his policies and therefore his government were dependent on the approval and support of the National Liberal Party in the *Reichstag*. He wished to escape from this reliance on a particular party, and in so doing to demonstrate his superiority to the whole system of parliamentary government, by throwing over the National Liberals and devising a new *Reichstag* grouping which would be at his beck and call (Doc. 53). This coalition was to consist of the two conservative parties plus the Centre. The relaxing of the *Kulturkampf*, together with the Conservative Party's abandonment of its Prussian particularism, were essential prerequisites to the forming of such a pro-government coalition, but they were not by themselves sufficient: for such a coalition could not maintain a stable majority unless the National Liberals were first weakened.

To achieve this objective—which would, incidentally, also protect him from an alliance between the National Liberals and the supposedly liberal crown prince, whom he imagined to be plotting to institute a 'Gladstone ministry'—therefore became Bismarck's immediate task, and to it he applied the simple maxim 'divide and rule': in other words, he proposed to weaken the National Liberals by splitting them, or rather by widening and taking advantage of splits which were already latent within the party. His first move (his reputation for infallibility notwithstanding) failed. One of the most respected leaders of the National Liberal Party was Rudolf von Bennigsen, a Hanoverian and one of a number of non-Prussians who, not being burdened with the memory of the constitutional conflict, found it easier, despite or because of Prussia's seizure of Hanover in 1866, to support Bismarck's domestic policies than many liberal Prussians. Throughout the second half of the year 1877, Bennigsen was under intermittent pressure from Bismarck to enter the Prussian ministry, exerted in the belief that if Bennigsen accepted a time would come, sooner rather than later, when the left wing of the National Liberals would repudiate Bennigsen's participation in some government action or decision, and a split in the party would result. Bennigsen, however, while not seeing Bismarck's game as a whole was nevertheless aware of the degree to which, as a party man, he would be isolated in a Cabinet consisting of administrators, and stipulated that he could accept only if two of his National Liberal colleagues (both on the left wing of the party) were also invited to join the government. For his part, Bennigsen also had a larger purpose behind his request, namely that the presence of three National Liberal *Reichstag* deputies in the Prussian Cabinet would lead to a greater degree of genuine parliamentary and responsible government. Bismarck, however, would not take this bait, abandoned his negotiations with Bennigsen, and launched on two larger-scale operations to outwit the Liberals. Both of them, at the same time, were designed to achieve ends which were independently desired by Bismarck: policy and parliamentary strategy were made to coincide.

The first of these objectives was to defeat and suppress the growing socialist movement in Germany; the second was to abandon the low tariffs (for revenue only) traditionally in force in Prussia—and adopted by the *Zollverein* at its inception—in favour of a system of high protective tariffs. Bismarck's fear of the revolutionary nature of German socialism was genuine enough and, in view of the ostensibly radical and Marxist slogans propagated by the Social Democratic Party, understandable enough. It was certainly a fear shared, on economic as well as political grounds, by the National Liberals in the *Reichstag*, especially by the businessmen among them, and by their electorate. Bismarck was given a golden opportunity to exploit this fear when in the spring of 1878 an attempt was made on the life of the aged and revered emperor. By alleging that the assassin was linked with the socialists, and by deliberately inserting excessively harsh repressive measures into a bill to outlaw socialism, Bismarck hoped to split those National Liberals whose consciences would not allow them to accept the latter from those whose fear of socialism outweighed their liberal scruples. Once again, however, Bismarck failed when the hastily drafted bill proved to be defective and was easily defeated, only the conservatives among the large parties voting for it. It took a second assassination attempt on the emperor to bring Bismarck success: he dissolved the *Reichstag* and in the ensuing election campaign capitalized on the agitated state of public opinion by accusing the National Liberals of responsibility for the miscarriage of the bill (even though no more evidence of a socialist conspiracy was produced in the case of the second assailant than in that of the first). In the result, the strength of the two conservative parties in the new *Reichstag* had risen from 78 to 115, while the National Liberals had slumped from 127 to 98 and the Progressives from 44 to 31. With the Centre maintaining its numbers at 93, this party could now form a majority in combination with the conservatives in accordance with Bismarck's long-term political strategy.

The National Liberals, for their part, were not only reduced in numbers but in a state of disarray which was evinced rather than concealed by the fact that they voted solidly for a new and almost equally harsh law against the socialists. They had bound themselves to do so, in the hope of preserving their electoral strength, without securing any *quid pro quo* from the government. They were therefore confessing the weakness of their position even before the election, and in so doing provided moral as well as practical grounds for those members to whom the radically illiberal nature of the anti-socialist law was repugnant to voice their dissent again. A particularly poignant as well as illuminating sidelight was cast upon the whole episode by the attitude and experience of the government of Baden, long the most liberal of all the German states. The grand-duke and his ministers, though like almost all non-socialists in Germany convinced that energetic measures must be taken against the spread of socialism, at the same time were quick to recognize the political significance of the sort of exceptional legislation that Bismarck was pressing for. They sought to use Baden's moral influence as perhaps Prussia's oldest and staunchest ally in Germany to keep federal policy on liberal lines and to prevent the rift between the National Liberals and Bismarck at which the latter was aiming. They soon discovered, however, that moral influence was a negligible quantity with Bismarck when he had his sights set on something. Then they tried, hesitantly and late, to use Baden's votes in the Federal Council instead, only to be completely outmanoeuvred by Bismarck's greater diplomatic skill and ruthlessness. In the end they not only found themselves supporting Bismarck's policy after all, but also saw their own internal policies threatened by the Baden electorate's defection from liberalism. The grand-duke, at least, may have had some sort of revenge twelve years later in bringing his influence to bear in obtaining Bismarck's dismissal.

But for the present the chancellor was riding the crest of the wave. He had secured his law against the socialists, and on his way to it had sown dissension within the ranks of the National Liberals. The party's renewed disavowal of liberal principles engendered or increased among deputies on its left wing a hankering after joining the Progressives, while at the same time the party as a whole was exposed to pressure from its electorate in the opposite sense. As the pace of German industrialization increased, the National Liberal parliamentary Party slowly began to reflect the accompanying social changes. In 1871, after more than a decade of intensive industrialization, the first imperial *Reichstag* was still dominated by the traditional *élites* of a pre-industrial society. The liberal delegations, in particular, showed remarkably little change in composition from the deputies to the Frankfurt Parliament in 1848. National Liberals and Progressives together still contained only 10% of merchants, bankers, and industrialists, the same proportion of university professors, but twice as many large landowners; 17% were government officials and 25% exercised functions connected with the administration of the law. In the Conservative Party, predictably enough, two-thirds of the deputies were large landowners, about half were high officials, and one-third were jurists, mostly to be found among the high officials (obviously there is overlapping among all these categories); but even the Centre Party delegation contained 40% jurists and 30% large landowners. Most striking of all, 40% of all *Reichstag* deputies were nobles; the next largest social group consisted of the old professional and academic bourgeoisie, while only 8% were businessmen. Even in the *Reichstag* elected in 1878 (which first met in the following year) this proportion had risen to only 13%, but the National Liberal delegation contained double the average percentage.

Even so, the National Liberals were relatively unresponsive to the national trend on the great economic issue of the day, the question of free trade (or, rather, low tariffs *vs.* protection). While the national pressure-group for protective tariffs could count among its members 61% of the Conservative deputies in the new *Reichstag*, 69% of the Free Conservatives, and over 90% of the Centre Party, only just over a quarter of the National Liberals were avowed protectionists, and these were by no means identical with the group of businessmen who were, in fact, far from united on the matter.

Since free trade was perhaps the last great principle of classical liberalism that the National Liberals had not yet partially or completely abandoned, the national swing toward protection was an ideal instrument for the third and decisive blow that Bismarck struck at the party. By exploiting this issue he not only exposed the disparity between liberal economic principles and the economic interests of a relatively small but important group of National Liberal deputies but also helped to convert the *Reichstag* of 1878 into what the novelist Gustav Freytag called 'a large assembly of delegates at a conference on tariff and transport problems'. In political language, Bismarck was subverting the ideological basis of parliamentary government by encouraging the political parties to become economic interest groups.

The question of protective tariffs would have been complicated enough on its own merits. Indeed it could lend itself to Bismarck's political manoeuvring only because economic circumstances and therefore the climate of opinion in Germany had entered a period of rapid change. The central fact behind this change was the world depression of 1873 which halted and then reversed the expansion of the German economy. The policy of free trade, of which the most eloquent theoretical exponent was the naturalized Englishman John Prince-Smith (Doc. 42), offered itself as a natural target for those who were hardest hit by this development, especially the iron and steel manufacturers who had tended to resist it even before 1871 and who could now legitimately point to the aggravating effects of easy entry for foreign goods on a shrinking home market. Very quickly the campaign for protective tariffs spread to other branches of industry, and then to farmers as well, including the *Junkers* of eastern Prussia. This latter phenomenon had less to do with the depression than with the scale and efficiency of North American agriculture, which with the help of greatly improved transport and communications could suddenly undersell German produce in world markets. German farmers, traditionally exporters, therefore became susceptible to the argument put forward by the Free Conservative Party that they ought to concentrate on the domestic market instead and to take an interest in the prosperity of German industry and of the national economy as a whole. This argument amounted to a revival, in a new form, of the economic nationalism of Friedrich List including its protectionism, for without high tariffs grain from eastern Prussia could not meet foregin competition even in western areas of Germany. In fact, as shown above, the conservative parties, the chief political representatives of agrarian and especially *Junker* interests, swung far more violently towards protection than the National Liberals, the representatives of a variety of economic interests and of none.

This rapid evolution among the Conservatives was basic to Bismarck's scheme for switching for parliamentary support to that party and away from the National Liberals, and also for undermining the latter as a means to that end. In the long run he hoped to replace party interests and political ideologies by the common interest of agrarians and industrialists, as members of the ruling class, in a politically and socially conservative policy, an idea which came to full fruition only after Bismarck's dismissal in the 'Åra Stumm' (see Doc. 51). In the short run, Bismarck and the agrarian conservatives had a common political interest in destroying the liberals which was even stronger than their economic motives,[1] and the conservative gains in the 1878 elections at the expense of the liberals made it possible not merely to pass protectionist legislation but in so doing to put intolerable pressure on the already weakened and demoralized National Liberals. If the majority of the parliamentary party agreed to resist protection, the industrialist deputies and those who represented industrial constituencies would be likely to revolt. If they agreed to accept protective tariffs, the left wing and those who valued economic liberalism would be restless, to say the least. If they agreed to abstain, both wings might break away. This, in fact, is what happened. The majority of the party, by opting for neutrality on the issue of protection while protesting their loyalty to the government and to Bismarck in particular, got the worst of both worlds. The right wing voted for the tariffs, aligning themselves with agrarian protectionist interests; the left wing voted with the Progressives against the tariffs and in the following year seceded from the party (see also Doc. 57). The tariffs had, in fact, far more political and social than economic significance: they constituted a subvention from public funds for the large landowners of eastern Prussia, while exercising a retarding rather than a beneficial influence on German agriculture. 'In the period of the Great Depression the large landowners of Prussia redoubled their *political* efforts to be allowed to indulge in the luxury of *economic* apathy . . . at the expense of the German people and of foreign competitors.'[2]

The confusion into which Bismarck had succeeded in throwing the National Liberals becomes even more noteworthy when it is contrasted with the role played by the Centre Party in the tariff issue. While committed to protectionism, that party, having emerged unscathed from the *Kulturkampf* and with its secure electoral base in the Catholic population, could afford to bargain for its votes. The *quid pro quo* that the Centre leaders demanded, and got, from Bismarck was a provision in the law (the 'Franckenstein clause') that the revenues from the new tariffs could not be used to gain for the Empire increased financial independence from the federal states as well as from budgetary control by the *Reichstag*. Bismarck, as we have seen, valued the federal nature of the Empire only in so far as it was essential to maintain Prussian hegemony in Germany and his own supremacy in both Prussia and Germany: otherwise he used

---

[1] One recent researcher maintains, indeed, that there was no objective *economic* warrant for demanding tariffs at all: Karl W. Hardach, *Die Bedeutung wirtschaftlicher Faktoren bei der Wiedereinführung der Eisen-und Getreidezölle in Deutschland 1879*, Berlin, 1967.

[2] Hans Rosenberg, *Grosse Depression und Bismarckzeit*, Berlin, 1967, p. 186.

federalism and centralism as it suited him on specific occasions, and on the issue under discussion he wished to strengthen the central government against the several states. The Centre Party, however, had always stood for state particularism, had opposed *kleindeutsch* unification, and since 1866 had defended the federative principle and 'states' rights' as a means of checking Prussian hegemony in Germany. The party's success in holding out on the tariff issue, though not a famous victory, compares extremely well with the failure of the government of Baden to make any impression on Bismarck, to say nothing of the discomfiture of the National Liberals. The latter, indeed, continued to go from bad to worse. In the elections of 1881 they lost half of their remaining seats. (The *Reichstag*, in fact, presented the intriguing position that the parties whom Bismarck had at one time or another called 'enemies of the *Reich*' constituted a majority.) When in 1884 the secessionists of 1879 joined the Progressives—as was politically only logical—they were promptly rebuked by the electorate and in their turn lost half their seats; but most of them went, not to the National Liberals, but to the Conservatives who increased their seats by more than 50%, and on the other hand to the Social Democrats (SPD) who doubled theirs.

Although the absolute numbers involved in the latter phenomenon were still small, it was perhaps even more remarkable than the disarray of the liberal parties. The SPD displayed a resilience under the anti-socialist law of 1878 even greater than that of the Centre at the height of the *Kulturkampf*. Bismarck was not unduly perturbed at election results, since he cared nothing for political parties or the *Reichstag* itself in the first place and usually found ways of stultifying them. Nevertheless, the steadfastness of Centre and SPD voters should have given him pause. The SPD leaders, for their part, had also to overcome certain prejudices against participation in the political processes of Bismarckian Germany. The SPD as a political party dated only from 1875, when the two previously existing socialist groups agreed at Gotha to merge their differences, which had been considerable. Both of these groups, in turn, had originally been founded in 1863; one by Ferdinand Lassalle, which after his death in the following year was led by J. B. von Schweitzer; the other by Wilhelm Liebknecht, who in 1869 tightened up his rather loose organization and associated August Bebel with himself as joint leader. In the early years it was the Lassallean group that was more outspokenly socialist, despite Lassalle's advocacy of German unification by Prussia and his admiration of Bismarck, which extended to a willingness to collaborate with him in defeating the liberals, the common enemy. Lassalle's immediate aims were equal suffrage to give the workers a political voice and the reorganization of factories on co-

E

66   GERMANY IN THE AGE OF BISMARCK

operative lines to give them an economic stake (Doc. 40). After 1866
the Lassalleans, while becoming more emphatically socialist, also
became reconciled to the *fait accompli* of the North German Confederation as a national unit and to its *Reichstag* as a political platform.
It was for this acceptance of Bismarckian Germany that the
Liebknecht-Bebel group (the so-called 'Eisenach party'), unwilling
to put unity before freedom, condemned Schweitzer. Liebknecht and
Bebel, unlike Lassalle and Schweitzer not Prussians but Saxons,
'appealed in Saxony and the South to all democrats and Prussian-
haters,' and in their public speeches 'the economics of socialism took
second place to the politics of anti-Prussianism.'[3] It was therefore on
the issue of nationalism rather than on social and economic problems
that the Eisenach party were more radical in their opposition to the
status quo than the Lassalleans; and it was to help them to pass
muster as socialists at all that the Eisenach group affiliated themselves
with the Marxist First International rather than from any strong
Marxist convictions, and certainly with no desire to order their party
or its programme in accordance with the views of Marx or the pre-
scriptions of the International.

Nevertheless, the notion that the Eisenach party was Marxist, and
that its victory over the Lassalleans at Gotha in 1875 represented a
victory for Marxism over less radically socialist Lassallean principles, is not merely a myth. Whether they intended it or not, by their
contacts with the International the Eisenach leaders laid their group
and, later, the SPD as a whole open to greater exposure to Marxist
ideas than would otherwise have been the case. The international
solidarity of workers; the necessity of a class-conscious workers'
party; the impossibility of improvement in the workers' lot within
the capitalist system, and hence the need to overthrow the latter;
and the substructure of dialectical materialism and Marxist philosophy in general—these ideas gained easier access to the German
labour movement for its affiliation with the First International. But
'these doctrines were such as to encourage the socialist movement in
the line it was already taking, and they were in no way contradictory
to the main source of German socialism, which continued to be
Lassallean.'[4] Liebknecht and Bebel themselves were very far from being
simply Marxists. This fact can be illustrated, for example, by Bebel's
attitude toward religion. Brought up in the Evangelical Church, Bebel
became first indifferent and then actively hostile to institutionalized
Christianity. This change took place, however, in response to ex-

[3] Roger Morgan, *The German Social Democrats and the First International,
1864–1872*, Cambridge, 1965, p. 3.

[4] *Ibid.*, p. 234.

posure to the ideas of liberal freethinkers, not to those of Marx. Indeed, Bebel in his militantly atheistic phase ignored Marx's tactical advice that organized religion should be allowed to wither on the vine and not frontally attacked. Bebel understood Marx only as an economist, and to the Marxist economic analysis he added from the stock of freethinking ideas popular about 1870, especially from Darwinism, to produce his own rather simplistic version of inevitable evolution toward socialism.

But if the ideas of Marx in reality had only a limited impact on German socialism, the formal victory of the Eisenach party at Gotha and the SPD's adoption of much of the language of Marx and of the First International nevertheless served to arouse the susceptibilities of *bien-pensant* German society. Bismarck, in particular, was extremely anxious not only about the domestic aims but especially about the apparent international affiliations of German socialism which contributed to his *cauchemar des révolutions*. It was on these grounds, even apart from his tactical use of it against the Nationalist Liberals, that Bismarck pressed so hard for the anti-socialist bill in 1878. This law prohibited all 'social-democratic, socialist, or communist' associations, assemblies, and publications, and imposed other disabilities on the labour movement. One measure on which the political police particularly and successfully continued to insist, despite meagre results, was the right to evict socialists from their home areas. The police, who in this respect formulated government policy, argued that by this means the party would be deprived of its leaders and run short of money. The opposite argument, that socialists evicted from one area would agitate no less in the area to which they went, with the result of spreading socialist propaganda to places where it had not reached before, went unheeded despite its evident basis in fact. It was this power to evict, however, that caused the whole law to lapse in 1890. Meanwhile, in any case, despite all the disabilities imposed on it and all the pressure that the state could bring to bear, the SPD not only continued to get deputies elected to the *Reichstag* (who were then covered by parliamentary immunity) but even succeeded in increasing its votes at every election save one throughout the eleven years that the law was in force. Its parliamentary leaders, given unaccustomed power within the party by their immunity, managed to keep the more radical forces at bay and to insist that the party must prove its respectability by obeying the law. Adoption of these tactics did not mean, of course, that the rank-and-file all accepted the desirability of integration into a society that despised and rejected them; nor did it mean that the leadership did not have to engage in frequent agonizing reappraisals of their position. A particularly difficult problem was posed for them by Bismarck's

68 GERMANY IN THE AGE OF BISMARCK

campaign of 'state socialism'[5] whose practical benefits some of them were inclined to accept regardless of its source and of its purpose, which Bismarck quite openly avowed was to deprive the socialists of a *raison d'être.*

Bismarck's fear of socialism was also a principal motive behind one of the fundamental changes (perhaps the most fundamental of all) that took place in German society during the last decade of his chancellorship, the so-called 'feudalization of the bourgeoisie'. This phenomenon constituted a remarkable essay in halting one of the great secular tendencies of European history since the French Revolution, the gradual eclipse of the nobility by the middle class, and should give pause to any devotee of historical inevitability. Here is one case, at any rate, where determinism yielded to determination, where the seemingly inexorable course of 'progressive' social change was reversed by the actions of a resolute statesman. In this campaign, 'reactionary' in the truest sense of the word, Bismarck's chosen agent was Robert von Puttkamer, an orthodox conservative who was appointed Prussian minister of the interior in 1881, as much for his religious as for his political views: significantly, his previous post had been the ministry of public worship in which he had succeeded Falk in 1879 when Bismarck decided to soft-pedal the *Kulturkampf.*

Puttkamer's mandate from Bismarck was to complement, in the social and administrative fields, the dissolution of the liberal bourgeoisie that the chancellor himself was achieving in the political arena. Bismarck's premise was that the liberal bourgeoisie, and therefore the traditionally liberal and bourgeois Prussian civil service, were (to adapt a more recent phrase) 'soft on socialism'—not, of course, because they were vulnerable to socialist doctrines, but because they were intellectually obliged to tolerate socialism. In the era of the anti-socialist law, when socialism was by definition not to be tolerated, Bismarck believed that the traditional civil service was not to be relied upon to carry out the government's policies, particularly at a time when new economic and social problems of every kind were crowding in. If it was to retain its full measure of power, the Prussian monarchical power-state had to reconstitute the civil service and, not least, to give it a new intellectual basis and orientation. Liberalism was to be replaced by traditional Christianity and the Church. As William I said: 'The people must have their religion preserved for them'; but this religion was conceived in purely formal and external terms, and the Church as a mere instrument of the state in its battle against liberal idealism, deprived of all autonomy.

Intellectual re-fashioning was accompanied by social: the cam-

[5] See pp. 70–71.

paign was predicated not only on the waning of the *Kulturkampf* but also on Bismarck's winning the Conservatives over to support of the government. The nobility, who since the beginning of the century had seen control of the administrative machinery of the state fall more and more into the hands of an increasingly bourgeois and liberal central civil service, at least regained much of their lost ground. This victory did not take the straightforward form of civil service appointments being given wholesale to members of the nobility, who were in any event not numerous enough. Instead they were given, by a process of rigorous screening, to members of the middle class who were willing to adopt, or at least to serve, the social and intellectual values of the nobility. Moreover, the nobility themselves were rapidly increasing the rate of their infiltration into urban society and industrial economy. The picture, then, is one of the nobility inserting itself at the top of bourgeois society and setting its standards, 'feudalizing' it.

An interesting aspect of this general process, and of the particular process of screening for the civil service, was the role of the army. The relationship of the standing army with the reserves had been a crucial political as well as military problem in Prussia during the first half of the century, and the government's proposals for a drastic cut in the reserves had been one of the sources of the constitutional conflict of the 1860s. Just as the reserve army (*Landwehr*) had been regarded by the liberals as a bulwark against 'militarism', conversely the government viewed the 'citizen in uniform', especially in the uniform of a reserve officer, with deep suspicion as a threat to military discipline. Under the Puttkamer dispensation of the 1880s the process begun twenty years earlier was completed: the reserve officer now represented the infiltration of military discipline and monarchical loyalism into the bourgeoisie. The highest places in the civil service were usually given to reserve officers, vouched for, in turn, by the officer corps of the regular army. To achieve this end the personnel division of the army was removed in 1883 from the ministry of war, and hence from budgetary control and inspection by inquisitive members of the Diet, and incorporated instead into the king's 'military cabinet' which was responsible to nobody else. One by-product of this transfer was that *all* officers were in effect deprived of the protection of the constitution and were linked to the king by a special loyalty reminiscent of that of vassal to overlord: it was a 'feudalization' in the military field parallelling that in the civilian, and like it devized with social and ultimately political purposes in mind. The entire Bismarck-Puttkamer policy represented, one might say, the withdrawal of the Prussian nobility and their rapidly increasing allies into their richly stocked baronial castles, leaving stubborn bourgeois liberals, democrats, and socialists, and of course the proletariat itself, helpless and without resources on the wrong side of the drawbridge.

The image must not be pressed too hard, of course. Bismarck retained his interest and control over the whole country, and he and many others in Germany, both in and out of office, were concerned to counter the threat of socialism not merely by repression but by constructive measures of one kind or another, that is to say, to grapple with the 'social problem' which was recognized as an inevitable companion of rapid industrialization compounded by depression (Doc. 48). Some of the worst symptoms of the problem included the suddenly sharpened contrasts and antagonisms between capitalists and workers, the widening gap between rich and poor, the dissolution of the home, family, and guild ties of manual workers, and the pressure of big business on small entrepreneurs and artisans, many of whom were forced to become wage-earners and felt themselves being depressed into a 'proletariat'. Bismarck himself, as usual, took an entirely tactical and pragmatic view of the situation. He had no strong convictions of his own on social problems any more than on tariff problems. His memoirs, for example, not only otherwise very detailed but also skilfully written to put himself in the best possible light, contain nothing on the subject of social legislation. In so far as he had any *personal* views on these matters, they were determined by general considerations of Christian ethics on one side and by his experience as a landowner and timber-producer on the other. But mainly he was guided by his political intuition, which told him in a general way that 'revolutionary socialism' could be combated not only by way of repression and suppression but also by way of a rival system of 'state socialism' which would supply in a new paternalistic form the security that the workers might otherwise be tempted to reach out for on their own. It can be plausibly argued that here, as in the case of the *Kulturkampf*, Bismarck's political intuition misled him. His attempt to reconcile the workers to the Hohenzollern monarchy by means of social and economic paternalism failed precisely because the problem of integrating the workers was more political and psychological than economic and social. (For example, the rise in real wages in the deflationary economy of the 1880s made no psychological impact on the workers.) After 1870 and especially after 1878, both wings of the working-class movement by and large rejected the state created and run by Bismarck because it rejected them, because it offered no hope of democracy or political freedom, and because it excluded the Germans of Austria. It is true that some of them were tempted in the 1880s to accept 'state socialism' at Bismarck's hands, just as some of them had been tempted between 1866 and 1870 to accept German unification at his hands. But on both occasions they did not prevail within the movement and were soon disillusioned themselves.

The fact that Bismarck's 'state socialism' ultimately failed in its political purpose should not, however, detract from its intrinsic merits. The system of social security that Bismarck built in the 1880s, including accident, medical, invalid, and old-age insurance and limited factory inspection, was the first of its kind in Europe. On the details of the system Bismarck was amenable to advice, just because he held no strong views of his own; but he would not accept suggestions which tended to damage employers economically or to turn social reform into an end in itself and to elevate it above the preservation of the existing structure of society and power. For example, he refused to countenance a complete system of factory inspection on the ground that it would interfere with the employers' right to be 'masters in their own house' and would lower their social standing. Bismarck's favourite advisers, in fact, were drawn, not unnaturally, from the ranks of the conservatives, whose paternalism was evolving a 'social' wing. Typical of this group was Hermann Wagener, who saw that for better or for worse the pre-industrial structure of society was irrevocably destroyed and proposed to replace it by a new class structure responsive to the will of the state. He combined such semi-corporatist ideas with far-reaching proposals for social reform and state intervention in the economy which he had pressed on Bismarck ever since 1862. He was one of the few conservatives to oppose the anti-socialist law of 1878, and considered Bismarck's social legislation in the 1880s to be too little and too late (Doc. 44). Yet, at bottom, what bound Wagener to Bismarck was more important than what separated them: an active, aggressive conservatism in place of the traditional passive type represented by such a figure as Ludwig von Gerlach; above all, a willingness to consider unorthodox methods to attain conservative ends—in other words, *Realpolitik*—instead of the ethically and ideologically circumscribed world of Gerlach.

The affinity between Wagener and Bismarck, despite their differences, becomes clearer when their views on the social problem are compared with those of two other groups: the liberals and the Christian socialists. Among the latter, Catholics were far more prominent than Protestants, the tradition of social consciousness having always been weaker in the Lutheran Churches in Germany. The development of this tradition among Catholics owed a great deal to the bishop of Mainz, Wilhelm Ketteler, the 'social bishop' as he was called, who exercised an influence out of all proportion to his station. Starting out from his conviction that the care of souls must include the care of the bodies which they inhabited, he set out to 'sharpen the social conscience of German Catholics' on such problems as unemployment, disability, and the consequences of what he admitted to be the 'iron law' of wages which frequently kept the workers below subsistence level and turned them into 'slaves' of the prevailing price of labour, like a piece of goods. Particularly striking was Ketteler's recognition of the psychological as well as the social and economic dimension of the problem: the 'proletarization' of larger and larger groups of workers as well as of small artisans deprived of their living and their independence by the machine. To remedy these various ills, Ketteler demanded institutions for the disabled, better education for workers to raise their moral standards, the strengthening of unions and cooperatives, factory legislation, and (perhaps self-contradictorily) higher wages (Doc. 43). He had a great influence in bolstering the left wing of the Centre Pary and causing the party to adopt a policy of social reform in principle (while mistrusting it in Bismarck's hands). Such leaders of Christian trade unions as Georg von Hertling (later prime minister of Bavaria and, briefly, German chancellor) and Franz Hitze owed much of their initial inspiration to Ketteler.

By contrast, the Protestant Church, to the extent that it took any interest in social questions at all, remained for the most part committed to the philanthropic approach to their solution. Certainly there was nobody of Ketteler's stature to take up the cause. There was one Lutheran minister, Rudolf Todt, who took a prominent initiative in declaring socialism, as such, to be compatible with Christian teachings, and demanding that it should be introduced by reform, through the agency of the state, instead of by revolution and class war. Whether in doing so Todt departed from Lutheran theology, taking on both Catholic and Calvinist ideas of social obligation, is less important than his failure to make any direct impact on politics at all, confining himself instead to founding a society for theoretical discussion of social problems. An attempt, at least, to transform Todt's initiative into a political one was made by the curious figure of Adolf Stoecker, a man of humble origins himself who had attained to the appointment of court chaplain to the Hohenzollern and had the royal family's financial backing in trying, in 1878, to found a Christian-Socialist party. Stoecker, like Todt, was convinced that charity was an insufficient sop to the worker who had a right to a decent living, and that for the Church to take an initiative in giving it to him was also the only way to wean him away from the SPD, the Antichrist, and win him back for the Church and, incidentally, for the monarchy too (Doc. 47). But this kind of scheme was too clever by half; the German worker, imbued with socialist ideology, would not accept the leadership of a preacher, least of all of a court chaplain whose stock-in-trade was throne-and-altar demagogy. Stoecker thereupon abandoned the workers and turned to the petty bourgeoisie in whom he found a more sympathetic audience, especially for the anti-semitism which he now dispensed in the belief that the Jews were responsible for propagating the rationalistic and scientific materialism to whose prevalence he attributed his failure. When William II, with whom as crown prince he had been friendly, ascended the throne, Stoecker believed that his hour had struck at last and founded a Christian-Social Congress, designed to embrace all shades of Protestant opinion, to discuss social questions; but, like so many others, he was soon disappointed in the unstable young monarch.

Stoecker's Christian-Social Congress was consciously modelled on the *Verein für Sozialpolitik*[6] founded almost twenty years earlier by a group of economists who became known as Academic Socialists. Among their more remarkable features is the fact that they were almost all liberals, mostly National Liberals, set apart by their Tory paternalist leanings from the majority of German liberals who even when they abandoned free trade (Docs. 41, 46) remained committed to the principles of the Manchester School in domestic economic questions. The orthodox National Liberals' definition of 'industrial freedom' which the *Reichstag* of the North German Confederation adopted in 1868-69 characteristically did not include the right to strike, which they had advocated as late as 1866. In a way, their switch on this issue was as indicative of their new posture as their acceptance of Bismarck's indemnity bill.

It was precisely the conversion of the political parties, including the National Liberals, into interest groups that the Academic Socialists (the name, as so often, was originally a term of abuse which stuck) wished to combat. In so doing they played into the hands of Bismarck who, as we have seen, encouraged the parties in this direction in order to neutralize the *Reichstag* altogether. The Academic Socialists' concern for the strength of the national economy as a whole had, of course, clear political implications: preservation of the political *status quo,* support for strong authoritarian government with increased economic functions, a view of the monarchy as above parties and above politics, and a view of the state as the organ of the 'moral solidarity' of the nation. They were historically-minded scholars, prepared to break away from the hold that the Natural-Law, *laissez-faire* doctrines of Adam Smith had exerted on German economics— but prepared also to break out of the world of scholarship into that

[6] This term it is impossible to translate adequately. Perhaps the sense is rendered best by 'League for Social Reform.' See also James J. Sheehan, *The Career of Lujo Brentano: a Study of Liberalism and Social Reform in Imperial Germany*, Chicago and London, 1966, esp. p. 46.

of social propaganda. This they attempted mainly through the *Verein für Sozialpolitik,* dedicated principally to working for social reform and combating Manchester liberalism. The keynote was struck by the man who became the leading spirit in the *Verein,* the distinguished economic and administrative historian Gustav Schmoller (Doc. 45). At a preparatory meeting Schmoller said: 'What we seek here is a basis for the reform of our social conditions and a general agreement for ideas which have been frequently expressed, but which have still not found acceptance by the public'.[7] Schmoller and his fellow-organizers deliberately cast their net wide in order to attract anyone interested in the cause of social reform. The result, predictably, was disagreement within the association on economic theory and still more on its application. Schmoller was cast in the role of leader not only, no doubt, because of personal qualities but also because he occupied a moderating position between the extremes. One of these extremes was represented by Lujo Brentano, who fundamentally clung to the classical economic liberalism in which he had been trained, seeking a synthesis between it and cooperative unionism such as he believed was being worked out in England. He differed from Schmoller and the central current within the *Verein* in placing little emphasis upon historical method and in regarding social tensions as healthy and necessary, rather than wishing them to be reconciled through the agency of the state. At the other extreme stood Adolf Wagner, whose devotion to the cause of state intervention and to Bismarck in particular was so great that Brentano regarded him with more suspicion and hostility than he had for the Manchester liberals. What held such disparate elements together in the same organization at all was their agreement that solutions to new social and economic problems must be found within the framework of the existing social order. More fundamentally still, what united them was what might be called counter-revolutionary nationalism. Glaringly obvious in Wagner, this idea was also clear in Schmoller's combination of economic nationalism and social and political conservatism. Even Brentano had not only, like so many liberals, become reconciled to the unification of Germany by Prussia and (although he was a Catholic as well as a liberal) to the exclusion of Austria, but he was always responsive to appeals to patriotism. (This streak became clearest in the years just preceding the first World War.)

It would be wrong to identify the strength of this sort of appeal, even for liberal professors, with Germany alone. 'Integral nationalism' was characteristic of most western states after 1871. Nevertheless, it would be equally wrong to ignore the extent to which, for intelligible

[7] Quoted by Sheehan, *Brentano*, p. 71.

historical reasons, nationalism tended to transcend and to complicate other issues in German public life. Just as nationalism united the members of the *Verein für Sozialpolitik,* nationalism separated the Lassalleans from the Eisenach party among the socialists. It is no wonder, then, that in the field where nationalism can be said to have its proper place, that of foreign affairs, the growth of an articulate public opinion which at the same time was amenable to discreet guidance by an official and semi-official press was a greater boon to Bismarck, perhaps, than to any other contemporary statesman.

7

Aspects of Bismarck's
foreign policy, 1871-1888*

THE pervasiveness of the issue of nationalism and the responsiveness
of German public opinion to appeals to patriotism were of inestimable
value to Bismarck not only in his constant manipulation of the
precarious European balance of power but also in the equally inexhaustible changes that he rang in the domestic constellation of
forces. It is a mistake to attribute more than convenience of treatment
to any separation between Bismarck's domestic and foreign policy.
In fact, although he himself felt perhaps more at home in foreign
affairs, there is reason to cast doubt on that 'primacy of foreign policy'
which generations of historians have attributed to him. At the very
least, domestic and foreign policy exerted reciprocal influence;
usually both were conceived together as essential elements in a total
posture designed to maintain the inviolability of the monarchy in
Prussia, the hegemony of Prussia in Germany, and the control of
Germany over the diplomatic alignments of Europe, with Bismarck
himself as the dominant influence and authority throughout. In constitutional terms, his accumulation of the offices of imperial chancellor
and prime minister and foreign minister of Prussia usefully symbolized
this interconnection of his interests.

It found expression from the very beginning of the existence of the
German Empire, and because of its creation. Bismarck was quite
patently sincere when he described Germany in 1871 as a satiated
power, and he was determined to chart a correspondingly cautious
course in foreign affairs which would preserve a *status quo* that was so

*It would be tedious as well as unnecessary to recite here the full catalogue
of diplomatic moves and counter-moves in which Bismarck participated in the
period under discussion, involving as it would still another survey of the entire
international scene from the points of view of all the governments concerned
that would not differ significantly from the many that are already available.
This chapter is therefore confined to an analysis of Bismarck's policy with only
as much narration as will (I hope) serve to support the analysis.

favourable to Germany.[1] But by the same token the other powers of continental Europe could not fail to react to the massive change in the balance of power represented by the existence of a formidable new entity in their midst. The hostility of France after the annexation of Alsace-Lorraine was regarded by Bismarck, for the time being at least, as unavoidable. His atttention was therefore concentrated mainly on the two other great continental powers, Russia and Austria-Hungary. Both of these states possessed a potentially powerful weapon against Germany which pertained to the position of Poland. Russia could exert military pressure on the indefensible eastern frontier of Germany with 'Congress Poland'; Austria could cultivate 'Galician Polonism', that is to say the nationalism of her Polish population, with a view to creating an irredentist problem in Prussian Poland (although this, of course, might prove to be a dangerously double-edged sword for the multi-national Habsburg empire). Most menacing of all, Russia and Austria-Hungary might combine on the Polish question against Germany, who would then be completely isolated.

Bismarck's response to this possible threat was two-pronged. On the domestic front he launched what became known as the *Kulturkampf*, directed in the first place, as we have seen, against Polish nationalism and the Centre Party as its potential ally. In this way Bismarck hoped, among other things, to reduce the dimensions of Polonism within Germany's borders as a target for foreign agitation. In the diplomatic field he tried first to keep both Russia and Austria-Hungary as allies by means of the Three Emperors' League of 1873, and then, when this threatened to break apart, to ensure that at least one of the eastern powers would be friendly toward Germany by offering Russia, in 1875, a division of Europe into two spheres of influence. The danger which he was attempting to parry was, however, of Bismarck's own creation, for it was he who had raised a war scare by allowing German diplomats to make equivocal statements, and the inspired press pretty unequivocal ones, about the desirability of a preventive war against France in view of repeated increases in the French military establishment (Doc. 54). It was this attempt to intimidate France that gave the French government a basis for appealing to others, and it was Russia's response to this appeal that, in turn, caused Bismarck to try to buy Russia off. But he was not as successful in obtaining Russia's good will as he had been, right at

---

[1] There is some ground for holding that this caution was also a result of the pressure of domestic considerations in still another respect: that a period of potential social crisis induced by the depression was in Bismarck's opinion no time for risky foreign adventures. See Hans Rosenberg, *Grosse Depression und Bismarckzeit*, chapter 7, especially the quotations from Bismarck on pp. 262-5.

the beginning of his period of office, in the Polish crisis of 1863: the tsar announced that he was going to Berlin, the clear suggestion being that he intended to persuade William I to abandon his bellicose line. At the same time the German spheres-of-influence offer was by implication turned down, a day before the tsar's arrival in Berlin, by the publication in a semi-official Russian newspaper of an article declaring that the maintenance of peace was not, so far as the Russian government was concerned, a matter for bargaining, an article which was greeted with satisfaction in Paris. At this point 'Bismarck found it expedient to protest that Germany's intentions were entirely peaceful and that the crisis was an imaginary one; but there were many who agreed with Disraeli's foreign secretary, Lord Derby, who said tartly: "It is really imposing on our supposed credulity to tell us now that our ears have deceived us and that nothing was said or meant against France".'[2]

This quotation serves to remind us that Britain was also, as always, vitally interested in the continental balance of power and entered very much into Bismarck's calculations. In fact, the Europe in which Bismarck saw himself as manoeuvring was a Europe of five powers that counted. Taking French hostility for granted, he posited two primordial necessities for Germany: to avoid a simultaneous war on two fronts, against one of the eastern powers as well as against France, which dictated that one at least of the eastern powers must be Germany's ally, in which case the other would not dare to attack her; but secondly, if only one of the eastern powers could be aligned with Germany, then Britain must at all costs be friendly. In a constellation of five, Germany must always be one of at least three. It was because of this analysis of the situation that Bismarck was so much alarmed when Britain as well as Russia, in fact, intervened on France's behalf in 1875. He had on this occasion escaped with nothing worse than loss of face; but the lesson was clear that further provocative actions on his part might easily set in motion against Germany the balance-of-power mechanism that had traditionally operated in Europe against any power that threatened to become dominant.

That this reaction had not been elicited already by the very fact of German unification itself perhaps followed from the introduction of irrational factors into European politics and society which reduced the role of such straightforward conceptions of foreign policy as counterbalancing and compensation. (It is only in the computer age that such ideas have regained ground.) It was the strength as well as the weakness of Bismarck as a diplomat that he still thought mainly

[2] Gordon A. Craig, *Europe since 1815*, New York, 1961, p. 271. Chapter 11 of this book provides an admirable introduction to the general diplomatic history of the period.

in terms of old-fashioned 'cabinet diplomacy'. It was his strength to the extent that he consciously (though not always successfully) strove to exclude from his plans and actions all considerations that would tend to distract him from the central purpose of safeguarding Germany's security and integrity in her geographically vulnerable position in the middle of Europe; and the importance of this adherence to the strict and sober calculations of *raison d'état* becomes clear when Bismarck's statesmanship is contrasted with that of some of his successors. On the other hand, Bismarck's rationalism was his weakness because he tended to believe, either that his contemporaries and potential adversaries exercised the same sovereign control over popular movements and were as inaccessible to ideological promptings as he was, or that they ought to be so. At the same time he would sometimes try to manipulate ideological factors in Germany's favour. (Thus, notoriously, he was always happier when governments of the Left were in power in France because he thought the autocratic eastern empires would be less likely to enter into alliances with her.) But, though he could resist the pan-German blandishments of those on both sides of the Austro-German border (most prominently, on the Austrian side, Georg von Schönerer) who advocated Austrian union with Germany, he probably had only an imperfect appreciation, for example, of the force and nature of pan-Slavism.

It is true that he was aware of changes taking place in Russia; it was not for nothing that his period 'on ice' as ambassador in St Petersburg had coincided with Alexander II's emancipation of the Russian peasants. He noticed, moreover, that this had been an act of weakness; he noticed, also, that the peasants were disappointed, and that revolutionary tendencies as well as widespread corruption might further undermine the stability of the tsarist régime; but he continued to regard the peasantry as basically healthy and as the mainstay of that régime, and he had confidence in the skill of Russia's statesmen as adequate to overcome the forces making for instability. Nevertheless he did not discount the possibility of revolution, and his attitude toward Russia, therefore, was as undogmatic as any other aspect of his foreign policy. Bismarck himself referred to this flexible, patient policy as one which allowed him to keep his options open. An ill-intentioned critic might say, instead, that it was a policy of stopgaps, of living from hand to mouth. Whichever of these is true—probably it was a mixture of both—it is hard to deny that over the years Bismarck was driven to employing ever more resourceful methods (or desperate expedients) in order to keep all the five balls with which he was juggling in the air at the same time. And it is also hard to deny—to revert to the subject of Bismarck's rationalism—that it was a pretty simplistic mistake to conceive of the five powers that he defined as great as more or less equally great without making, most of the time at any rate, further qualitative distinctions among them. He was clear enough that Italy was not a great power; but he was a good deal less clear that Austria-Hungary was significantly weaker than the other four great powers.

Both his rather sanguine estimate of the strength of the Habsburg empire and his defective appreciation of the impact of pan-Slavism were in evidence in Bismarck's handling of the tension between Germany's partners in the Three Emperors' League, which continued to mount after the war scare of 1875. The immediate cause of the crisis was the series of risings throughout the Balkan areas of the Ottoman Empire suppressed with notorious brutality by the Turkish government. It was highly significant, and not only of the changing scene within Russia, that the Russian government, which had based its previous attitude toward the subject populations of the 'sick man of Europe' on a policy of safeguarding the interests of the Orthodox Church, now took its stand predominantly on the ground of pan-Slavism. Nevertheless it sought general European diplomatic support for measures to protect the subjects of the sultan from further atrocities. Bismarck, still intent upon preserving the friendship of both eastern empires and therefore upon maintaining a passive attitude in eastern Europe, declined to commit himself; Austria-Hungary, however, concluded the Convention of Reichstadt (1876) with Russia which provided for the division of European Turkey into spheres of influence between them and for the continued independence of Serbia and Montenegro. But Serbia, which had declared war on Turkey over the atrocities, suffered such crushing defeats in the field that Russia recognized the necessity for active military intervention on her behalf which was likely to arouse Austrian susceptibilities and thereby negate the agreement just reached. The Russian government therefore once more asked for German support in the event of an armed clash with Austria-Hungary in the Balkans, reminding Bismarck of Russia's benevolence during the Franco-Prussian war. Bismarck, however, without interests of his own in the Balkans, and faced once again with the unpleasant prospect of having to make a choice between Russia and Austria-Hungary, devoted himself instead to preventing a confrontation between them. He evaded the Russian request and made speeches at home in praise of neutrality, about the necessity of safeguarding the integrity of Austria-Hungary, and about his willingness to support Russia in Turkey but not to give her a general 'blank cheque' (an interesting phrase, having regard to the events of July 1914). He was beginning to regard the relationship between Germany and Russia as problematic and to look with favour upon closer collaboration with Austria-Hungary while maintaining the 'wire to St Petersburg'.

Meanwhile, on the battlefield, Russia forced Turkey to the Treaty of San Stefano (1878) which imposed considerable territorial losses on her and created an autonomous Bulgaria under Russian protection. These provisions gave Russia a sphere of influence greater than that agreed at Reichstadt, and accordingly Austria-Hungary called for a European congress to settle the affairs of south-eastern Europe. The British government was also roused to intervene by sending the fleet to the Sea of Marmora, much to the satisfaction of a public opinion among which the term 'jingoism' was coined at this time. Russia, unwilling to risk active British hostility, grudgingly accepted the proposal for a congress, doing what it could to save face by refusing to meet in Vienna, as the Austrian government had suggested. Thus it came about that the congress met in Berlin, giving Bismarck, as host, the opportunity to act as the 'honest broker' who arranged that Britain, Russia, and Austria-Hungary all went away satisfied—and that Germany, therefore, would still be able to avoid choosing between the last two while at the same time acquiring British goodwill by declining to charge a 'commission' for his services, as Disraeli and Salisbury had feared he would. The British ministers were now inclined to accept Bismarck's assurances that Germany was a 'satiated power'.

It was Russia, understandably enough, that was the least contented of the parties to the Congress of Berlin. Though still retaining enough of her acquisitions to repair the losses of the Crimean War, Russia had had to disgorge much of what she had gained at San Stefano and tended to reproach Bismarck for it. Alexander II, in fact, did so explicitly in a letter to William I which, temporarily at least, had the desired effect of making William extremely reluctant to agree to an alliance between Germany and Austria-Hungary that Bismarck had begun actively to consider. The chancellor was now prepared to make the choice between the two eastern empires; and, if his emperor was affected by the appeal to his dynasty's established friendship with the Romanovs, Bismarck's own option was perhaps not dictated purely by considerations of *Realpolitik* either. In addition to fearing the possibility of an alliance between Britain, France, and Austria-Hungary if the latter were not given sufficient security elsewhere, he found it emotionally difficult to come to terms with a government influenced by such a movement as pan-Slavism and placed more confidence in Vienna. On such a basis the famous Dual Alliance (1879) between Germany and Austria-Hungary was concluded.

'Because of his emperor's strong predilection for Russia, Bismarck

F

hoped to make this a general treaty, calling for mutual assistance if either partner were attacked by a third power. The Austro-Hungarian foreign minister, Count Andrassy, felt that this might be interpreted as anti-French and, his own relations with Paris being good, insisted that the new treaty mention Russia explicitly. It is a measure of Bismarck's feeling of insecurity that he gave way, agreeing to a treaty which called for mutual assistance if either signatory were attacked by Russia and for benevolent neutrality if either were attacked by another power. The completed treaty (which Bismarck persuaded his sovereign to ratify only by threatening to resign if he refused to do so) was a landmark in European history. While previous treaties had usually been concluded during or on the eve of wars, or for specific purposes and restricted duration, this was a peacetime treaty and, as is turned out, a permanent one, for it did not lapse until 1918. It was, moreover, the first of the secret treaties, whose contents were never fully known but always suspected and which encouraged other powers to negotiate similar treaties in self-defense, until all Europe was divided into league and counterleague.'[3]

So far as Bismarck was concerned, the long-range worry extended only to the possibility that Austria-Hungary would construe the alliance as encouraging aggression on her part in the Balkans. His more immediate worry, in any event, concerned the reactions of Great Britain and Russia even to the public parts of the treaty. He inquired in London what reaction he could expect if, because of his friendly relations with Britain and Austria-Hungary, Germany became involved in difficulties with Russia in the Near East. Disraeli replied that in that event he would ensure the neutrality of France and Italy. Bismarck noted: 'Is that all?' A few hours later the Russian ambassador appeared to suggest a renewal of the Three Emperors' League. Bismarck thereupon dropped his initiative in London and made no reply when Salisbury later offered to join the Dual Alliance. He did not want to become too dependent on Great Britain in case of a clash with Russia and thought it wise to play hard-to-get. He was also afraid of a return to power by Gladstone, whose Christian principles, he thought, would not allow him to support Turkey against Russia and whose liberalism would render him an unsympathetic and therefore unreliable ally.

It was more than a year before the renewal of the Three Emperors' League suggested by Russia could be completed, such were the mutual suspicions between that country and the Habsburg empire. The renewed treaty obliged all three powers to take a position of benevolent neutrality if any of them were involved in a war (whether

[3] Craig, *Europe since 1815*, p. 277.

offensive or defensive) with a fourth power other than Turkey. A secret treaty, also containing complicated provisions concerning the Turkish Straits, it ran for three years and was renewed in 1884. Its value, however, was always doubtful owing to the persistent Austro-Russian antagonism and the growth of pan-Slavism, and it could not be renewed again in 1887. Meanwhile, different trouble spots had appeared in other parts of the Ottoman Empire. Tunisia and Egypt, still nominally ruled from Constantinople, were bankrupt and were in fact completely dominated by the countries whose money kept them going, France and Great Britain respectively. These two states had agreed to ratify the *fait accompli* by treating the two areas as parts of their respective spheres of influence. Bismarck's interest in the matter was indirect. Although he was not happy to see Britain and France enter into any kind of accord, he hoped nevertheless that colonial enterprises would at least take the attention of the French government away from ideas of *revanche* in Alsace-Lorraine, and might even embroil her in difficulties. He therefore encouraged the Anglo-French *démarche*. France sent troops to Tunisia and declared the country a protectorate in 1881; Britain, in spite or because of Gladstone's Christian scruples, did likewise in Egypt in the following year.

But even if Berlin acquiesced in these procedures, Rome did not. In Italy, Tunisia was regarded as an Italian 'sphere of influence', partly because ten thousand Italians had settled in Tunisia and partly because of that country's strategic location across the water from Sicily. The Italian government therefore turned to Germany and Austria-Hungary for help and obtained the Triple Alliance (1882), which guaranteed German and Austrian support for Italy against an unprovoked French attack and provided for benevolent neutrality by the other two if the third were involved in a war with any one other European power and for active support if with more than one, always excepting Great Britain against whose Mediterranean fleet, it was recognized, Italy could not be defended. Bismarck's motives in entering into this complicated agreement, which was highly unlikely to prove of any military benefit to Germany, were again of an indirect nature. He hoped, as Italy's alliance partner, to be in a position to prevent that country from disturbing the precarious peace of Europe by making any moves against either France, which had seized Nice and Savoy during the war for Italian unification, or Austria-Hungary, in pursuance of irredentist claims in the Tyrol. It does seem, in retrospect at least, that Bismarck was giving a lot of diplomatic hostages to fortune.

The Anglo-French agreement on Egypt and Tunisia, followed by the actual dispatch of troops to those areas, was the signal for the beginning of a new phase of European imperialism overseas. With the shrinkage of territories still available for colonization, the imperial powers found themselves in growing danger of serious collisions. Great Britain, in particular, as the power with the widest range of interests overseas, was beset by problems of this kind: in Egypt, the Sudan troubles of General Gordon and French interference, at international conferences, in British administration of the country's finances; on the frontiers of India, Russia's infiltration into Afghanistan. The obstructiveness of the French, during the premiership of the colonial-minded Jules Ferry (1880–81, 1883–85), had been actively encouraged and supported by Bismarck; but the latter was prepared to exploit even those crises that he had not connived at creating. Although not interested in colonies *per se*, Bismarck at this point inserted Germany into the 'scramble for Africa'. On the basis of the venturesomeness of private German citizens (in one case arriving on the scene only five days before British agents), the government proclaimed and secured international recognition of protectorates in Togoland and the Cameroons in the west, Tanganyika in the east, and what became known as German South-West Africa. Bismarck was induced to enter this field of activity for a variety of reasons, of which promotion of the activities of German traders was the weakest; certainly he expected no direct financial gain for the government. There were diplomatic aspects: by opposing a British monopoly of Africa south of the Sahara (expressed also in German support for Belgium in the Congo) Bismarck hoped to cement his friendship with France. But this tension with Great Britain also played a role in the domestic German considerations which were paramount with Bismarck: it was designed to frustrate the putative Anglophilia of the crown prince. William I, who despite occasional difficulties had for a generation sheltered Bismarck under the mantle of his increasingly legendary authority, had been born in 1796, and the chancellor expected a less easy ride after the change of rulers that seemed imminent from day to day. The crown prince Frederick William and his English wife, the eldest daughter of Queen Victoria, were suspected of harbouring designs to abandon the 'sham constitutionalism' of the Bismarckian system by converting the *Reichstag* into a proper working parliament to which ministers would be responsible. The colonial issue was calculated to serve as a bone of contention between Germany and Britain that would make it more difficult to introduce such an 'English' political system. But German colonial enterprise could contribute to the same end in another way too: by strengthening the right-wing parties, always the most susceptible to nationalistic appeals, Bismarck hoped to confront the crown prince with a hostile *Reichstag*.

This analysis is confirmed, rather than denied, by the fact that, the issue having been created, Bismarck abandoned the colonial scene as soon as Ferry was overthrown. He would even have given away the rather unattractive territories that Germany had acquired but for his domestic calculations and considerations of prestige. Meanwhile William I still lived on, and Bismarck had other aspects of European international affairs to deal with. The dismissal of Ferry was a double blow for him: not only could colonies no longer be counted on to distract the attention of Paris, but Ferry's successor Freycinet[4] had had wished upon him, by Georges Clemenceau and the Radicals who put him in office, the bellicose and violently anti-German General Georges Boulanger as minister of war. More than at any time since 1871, Bismarck now had to fear a war in the west. A still greater danger loomed as a consequence of the estrangement between Russia and Austria-Hungary, and this was the possibility of an alliance between Russia and France and therefore of an attack on Germany on both flanks at a time when Great Britain was unfriendly. Once more, Bismarck drew upon his seemingly inexhaustible fund of ingenuity and devised a series of counter-measures. He took steps to strengthen the Germany army;[5] he did what he could to soothe the French; most important, he gladly accepted the Russian proposal for a new bilateral agreement when it proved impossible to renew the Three Emperors' League in 1887. The result was the celebrated Reinsurance Treaty, which in part merely repeated *verbatim* the purely defensive provisions of the Three Emperors' Pact, excluding the Habsburg monarchy. But it also contained a secret protocol which bound Germany to support Russia (but not vice versa) in certain situations in which she might not be the innocent party. Bismarck was contemptuously indifferent to the fact that this protocol, and therefore the treaty as a whole, set at naught both the Dual and Triple Alliance. For him such considerations were completely outweighed by the value of the treaty in checking any Russian moves toward an alliance with France; in preventing Russia from feeling isolated in the Near and Middle East by the Mediterranean Agreements just concluded between Britain, Austria-Hungary, and Italy; and, indeed, in encouraging Russian activity in those areas, which would keep Britain engaged and cause her to seek German goodwill. In the still longer run, Bismarck calculated that Russia would launch another venture against Turkey intolerable to Britain, which would therefore align herself with Austria-Hungary to repulse it. By this devious road, Bismarck could argue, the Reinsurance Treaty was really a trap for Russia,

[4] Not counting a short-lived caretaker administration.

[5] See pp. 88–89.

which would be lured into a diplomatic *cul-de-sac*, and therefore really a support for his true ally, the Habsburg monarchy.

The impartial observer, even without the light of hindsight and disregarding the merits of Bismarck's successors who dropped the Reinsurance Treaty, may be inclined to think that Bismarck's diplomatic webs were getting both so speculative that they were unlikely to stand any strain put upon them and so intricate that he was liable to be caught up in them himself. There may, after all, even in diplomacy be such a thing as being too clever by half. Was Bismarck not by now in the position of devising ever more ingenious expedients for dealing with ever more desperate situations? He thought he was playing a canny multiple game of chess, but his opponents were making the moves expected of them less and less often. In this particular case, it was not much more than wishful thinking to suppose that Russia would go down the 'blind alley to Constantinople'. The specific constellation into which the Reinsurance Treaty fitted—the Mediterranean Agreements—was in any event a temporary one. Bismarck would no doubt retort that the Reinsurance Treaty itself, equally, was a temporary stratagem; but it was capable of conjuring up ghosts that might (at best) take a long time to exorcize. Meanwhile it might not even prevent Russia from moving toward an alliance with France. Bismarck himself admitted as much when he attempted to revive the project of a British alliance, this time by a public treaty to deter the French from the idea of making war against Germany; but Lord Salisbury, though fundamentally pro-German and afraid of French domination of the Continent, no longer had the confidence in Bismarck that he had placed in the 'honest broker' of the Congress of Berlin. This is at any rate one measure of the success of Bismarck's diplomacy.

Yet the question must be asked whether, given his aim, and then the *fait accompli*, of a unified and independent great power in the middle of Europe, Bismarck had in fact any choice. Was he not condemned, having once upset the European balance of power, to walk a tightrope on which sooner or later he would lose his own balance? Is he not rather to be admired for staying on it so long, for keeping a cool head and refusing to be distracted by the clowns below? If that is so, then criticism of Bismarck's foreign as well as of his domestic policy must properly be directed not at his means but at his ends, in other words at the creation of a Prussian-dominated, tightly federated Germany in the first place. But here too, as in the area of domestic policy, it is difficult to envisage a more attractive alternative. Such advocates of a loose confederation including Austria as Constantin Frantz (Doc. 25) had ideas of their own in the area of power politics. A Central European federation (*Mitteleuropa*) focused on the Danube would have been as vulnerable militarily as Bismarckian Germany, if not more so, and would therefore have needed defence, particularly against Russia.

The fact remains, however, that Bismarck set the tone for the deteriorating quality of diplomacy, as well as for the growing thicket of international suspicion, during his period in office. Although the chickens did not come home to roost until afterwards, still it was Bismarck who had hatched them.

8

Bismarck's last years in power

BISMARCK'S personal chickens came home to roost earlier than that. He had staked his own position as master of the German political arena on the unassailable authority and prestige of the Hohenzollern king-emperor, and on his own constitutional responsibility to him alone. We have already seen how Bismarck tried to anticipate the problems that would arise when the throne ceased to be occupied by the venerable William I. By the time this finally happened, in 1888, the crown prince whose 'English' proclivities Bismarck so much feared was already mute with cancer of the throat and clearly close to death. That did not prevent Bismarck from making things difficult for him in various ways, mainly petty; not did it prevent Frederick III, for his part, from dismissing Puttkamer, Bismarck's minister of the interior. This was enough to indicate that the dying emperor, though by no means the liberal for whom Bismarck mistook him, did not countenance the intensely reactionary outlook on the domestic scene that Puttkamer's policies represented. Although this outlook was Bismarck's own, and although Puttkamer was his agent, the chancellor remained passive, characteristically allowing the fallen minister to serve as scapegoat.

Puttkamer's dismissal was the only important political action of Frederick's short reign (all the more tragic for the very long time he had spent as heir apparent), and Bismarck in any event could feel that his position was abundantly secure. He had taken measures to protect himself against the 'liberal' emperor in the domestic political field even more specific than his moves in the area of colonial rivalries; or, rather, he had, again characteristically, used foreign affairs for domestic purposes, the link between them being, once more, the army. The *Reichstag's* seven-year block vote of army appropriations was due to expire in 1887. Bismarck proposed to the *Reichstag* a new seven-year commitment (*Septennat*), this time to a peacetime establishment increased by 10%. The increase was deliberately designed to aggravate the irritation felt by the Progressives and the Centre (the SPD always voted against all military appropriations anyway) at the seven-year blank cheque, and they duly voted against the seven-year term. This gave Bismarck the pretext he wanted for dissolving the *Reichstag*. Invoking the danger to Germany allegedly posed by the bellicose stance of General Boulanger,[1] he accused the recalcitrant parties of lack of patriotism and supported a vigorous electoral campaign on behalf of the 'reliable' parties of the Right. It is of more than incidental interest to note that, in the twenty years since its formation in the cause of *kleindeutsch* unification, the National Liberal Party had become unequivocally one of the parties of the Right. Shorn of its left wing (which had first seceded and then joined the Progressives), espousing conservative social policies and protective tariffs as well as unquestioning nationalism, the party was indeed much closer to its conservative partners in the new coalition (*Kartell*) forged by Bismarck than to its former partners in liberalism, the Progressives. The National Liberals, remembering their discomfiture of 1879, now eagerly grasped at the opportunity to be once again a 'governmental' party and in Bismarck's good books. The electorate, for its part, did Bismarck's bidding and almost doubled the National Liberal seats in the *Reichstag* at the expense mainly of the Progressives. The resulting new majority passed the *Septennat* and was available for any further projects of Bismarck's. Having achieved his immediate tactical objective, though, the chancellor put no constructive proposals before this presumably docile *Reichstag* purged of many of the 'enemies of the *Reich*', and seemed content with its mere existence.

His calculations went awry, however, because danger turned out to threaten him from a quarter from which he had not expected it. The death of Frederick III brought to the throne his son, William II, against whom the prophylactic measures taken by Bismarck to counter the possibility of royal interference were inappropriate. The impetuous and vain young emperor, eager to cut a popular figure, strained at the leash from the beginning. The first field he selected in which to display his concern for his people's welfare was that of social policy. Here he was stimulated by a spontaneous strike of coal miners in the Ruhr in the spring of 1889, the first major strike in German history (Docs. 49–50). Directed not only at specific conditions and hours of work in the mines but also, perhaps above all, at the deterioration in the miners' status and at the employers' treatment of them, the strike could be taken as an indication of general unrest among the workers and hence of the inadequacy of Bismarck's social policy.

[1] In fact, Boulanger fell from power in France a few months later, but this could not have been foreseen.

William II therefore did not confine himself to personal intervention with a view to settling this particular strike, but went on, in January 1890, to propose a rather modest extension of Prussian factory legislation (Doc. 58).

On this issue Bismarck beat a skilful tactical retreat, thereby avoiding a direct collision, but the clear possibility of one had been publicly revealed. The actual confrontation had in fact been in the making for some time. Although the triennial renewal of the anti-socialist law was not due until 1890, as early as the autumn of 1889 Bismarck had submitted to the *Reichstag*, not a mere request for renewal, but a new Bill which would need no further renewal and would not lapse unless specifically repealed. It seems likely that this was a deliberate provocation on Bismarck's part of the National Liberals, who had always been restive about the eviction clause of the law and had made threatening noises about renewing it at all, let alone strengthening it.

To explain why Bismarck should have wanted to provoke the National Liberals (although this would not by any means have been the first occasion on which he had indulged in such manoeuvring), and why the National Liberals considered incurring Bismarck's wrath at a time when a general election was not far away, it becomes necessary to consider the personal tension between the aging chancellor and the young emperor in the context of German political life generally.[2] In the first place it must be stressed that the *Kartell* was in fact by no means such a docile coalition as it appeared to be on the surface, and was certainly not a homogeneous one. The extreme right wing of the Conservative Party was uneasy about association with the National Liberals, no matter how moderate and Establishment-minded the latter had become. The editor of the influential ultra-conservative *Kreuzzeitung*, Baron Hammerstein, acted not only as a dispenser of anti-*Kartell* propaganda but also as a collector of such disparate malcontents as General Waldersee, who had designs on the chancellorship, and Adolf Stoecker, who addressed to him a celebrated letter urging the lighting of figurative funeral pyres (*Scheiterhaufen*) around Bismarck in order to dislodge him from power. It was tactically natural for conservative opponents of the *Kartell* to be opponents of Bismarck and *vice versa*, since Bismarck had been the architect of the *Kartell*. But of far more than tactical danger for Bismarck were the National Liberals, who were unhappy about his pro-Russian foreign policy, his abandonment of further

---

[2] The importance of this aspect of the crisis has recently been reemphasized by the article of J. C. G. Röhl, 'The Disintegration of the *Kartell* and the Politics of Bismarck's Fall from Power, 1887–90,' *Historical Journal*, ix, 1966, 60–89, which I follow here.

colonial expansion, and various aspects of domestic policy too. 'By
the beginning of autumn, 1889, an open breach had occurred between the chancellor and the National Liberals.'[3] The *Kartell* was
therefore disintegrating, and Bismarck decided to discredit it and
look for the parliamentary support that he would need against William
II if it came to a showdown to the pre-*Kartell* coalition of Centre,
Free Conservatives, and Conservatives that was much more to the
liking of the extreme right wing of the latter.

For his part, William II was being encouraged in the natural inclination to challenge Bismarck that he had vividly expressed in a
remark passed on to Hammerstein in Stoecker's *Scheiterhaufen*
letter: 'I will give the old man six months' breathing space, then I
will rule myself.' For several years before he became emperor,
William had accepted advice from certain political figures, although
he preferred the company of Guards officers. These advisers included
Friedrich von Holstein, the famous but still somewhat shadowy
Foreign Ministry official; Marschall von Bieberstein, the ambassador of
Baden in Berlin and a faithful servant of his liberal ruler; General
Waldersee; and Count Philipp Eulenburg, a Prussian diplomat and
William's favourite. These men had little in common save a growing
hostility toward Bismarck, and even this for varying motives. Still,
a situation was taking shape in which, since Bismarck was alienated
from the National Liberals, the latter 'moved closer to the Kaiser as
the Kaiser moved further away from Bismarck.'[4] Conversely, the ultra-
conservatives gladly became reconciled with Bismarck, and the Conservative Party as a whole supported Bismarck's undermining tactics
against the *Kartell* of which they were members.

This was the constellation of forces when Bismarck refused to
accept a moderating National Liberal amendment to the new anti-
socialist Bill, with the consequence that the entire Bill was defeated
in January, 1890 by the votes of the conservative parties and the
Centre. 'Bismarck had thus succeeded in causing the disintegration
of the Kartell three weeks before the elections,'[5] and during the campaign he ostentatiously refrained from supporting the *Kartell* parties.
As expected, however, it was mainly the National Liberals who were
the losers, going even below their number of seats before the previous
election; and although the gains went chiefly to the Progressives and
the SPD, the Centre with its allies was placed in a commanding
parliamentary position. Bismarck had calculated that he could afford
to tolerate gains on the Left and 'hardly waited for the election results

[3] Röhl, p. 76.
[4] Röhl, p. 76.
[5] Röhl, p. 85.

to come in before making his first moves towards a Conservative-Clerical majority.[6]

At the same time as he played this electoral and parliamentary game, and true to his fundamental contempt for parliamentary institutions as well as to his habit of employing more than one means to an end simultaneously, Bismarck was also entertaining the idea of a *coup d'état*. This would have taken the form of a suspension of the constitution by the emperor, either cancelling the elections due to be held or, after the elections had taken place, dismissing the *Reichstag*. In either case the object would have been to enact the new law against the socialists by decree and generally to be able to pursue a rigorous anti-socialist and anti-worker policy unhampered by parliamentary procedures. For about a week after the elections William II seemed amenable to eventual resort to a *coup d'état*. It was, after all, he who had become committed to the *Kartell* which had just been resoundingly defeated, and Bismarck who had tacitly backed the new Conservative-Centre coalition; therefore a suspension of the *Reichstag* was tempting. But then William drew back. In the first place a *coup d'état* would represent an ineradicable blot early in the reign of a young emperor seeking popularity; in the second place a prolonged and intense domestic conflict would make him more and not less dependent on Bismarck.

This analysis, however, also reveals the essential inconsistency of Bismarck's own plans, because rather than in spite of their very ingenuity. His plans were inconsistent because his aims were incompatible. These included, above all, two: the maintenance of his own power position undiminished, and vigorous prosecution of his campaign to suppress socialism. The first of these contained some potential internal tensions of its own, since it required resistance on at least two fronts simultaneously, against the emperor and against the *Reichstag*; but this was a problem not unlike many that Bismarck had solved in the past by playing two parties off against each other. The second aim was far more difficult of realization, for *neither* the emperor *nor* the Centre Party, the essential element in a new *Reichstag* combination, was sympathetic to intensified persecution of the socialists. One or other of them would therefore have to be somehow bribed if cooperation was to be obtained, which would almost automatically reduce Bismarck's independence. This state of affairs is reflected in his tactics. On the one hand he was proposing to rely on a *Reichstag* majority including not only the Centre, which always sought and usually maintained its independence, but also the Centre's allies, the Alsatians, the Guelphs (Hanoverians unreconciled to the

6 Röhl, p. 86.

THE AGE OF BISMARCK

annexation of 1866), and above all the Poles, who took second place only to the socialists as Bismarck's *bêtes noires*. Their cooperation, above all on anti-socialist legislation, could presumably be bought, if at all, only at a high price, including Bismarck's self-esteem. On the other hand he was contemplating reliance on the emperor for a *coup d'état* to achieve, with the support of the army and the Conservatives, an aim with which the emperor did not agree. It is no wonder that William's advisers saw that a *coup d'état* would deliver him into Bismarck's hands and counselled him, if the worst came to the worst, to dismiss Bismarck instead. 'It is highly improbable that Bismarck could have stayed in office under Wilhelm II no matter what policy he ... had pursued with the young man. The policies he did pursue made his dismissal more certain, and the men around the Kaiser who hoped to profit by Bismarck's fall did not hesitate to exploit the ever more frequent differences between the Kaiser and his Chancellor.'[7]

Dismissal of the chancellor in the prevailing circumstances would not accord with the practice of responsible government, since the parties to whom Bismarck now looked for support had just won the elections. On the other hand his dismissal would not itself represent a *coup d'état* since the constitution which Bismarck had himself drafted did not call for responsible government but made the chancellor's tenure of office dependent solely on the emperor's pleasure. So far as William was concerned, if he had always regarded Bismarck as an obstacle to his pretensions to rule as well as reign, he now found him not merely politically dispensable but, in view of his *coup d'état* notions, a positive and specific danger. The emperor was therefore not only prepared to heed advice to let Bismarck go in the last resort but even to provoke him. The chancellor, for his part, though for the time being withdrawing the anti-socialist legislation in the face of William's adamant refusal, in a conference on 5 March, to countenance it, at the same time was pressing his military aides for the urgent preparation of a new bill for a further increase in the army beyond the provisions of the law of 1887 which still had four years to run. Apart from the direct military implications of a strengthened army in the event of a *coup d'état*, such a bill had grave political implications, for it could not be got through the *Reichstag* without such a considerable *quid pro quo* for the crucial Centre Party votes as William II and his anti-clerical advisers were unwilling to contemplate. Indeed, within a week of his audience with the emperor Bismarck in his

[7] Norman Rich, *Friedrich von Holstein: Politics and Diplomacy in the Era of Bismarck and Wilhelm II*, Cambridge, 1965, i, 244. See also p. 279: 'Given the characters of Wilhelm II and Bismarck, the ultimate break between them was virtually certain from the first.'

turn received the Centre leader Windthorst to discuss his party's co-operation with the government.

This interview then became the first bone of contention in a further confrontation between Bismarck and William II, who got the chancellor out of bed early in the morning to tax him with negotiating with parliamentary leaders without his, the emperor's sanction. Bismarck rejected the emperor's right to interfere with his choice of conversation partners. The altercation became heated, and now William reverted to another act of Bismarck's that he regarded, rightly, as designed to limit the emperor's authority. The chancellor had circulated to the Prussian ministers copies of a decree issued by Frederick William IV in 1852, with a covering letter requesting them to observe it (Docs. 59-60). This decree, originally brought about by the introduction of a constitution in Prussia, required the ministers to give the prime minister advance notice of any important matter that they intended to raise with the king, with a view to avoiding dissonant statements to the legislature. It had, with Bismarck's acquiescence, been for many years honoured more in the breach than in the observance, and he now revived it in order to prevent William II from intriguing with any of the other ministers against him. Understandably in the circumstances, William demanded its repeal and made Bismarck's refusal the immediate occasion for asking for his resignation.

This issue, however, would not have constituted sufficient substantive reason, any more than the Windthorst visit, for so grave a step. Nor yet would the disagreements between the emperor and chancellor over foreign policy have done so, despite the deliberate emphasis placed on this matter in Bismarck's letter of resignation (Doc. 61). Fundamentally, each of them wanted unfettered power for himself, and only one of them could have it. Bismarck, in spite or more probably because of his possession of that power for nearly thirty years, had overreached himself and resorted to ill-considered and contradictory, if not desperate, measures which made his position worse instead of better. Almost a year earlier a journal had carried a headline 'Nothing succeeds any more'. All the elaborate political machinery of balances and counter-balances that Bismarck had devised for his personal convenience no longer availed him. William II, on the other hand, in the full flush of admittedly naïve enthusiasm and supported by such former but now alienated admirers of Bismarck as the grand-duke of Baden, had at his disposal the one simple but effective device characteristic of the Prussian system of 'monarchical constitutionalism' that Bismarck had insisted upon preserving: he could with absolute propriety dismiss the chancellor who had made his grandfather emperor.

He could even do so to the applause of large sections of public opinion. Despite the appearance he had given of having secured the election results he wanted, Bismarck went at first largely unlamented. It was not long, however, before the young emperor and his new advisers appeared less capable of handling the increasing and increasingly complex problems of Germany. This was an impression which for eight more years Bismarck from his retirement strove vigorously to stimulate, by intrigue, by pronouncements, and above all by means of his memoirs, more revealing, often, of the light in which he wanted to be seen than of what he had actually done (Doc. 62). These memoirs have exercised and continue to exercise such a hold even on professional historians, however, that it is still not always easy to separate truth from fiction and to arrive at a just estimate of Bismarck's character and achievement. The difficulty is increased by the genuine contradictions and tensions within the man himself, which are perhaps the key to his strength and his weakness alike. He was willing to seek conservative ends by revolutionary means in both domestic and foreign policy. In this way he was able to escape from the inhibitions limiting traditional conservative statesmen, but exposed himself to the suspicions of men of all shades of opinion who could not accustom themselves to such an unorthodox approach to politics. This approach itself was in the main based, clearly, not on preconceived principles but on the assumption that the world is complex and requires flexible methods to meet unforeseen contingencies, the maintaining of options as mutually conflicting as those contingencies. The only unity in Bismarck's outlook consisted of a system of contradictions one or other of which could be carried to the surface by the stream of events. He was convinced that unity and harmony were to be expected only in the next world; the contradictions of this one must be borne in the confidence that with God's guidance and by the use of close observation and great care they could be dealt with. The state, like everything else in the world, was ambiguous and ephemeral, a makeshift means of keeping order of which it was dangerous to expect much more. Constitutions, therefore, must be elastic rather than consistent. There was, of course, a limit to the extent to which Bismarck was willing to apply this view, and this limit was defined by precisely that element in Bismarck's outlook that was based on prejudice or, if one prefers, on principle: his refusal to absorb into his system of weights and counterweights movements that he judged subversive (chiefly socialism and militant Catholicism), his *cauchemar des révolutions*. It may well be argued that this was his Achilles' heel, and the moral may well be that *Realpolitik* must be practised *à outrance* or not at all. What can hardly any longer be doubted by an unbiased observer (if indeed such exist) is that Bismarck's system, whatever its intrinsic merits, was too intricate and opaque for anyone else to operate, certainly anyone who had not been trained to do so; and since it was Bismarck's nature, and perhaps in the nature of the system, that nobody else could be admitted to its secrets, it was destined to collapse with him. This is perhaps the most interesting respect in which Bismarck resembled that other traditional hero of the Prussian past, Frederick the Great.

The two figures were indeed often linked by hero-worshipping historians of Bismarck's own and the two following generations. Quite apart from the effect of his memoirs, Bismarck's impact on his contemporaries, even on those who did not like him, was such that it was impossible for a long time to gain a true perspective of him; and the spell is not entirely broken even yet. Bismarck the realist, the educator of the German people to political realism, is an image which dies hard, whereas the truth is, rather, that

'he obscured the German people's view of reality. The reality that the Germans had before their eyes was surely far more one that he had created than one that would have emerged from any likely course that events would have taken without him. . . . He alone was responsible for the unique combination of various, even heterogeneous elements, and therefore the effects of his activity were to a great extent bound up with his person. . . . It is to say too little of Bismarck merely to assert his superiority in both will and intellect to all the politicians of his time. His conceptions and actions in the decade of the foundation of the *Reich* were of such an unusual nature that his enemies both foreign and domestic were confounded in their mental reactions before they could act at all. . . . He was not merely the incarnation of the common will of a nation which could not exist in view of its political divisions. He created the illusion of a continuity that was not there.'[8]

---

[8] This remarkable and subtle analysis of Bismarck and his role is translated from an article by Otto Graf zu Stolberg-Wernigerode, 'Gedanken zum hundertsten Geburtstag von Erich Marcks,' *Die Welt als Geschichte*, XXI (1961), 252–3. The first point is also made by Faber, 'Realpolitik als Ideologie,' p. 40.

PART II: SELECTED DOCUMENTS

A. The Prussian Constitutional Conflict and its Settlement after the Defeat of Austria

a. Bismarck in 1863 on the internal and external problems of Prussia

1. From a speech by Bismarck in the Prussian House of Representatives, 27 January, 1863: from ERNST RUDOLF HUBER, ed. *Dokumente zur deutschen Verfassungsgeschichte*, II, 49–53. Also partially translated in Anderson, *Social and Political Conflict*, pp. 218–20.

The draft laid before you by your committee has the undeniable merit of clarifying relations [between the House and the government]. Less than a year ago ... the assertion that the parliament and the Crown were disputing for control of Prussia was energetically disclaimed; but when you have adopted the Address as it is submitted you will no longer be able to maintain this disclaimer. This Address assigns to the House of Representatives rights which it either does not have at all or does not have exclusively. If, gentlemen, you had the unilateral right to determine the budget and its items definitively; if you had the right to demand of His Majesty the King the dismissal of those ministers in whom you have no confidence; if you had the right, by means of budgetary resolutions, to determine the size and organization of the army; if you had the right, which under the constitution you do not have but to which you lay claim in your Address, to exercise ultimate control over the relations between the executive power of the government and its officials—then you would indeed possess full governmental power in this country. Your Address is based on these claims, if it has any basis at all. I believe, therefore, that I can describe its practical import very simply: this Address claims to deprive the royal house of Hohenzollern of its constitutional rights of government and to transfer them to a majority of this House.

You advance this demand in the form of a declaration that the constitution is violated to the extent that the Crown and the House of Peers do not submit to your will; you level the accusation of violating the constitution at the ministry and not at the Crown, whose loyalty to the constitution you do not call into question. I have already rejected this distinction in the sessions of the committee. You know as well as anyone in Prussia that the ministry acts in the name and on the command of His Majesty the King, and that in particular it has undertaken in this sense the acts of government which you choose to regard as violating the constitution. You know that a Prussian ministry occupies in this respect a different position from an English one. An English ministry, whatever it may call itself, is a parliamentary one, a ministry of the majority in parliament; but we are ministers of His Majesty the King. If I reject the separation between ministers and the Crown which is assumed in the Address it is not, as was suggested from the rostrum a while ago, in order to convert the authority of the Crown into a shield to protect the ministry. We require no such protection, we stand firmly on the ground of our established rights. I reject that separation because it conceals the fact that you are contesting power in this country not with the ministry but with the Crown. You find a violation of the constitution specifically with respect to Article 99. If I recall the words correctly, Article 99 says: 'All revenues and expenditures of the state must be estimated annually in advance and must be included in the budget.' If it continued: 'the latter is determined annually by the House of Representatives,' then you would be quite right in your complaints in the Address, then the constitution would be violated. But Article 99 continues: 'the latter (i.e. the budget) is determined annually by a law.' Article 62 lays down with incontrovertible clarity how a law comes into being. It says that for the completion of every law, including, therefore, the budget law, the agreement of the Crown and both Chambers is necessary. The Article emphasizes that the House of Peers is entitled to reject a budget voted by the Lower House with which it does not agree.

Each of these three concurrent rights is in theory unlimited, one as strong as the other. If agreement among the three forces is not reached, the constitution contains no statement whatever as to which of them must yield. In earlier discussions here you have, to be sure, passed lightly over this difficulty. By analogy with other countries, whose constitution and laws, however, are not published and have no validity in Prussia, you have assumed that the difficulty is to be removed by the other two elements yielding to the House of Representatives; that if no agreement on the budget is reached between the Crown and the House of Representatives the Crown not only submits to the House of Representatives and dismisses the ministers in whom the House of Representatives has no confidence but also by mass appointments forces the House of Peers, if it does not agree with the deputies, to lower itself to the level of the House of Representatives. In this way, to be sure, the exclusive sovereign power of the House of Representatives would be established; but such exclusive power is not constitutional law in Prussia. The constitution holds firmly to the equilibrium of the three legislative powers in all matters, including budgetary legislation; none of these powers can force the other to yield; therefore the constitution points to compromise as the means to reach agreement. A statesman wise in constitutional matters has said that all of constitutional life is always a series of compromises. If compromise is made impossible because one of the powers involved wishes to enforce its own will with doctrinaire absolutism, then the series of compromises is broken and is replaced by conflicts. Since the life of a state cannot stand still, conflicts become questions of power; whoever has power in his hands then proceeds according to his will, because the life of a state cannot stand still even for a moment. You may say that this theory would enable the Crown to prevent the completion of a budget because of any insignificant difference of opinion. In theory this is admittedly undeniable, just as it is in theory undeniable that the deputies can reject the whole budget in order to bring about the disbandment of the army or of all government bodies. But in practice this does not happen. Such an abuse of an incontrovertible theoretical right of the Crown has not taken place in the last 14 years. We shall scarcely agree on whose fault it is that in the present case no compromise has been reached. But I remind you that after the dissolution of the previous House of Representatives the Crown voluntarily made considerable concessions to you: the budget was reduced by several million, the surtax of 25% was voluntarily dropped.

In response to your wishes, and despite the difficulties this caused the government, the budget was broken down into items. Your answer to these attempts at conciliation consisted in your resolution of September which enables me without hesitation to throw back at you the accusation of an abuse of power levelled against us in the tenor of your Address. You used your right to participate in the fixing of the budget to adopt a resolution which it was impossible to put into effect if Prussia was not to be rendered entirely defenceless, if the funds so far expended on the reorganization were not to be thrown away, I do not know how many million, only to have to start again from scratch next year. You expected of His Majesty the King, if indeed you expected your resolution to be carried out—and I cannot assume of this assembly that you would have adopted a resolution that you did not wish to have carried out—you expected the dismissal of half the infantry, a third of the cavalry, 119 battalions—I do not know how many regiments. The resolution as a whole was incapable of being carried out if only for the reason that it referred back to the past. . . .

You expect the Crown to give in, and we expect you to. ... The
House of Peers rejected the budget law voted by you as inadequate
for the state's needs, in the view of the royal government quite rightly.
It was the case that no budget was passed, although this was regarded
as impossible. The fact refuted the assertion that it was impossible.
The event which took place here could easily recur. ... It is no new
discovery that there is a gap in the constitution here. ... A number of
theories have been offered as to the legal position if no budget is
passed, but I will not go into their merits here. ... I am content with
the necessity of the state's existence, and that it cannot pass its time in
pessimistic reflections on what would happen if the flow of money
dries up. Necessity alone is decisive, we have taken account of this
necessity, and you yourselves will not wish us to have withheld interest
and salaries. ... No official has refused the government his cooperation,
none has declared that he wishes not to receive his salary from the
first of January. ... We are firmly convinced that we are not in conflict
with the constitution and firmly resolved, so long as we have His
Majesty's confidence, to resist steadfastly and energetically your efforts
to extend your competence beyond the limits allowed by the constitution. The rights granted to you by the constitution you shall enjoy in
full measure; what you demand beyond this we shall refuse, and we
shall untiringly defend the rights of the Crown against your claims.

It is a curious coincidence that the debate on this manifesto which
is to be handed to our royal master should fall on the birthday of the
youngest heir-presumptive to the throne. In this coincidence, gentlemen, we see a redoubled command to defend firmly the rights of the
monarchy and the rights of His Majesty's successors. The Prussian
monarchy has not yet fulfilled its mission, it is not yet ready to form
a mere ornamental decoration on your constitutional edifice or to
become a dead cog in the machinery of parliamentary government.

2. Bismarck to the Prussian ambassador in St Petersburg (24
December, 1863): from ROTHFELS, pp. 118-20.

... The question is whether we are a Great Power or a state of the
German Confederation, and whether, as would correspond to the
former, we are to be ruled by a monarch or, as would be permitted
by the latter, by professors, local magistrates, and small-town gossips.
The pursuit of the phantom of popularity 'in Germany' that we have
been conducting since the 40's has cost us our position in Germany
and in Europe, and we shall not win it back again by allowing ourselves to drift, but only by standing firmly on our own feet and by
being a Great Power first and a state of the Confederation afterwards.
This is something that Austria has to our cost always recognized and

she will not allow her European alliances, if indeed she has any, to be destroyed by the play-acting which she is conducting with German sympathies. . . . The twenty per cent Germans in Austria are not in the last resort a factor which would compel Austria to allow herself to be diverted from her own interests. . . .

If we were to turn our back on the Great Powers now in order to throw ourselves into the arms of the small states, caught as they are in grass-roots democratic politics, that would be the most miserable position that the monarchy could occupy both internally and externally. We should be led instead of leading; we should be dependent for support on elements that we do not control and that are necessarily hostile to us but to which we should have to submit for better or for worse. . . . We can gain strength not from the politics of legislative chambers or of the press, but only from the politics of a Great Power equipped with suitable weapons, and we have not sufficient power to be able to dissipate it on the wrong cause, or on phrase-making, or on the Duke of Augustenburg. You over-estimate the whole Danish question and you allow yourself to be deluded by the general uproar among the democrats who control the media of press and assembly and who are agitating this question which, in itself, is of no great importance. . . .

For the moment I regard it as the right policy to have Austria on our side; whether the moment for separation arrives and on whose part, we shall see. . . . I am not afraid of war, on the contrary; I am also indifferent to the labels revolutionary or conservative, as I am indifferent to all phrases; you will perhaps soon convince yourself that war is a part of my programme as well; it is only that I regard your method of reaching it as politically the wrong way. . . . If popular enthusiasm here impresses them in London and in Paris then I am glad, for this is all grist to our mill; but that does not mean that it impresses me and it will deliver not a single shot and very little money for a war. You may call the London Treaty revolutionary; the Vienna agreements were ten times more revolutionary and ten times more unjust with respect to many princes, Estates and countries, but European law is nevertheless made by European treaties. If these were to be judged by the criteria of morality or justice then they would practically all have to be abolished.

b. The liberals' struggle with Bismarck and their consciences

3. J. G. Droysen (Letters, 1863–66): from *Briefwechsel*, II, 813, 836–7, 871–2. Droysen, Johann Gustav (1808–84), noted historian, Liberal deputy to the Frankfurt Assembly 1848–49 and a leader of the *kleindeutsch* movement.

The Battle of Düppel (18 April) was a decisive victory for Prussia in the war against Denmark.

(*To Heinrich von Sybel, 19 October, 1863.*) . . . Even if, as I believe, the military reorganization was itself a good thing and in any event cannot be suspended now in view of the great dangers from abroad and in spite of all the many serious shortcomings of the army, that does not make Bismarck etc. [*sic*] any less intolerable. It is nothing short of revolting that this group should use this measure which is correct in itself to cover up its passage by arbitrary force. From the very beginning there has been a group who desired this measure not because it was good but because it was to cloak the way it was to be forced through. I do not know whether this brutality or that of the extreme Left will win the day in the end. In any case the Prussian state and freedom are finished. For me the absolutism of the democrats is as unacceptable as that of the courts. . . .

(*To Wilhelm Rossmann, 29 April, 1864.*) . . . I am certainly no Bismarck enthusiast, but he has the ability to act. . . . I look forward to the future with pleasure. There is something invigorating, after fifty years of peace, in a day like the battle of Düppel for the young Prussian troops. One feels as if all one's nerves had been refreshed. And what a blessing that in the face of all the manoeuvring of the princes and the grandiloquence of the true Germans, the Austrian project for reform, and the *Nationalverein*, the full force of real power and real activism should make itself felt. . . . It is time that the importance of the medium-sized and small states were kept within its real limits. . . . They will go on saying that Prussia under Bismarck is not to be trusted; they will denounce more loudly than ever Prussia's greed for annexations and use it as a pretext for dissociating themselves; they will continue to say that the real Germany is outside Prussia and menaced by Prussia. With God's help all this will not stand in the way of what has been begun. . . .

(To August von Haeften, 2 August, 1866.) ... At last Prussia's full significance is appreciated. I scarcely know anything in history that could be compared with this period of time. What has happened and how it has happened must convince even the most stubborn that we who did not cease even when things were going badly to talk about and to believe in the destiny, the power, and the right of this state were right after all. We have seen at last the triumph of the true German spirit over the false, of the spirit of 1517 and 1813 over Latin and Austrian oppression and scorn. And there is even more! Napoleon III thought that he could direct the fate of Europe at the head of the Latin world, and the thick-skinned English believed him. Now the spell has been broken, Caesar is gnashing his teeth, the Tsar is angry, the [Austrian] emperor is writhing on the ground, and England is in a hurry to shake us sincerely by the hand. ...

(To Rudolph Ehmck, 14 October, 1866.) ... There is no longer any getting away from the fact that Count Bismarck has a rare capacity for statesmanship which it would be unfair to judge according to so-called principles, that is to say, according to preconceived and hardened opinions and conclusions drawn from such and such precedents and ideas; whereas what is at stake is to take a step ahead, not merely to see new possibilities but to realize them. ... And this man, glowing coldly, passionately moderate, heedless of friend and foe, of parties and principles, entirely rooted in the facts, in the reality of this state, can act. If the nation had more understanding than indolence, more sincerity than deception, more recognition of its weaknesses and its misery than comfortable, lazy complacency in its humble and humiliating position, it would thank God that at last a Hercules has arrived to clean out the Augean stables that it has fouled. But many of them, above all our German brothers in the south, go on preferring to roll about in their own filth. ... And this is what my friends in Göttingen call the profound feeling of the German nation for justice. And I can already see how, when they have succeeded in obstructing what could now be accomplished easily, they will cry spitefully: you see, he couldn't do it either! And yet they ramble on about Germany and German might in every beer hall. ... In my estimation these stubborn Swabians, these beery Bavarians, these Catholicized Franks and Alemanni have lost not only their sense of humour but their common sense as well. For the first time we have in Germany a free reorganization without the direction of foreign powers, a truly national one. And in the meantime the honourable fragments of the German people exceed the much-scorned dynasties in their silly resistance to the greatest step forward that we have taken in centuries, since 1517. ...

4. Heinrich von Sybel to J. G. Droysen, 19 June, 1864:
from HEYDERHOFF, pp. 225–8. Sybel, Heinrich von (1817–95),
noted historian and liberal politician, author of the semi-official
history of German unification. (See also Doc. 39.)

... It seems to me that the lack of political morality and consistency
in which our rulers excel has been sufficiently demonstrated in the
actions and results of our policy already. I cannot but think that it is
only the justice of the cause and the bravery of our soldiers that
has kept our heads above water, despite the minister's craftiness. He
alone is responsible for the bad results of his frivolous lack of plan
and of principle....

I was as glad as anyone else that our government did not ... regard
war as the greatest of all evils ... [and] that the military success
hitherto achieved has for the moment raised our stature in Europe—
but I cannot ignore the fact that our rulers have constantly reduced
and endangered these results by their lack of consistency and of a
sense of justice, and still continue to do so.... Holding this opinion,
which I should be delighted to have refuted, I cannot speak so clearly
and unequivocally as you do about a healing upsurge of a feeling
of power, of a hope of victory, or of a rise of Prussia in Europe. I will
gladly do everything possible to support even this ministry in a force-
ful solution of the Baltic question, but I confess that I should be
happier if I saw these matters in hands as bold as Bismarck's but
rather more reliable.

I said that I would do everything *possible* to support our external
position even with this ministry in office. What I find absolutely and
unconditionally *impossible* at the moment is only one thing. Since the
doctrine and the practice of 'We take money where we find it' have
been openly formulated in the House and implemented in the
country I see no possibility of voting any money without an equally
firm and binding retraction on the part of the government. The legal
recognition of the legislature's right to control the budget and the
possibility of laying a complaint against a minister, if only for violating
this right, is the precondition for any re-establishment of parliament's
right to vote money. This seems to me so evident, and its contrary so
incompatible with the House's honour, the oath of its members,
and the nation's self-respect, that I cannot give up the hope that you
will also agree, and that *if* our foreign policy should suffer as a result
of such a conflict you will place the responsibility for it where it
belongs, on the men who leave the nation only a choice between
external stagnation and internal self-mutilation, ... that you will also
draw a line—perhaps a generous line, but an absolutely firm one—
beyond which right can no longer be sacrificed to might.

Within this line I, for my part, hope fervently that for the sake of external action an internal reconciliation will take place. I believe it possible that in such a mood the majority of the House will be ready to make important concessions in the objective causes of conflict during the last few years, that it will drop a number of the objections raised against the new army even though it cannot regard these objections as refuted, that it will vote money for the artillery, for fortresses, and for the navy as well, and that it will overlook the underhanded reorganization of the army, the introduction of a feudal partisan spirit into it, and the violations of the constitution that have taken place up to now. But one thing it cannot overlook, even if an angel from heaven promised Prussia the domination of Europe for it. ... I admit to you that the first interest of a state must be power. But equally I think you will admit to me that it must not be its only interest. Because it is the first I gladly make to it very important and very painful objective concessions. But since it cannot and must not dominate the world all by itself I cannot extend these concessions to the point of destroying the principle of law.

5. Karl Twesten (Letters, 1865–66). Open letter to the *National-Zeitung*, 28 September, 1865: from HEYDERHOFF, pp. 255–6, 306–7. Twesten, Karl (1820–70), jurist, Progressive deputy in the Prussian House of Representatives, National Liberal deputy in the *Reichstag* of the North German Confederation.

... I regard the present moment as an unfortunate choice for a meeting of delegates from German legislatures. I regard it as a deception practised on the German people who will look forward to this meeting with keen expectation. ... There is no legitimate reason to place any hope in the middle states, either singly or collectively, for action on behalf of the power and interests of Germany. There is just as little reason to believe that in the present situation any resolutions of such a meeting of delegates would have the slightest influence. ... I do not regard it as appropriate for a great assembly of members of German legislatures to meet in order to accompany facts in process of being accomplished with superfluous resolutions.

Moreover, the invitation [to the congress] ... as well as the mood among the spokesmen for the smaller states is directed exclusively against Prussia and her policy in the matter of the [Danish] duchies. The majority of the Prussian House of Representatives did not want this policy. ... We can still not accept that a German province should be disposed of without its agreement, that it should be treated as an impotent object of Cabinet diplomacy. But we must keep in mind not only the right of self-determination of German people, not only the rights of the people *vis-à-vis* the governments, but also the power position of our state, and we can never take part in proceedings directed not only at the present rulers but against the Prussian state itself, with the object of preparing a defeat for Prussia. . . .

We would prefer anything as an alternative to a defeat of the Prussian state. We do this in the interests not only of Prussia but also of Germany, since we are strengthened by recent events in the conviction that no other Power can do anything for Germany but Prussia. . . .

(*To Gustav Lipke, 10 June, 1866*.) . . . If, by a real recognition of the parliamentary control of the budget, we are given the legal and moral possibility of voting funds, we shall scarcely be able to refuse them once war has broken out. In any event the government is preparing to wage the war without us if necessary, and there is no doubt that it can do it—and not only for a year. It could therefore easily come about that we would have a greater interest in being able to vote funds than the government has in getting them voted.

If we arrive at no understanding on money matters I expect a general state of emergency and suspension of the constitution, but I have no hope at all of resistance.

In case of serious defeats there would probably be an early peace treaty, in case of minor setbacks there would probably be no change, in case of a quick victory the government would be in complete control of the situation . . . —only in the event of a prolonged war would the government perhaps be inclined to serious concessions, and then not so much under compulsion as from considerations regarding the course of the war and the position during peace negotiations. . . . What is likely to happen in Prussia and Germany after the war is hard to predict; the most probable outcome is economic dislocation and political apathy for a prolonged period. In my opinion all the signs favour absolutism and the *Junkers*. Whether Prussia is defeated or whether she wins without our participation, we shall be the sufferers in both cases. . . .

Our programme must, of course, continue to be directed at a change of system and persons, and we must hold absolutely to the refusal to vote money without recognition of our rights concerning the budget; farther than that I do not want to commit myself, . . . as the shape of the future is unpredictable. A call for peace at the moment certainly makes no sense, and much discussion of who is responsible for the war is superfluous. Still, I would not like to declare the war fought because of and under Bismarck as just and useful; our situation might in any event be improved if, with full justification, we could explain that Bismarck had unnecessarily brought about the war for the sole reason of accomplishing the very annexation which he had himself caused the duchies to abominate. . . .

6. Letters and writings of Rudolf Haym: from ROSENBERG, pp. 244, 303, 323–4. Haym, Rudolf (1821–1901), philosopher and historian, biographer of Hegel.

(*To Max Duncker, 18 April, 1866.*) . . . Even admitting all the factors to which you draw my attention, there is still a large error in his [Bismarck's] calculation—I mean the paradoxical contradiction between his internal machinations and his proclamation of ultra-liberal ideas for foreign consumption. Diplomatically, to be sure, this is correctly reasoned. On the one hand he will make the idea of a German parliament and direct elections palatable to the king from a specifically Prussian and conservative point of view, and on the other hand he wins pro-parliamentary south German public opinion over to his side. . . . But how long can this go on? Will imperialism or revolution hatch out the egg? How will he balance the two off against each other? I cannot get rid of the painful feeling that liberal ideas deserve a better fate than to be used as means to an end, and I am afraid that this misdeed will be punished. We should be indeed fortunate if we succeeded in using Bismarck's foolhardy ventures to the advantage of both an expansion of Prussian power and the cause of internal freedom. That would be the task of a constitutional party if one existed. . . .

(*To Wilhelm Schrader, 16 May, 1866.*)* . . . For about a fortnight now I have once and for all accepted the idea and the feeling that a tragic era has opened in Germany whose end, perhaps, and whose full consequences, certainly, we will not live to see. . . . [The imminent German] struggle was bound up, in the last analysis, with the nature of things, it represents a pathological crisis in the stunted and misshapen body of German political life; finally, the dualism between Austria and Prussia must cease, the former if possible ejected from Germany, and the latter led towards its destiny as the sole German power. That this necessary event should occur just now, and at the hands of this particular agent and in this manner, gives cause for many misgivings, ethical, legal, and practical. The catastrophe has been provoked by the arrogant minister in a manner which may be punished as *hubris* by the gods if they do not pay more attention to the justified ideal end than to the means. . . . Who else

*HEYDERHOFF, pp. 285–7.

could have so firmly won over the king and carried the Conservatives with him to such revolutionary actions . . . ? No liberal ministry would have been capable of it. . . . It is a splendid position: the alliance with Italy, Russian neutrality, the understanding with Napoleon. . . . But this contrasts sharply with the lack of moral support at home. People cannot fathom why it should have been impossible for Bismarck, in view of the way he is feared and of his irresistible energy, to win over a part of Germany and his own people by some sort of liberal concessions. . . . It would be incomprehensible if it were not for his evident lack of any sense for these moral forces. . . . I had hoped that time would be allowed for a patriotic-liberal party to gather strength and for the other side to come to their senses and be ashamed of themselves, especially if in the meantime the danger to the fatherland moved closer and the sound of guns worked on men's hearts. Instead we are driven into an election at the most unfavourable moment, when indignation at the military levies is increasing people's anger at the reactionary régime and the common people cannot find any *casus belli*. I am still hoping in the next few weeks for a royal proclamation, for any kind of conciliatory move or popular measures, and finally for the swing in sentiment that the sound of the guns must unfailingly bring about. . . . We must at any price get a section of the Progressive Party to come over to us. And I see no other means to this than what in any event corresponds to my desires and follows from my assessment of the situation: firm insistence on the country's right to re-establishment of its constitution. In my opinion the attempt must by all means be made to bargain the voting of funds, which will be demanded of the Diet and which in the last resort must be conceded, against a guarantee of parliamentary control of the budget. To act otherwise is simply to go over into the reactionary camp, and to miss an opportunity which will perhaps never return to give the country internal peace and the government the greatest conceivable moral support. . . .

7. From two letters of Rudolf von Ihering, 1866: from *R. v. Ihering in Briefen an seine Freunde*, pp. 196–8, 205–7. Ihering, Rudolf von (1818–92), jurist, early leader of the school of legal positivists.

The Austro-Prussian war broke out on 14 June; the decisive Prussian victory at Königgrätz (Sadowa) took place on 3 July; a preliminary peace was reached on 26 July, and the final Treaty of Prague was concluded on 23 August.

(*To J. Glaser, Giessen, 1 May.*) . . . Never, probably, has a war been incited so shamelessly and with such horrifying frivolity as the one that

Bismarck is currently trying to start against Austria. My innermost feelings are revolted by this violation of every legal and moral principle. God knows I am no friend of Austria; on the contrary, I have always been regarded as one of her enemies—that is to say of her political system, not of the Austrian people whom I have learned to love . . . —; I am devoted to the idea of Prussian influence in north Germany, even though I have little sympathy for the present political system in Prussia. But I would rather cut off my hand than to use it in such a disgusting operation as Prussian policy is now launching against Austria—the common sense of any honest man cannot even comprehend the depths of this perfidy. We ask ourselves in amazement: is it really true that what the whole world knows to be lies can be proclaimed from on high as the truth? Austria is supposed to be mobilizing against Prussia! Any child knows that the opposite is the case. . . . The saddest thing about it all is that once the struggle is under way principles of right and wrong must come in absolutely tragic conflict with interests. Whom should we wish victorious, Austria or Prussia? We have no choice, we must come down on the side of the *unjust* cause, because we cannot tolerate the possibility of Austria gaining the upper hand in Germany. Everyone here detests this war, nobody can be comfortable with the idea that it will have the result that we *must* desire—the hegemony of Prussia. That is our situation. Germans taking up arms against Germans, civil war, a plot of three or four Powers against one, with not even an appearance of legality, without popular participation, created by a few diplomats alone, a conspiracy against your poor country, which causes even the enemies of Austria to sympathize with her and in which they would have to desire her victory—if this victory did not mean our own ruin! . . . The war would be unthinkable if Austria had not for decades been doing everything to make it impossible even for her friends in Germany to take sides with her and putting the most menacing weapons in the hands of her enemies. . . . Everyone agrees on the crying injustice that is being done to Austria, and yet, as I say, thousands here would not lift a finger for her cause, people feel that that would mean turning against one's own cause; for with very few exceptions the general opinion here is that the free development of Germany would be incompatible with Austrian supremacy. This may be wrong, but I am merely stating the fact. There is just as little affection for the German princes: here also one finds the same collision between undoubted historical justice and a total inability to work up any enthusiasm for it. It is sad to be in conflict with one's own feelings—we ought to desire victory for the just cause in this instance too, but we cannot! . . .

(*To B. Windscheid, Giessen, 19 August.*) . . . I think I must be dreaming when I think of how much has happened in the short space of a few weeks; it seems that it must be years. I am only now gradually coming to my senses again; at one time I was quite dizzy from the pace of events. What a surging of emotions—of deep fear, anxious hesitation, joyous exultation, apprehensive suspense, furious indignation, profound pity, and in the end once more a rejoicing of the soul, an ecstasy of happiness such as my heart has never before known! Oh, my dear friend, what enviable luck to be living at this time, to have seen this turning-point in German history with which there has been nothing to compare for a thousand years. For years I have envied the Italians that they succeeded in what seemed for us to lie only in the distant future, I have wished for a German Cavour and Garibaldi as Germany's political messiah. And overnight he has appeared in the person of the much-abused Bismarck. Should we not think we are dreaming if the impossible becomes possible? Like you I was afraid at the prospect of war, I was convinced of the notion that the Austrians, experienced in the practical school of war, would be superior to the Prussians. Has intelligence and moral energy ever in history celebrated such a triumph over crude force? There is something wonderful about this spirit that animates little Prussia, this spirit that lifts us all out of a state of impotence and ignominy and gives to the name of Germany in Europe a lustre and a tone that it has not had for a thousand years. I bow before the genius of Bismarck, who has achieved a masterpiece of political planning and action such as are only rarely to be found in history. How marvellously the man spun all the threads of the great web, how firmly and safely so that none of them broke, how precisely he knew and used all the ways and means—his king, Napoleon, his army, the administration, Austria and her forces—in short, a masterpiece of calculation. I have forgiven the man everything he has done up to now, more, I have convinced myself that it was necessary; what seemed to us, the uninitiated, as criminal arrogance has turned out in the end to have been an indispensable means to the goal. He is one of the greatest men of the century; it is a real revelation to have lived at the same time as such a man; a man of action like that, not heedless action but action inspired and prepared both politically and morally, is worth a hundred men of liberal principles and of powerless honesty!

Nine weeks ago I should not have believed that I would write a paean of praise to Bismarck, but I cannot help myself! I leave it to my stubborn colleagues from Swabia and Bavaria to abuse him, to concentrate everything disgusting they can think of on the name of Bismarck. Incorrigible doctrinaires! For years they have yelled and drunk themselves hoarse for German unity, and when someone comes on the scene and achieves the impossible by transferring German unity from a book of student songs into reality they cry 'crucify him.' . . .

8. From letters of Hermann Baumgarten, 1866: from HEYDERHOFF, pp. 278, 281–4, 295–6, 315. Baumgarten, Carl August Ludwig Hermann (1825-93), south German historian and publicist.

(*To Heinrich von Sybel, 1 May.*) . . . Everything that I heard and saw indicated that Bismarck was in complete control of the situation. . . . Admittedly he stands on shifting ground, admittedly he lacks moral seriousness, admittedly he not only permits the silliest things to happen in internal affairs but he does them himself; nevertheless he is a man of impressive stature. I found it most interesting to compare the manner of government now with that of six years ago in the same offices. No greater contrast can be imagined, and unfortunately all the advantages are on Bismarck's side, particularly as regards the actual system and technique of government. You can have no idea how much he has his people under his thumb, how everyone fears him, how he has brought all diplomatic activity into line, and how closely he guards his secrets. . . . The Opposition of the Progressives etc. gave me an impression of utter impotence. . . .

(*To Heinrich von Sybel, 11 May.*) . . . Our friend . . . found Bismarck just as we would like him to be: determined, strong, shrewd, and convinced that the situation demands a different domestic policy. . . .

If Bismarck is victorious with the wholehearted support of popular forces it will be a victory for a liberal Prussia. If he is victorious while the people echo the clamour of the *Kölnische Zeitung* and of the Jewish *Volkszeitung*, then the Prussian people will turn its back on liberalism. If Austria is victorious the fate of the liberals is self-evident. . . .

No nation can go into such a war on the basis of a one-sided party programme. Prussia least of all can insult its nobility and its officer corps with a Progressive policy at a time when they are both supposed to fight a war which in itself negates the basis of their policy. Do you believe that a purely liberal ministry would bring this army into a war against Austria? And it is surely difficult to demand that at the moment of the outbreak of war a post-war state of affairs be stipulated that does not suit the officers very well. . . . The only conditions, it seems to me, that the liberal party in the Diet could make are the right to control the budget and the entry of a few efficient and unprejudiced men into the ministry. . . .

H

Prussia should surely be aware of the superiority in Europe that it enjoys today thanks to Bismarck, and that it would be suicidal to turn its wrath suddenly against the man before whom all the enemies of Prussia tremble. . . . A liberal ministry would hardly be able to carry this war with the dynasty, the nobility, and the military party, perhaps it would even shrink back from the responsibility. Since someone else has taken it on, we should surely accept the inevitable and take advantage of the best opportunity we are likely to get. . . .

(*To Karl Twesten, 27 May.*) . . . As things are now we must face the possibility that all of south Germany will be drawn into the Austrian camp. Hatred of Prussia is growing hourly. The governments, driven by fear of Bismarck and now also by the hope of being able to put paid to Prussia once and for all, are pushing forward energetically. . . . This sorry situation is due partly to the great misdeeds of the Bismarckian régime, in part to innate antipathy against Prussia, and at the moment to the attitude of the Prussian liberals. . . . I can understand that the men who for three years have fought in the front line against [Bismarck's] ruinous system should have as their principal purpose the breaking of this system. But surely it is their task really to break it, not to overthrow it at the price of humiliation and permanent damage for the Prussian state. In the present state of exernal conflict the battle can surely not be fought with the same means as in the recent peaceful years. In our opinion the policy of the Prussian liberals should long ago have been more explicitly adapted to the European situation. Today it must be decisive for them. If Prussian liberalism achieves its victory at the price of the elevation of Austria and the humiliation of Prussia the future will pronounce a grave verdict on it. It will judge that the men who for three years conducted the struggle with very carefully considered caution had no right to continue it now by such desperate means. . . .

Since [the Prussian liberals] indignantly refuse to join a government with Bismarck they must be in a position to form a ministry on their own. We are not unfamiliar with Prussian conditions and persons, but we know of no liberal who could in present conditions take over the Foreign Ministry. Of course one could say that the difficulties created by Bismarck are Bismarck's fault; let him take the responsibility for them. But is this of any help to Prussia? . . . The conflict would not be removed merely by Bismarck's dismissal. Or would a liberal government like to begin by giving up Schleswig-Holstein and to submit to the Diet [of the Confederation] led by Austria against Prussia? . . . I do not see how a liberal government would survive the storm [that would result]. I do not know any liberals who would have a chance of mastering such a terribly difficult situation, if only for the reason that hitherto they have had no opportunity of proving themselves in affairs of state and because nobody, not even a genius, can solve difficult political problems without practice and experience. If Prussian liberalism had any prospect of providing the solution—which admittedly is being sought at the moment on a mainly unjust basis—to the German question, including at the same time the internal Prussian question, we should all support it with all the means at our disposal. But all that we can see now as the probable result of its attitude in the recent crisis is the weakening of Prussia and the strengthening of Austria and of dynastic particularism. . . .

(*To Heinrich von Sybel, 23 June, 1866.*) . . . How Bismarck fulfils our hopes, how the Prussian people exceeds all our expectations! But liberalism, I fear, has spoiled its chances. If the good people in Berlin had heeded my warnings at the end of May something might have been saved. Now, I fear, my prediction will come true: the people will turn its back on liberalism. But these anxieties are now secondary. Once we have a great state everything else can wait.

9. Hermann Baumgarten's self-critique, Autumn 1866: from *Der deutsche Liberalismus: Eine Selbstkritik*, pp. 186–7, 193, 212–13. In May Baumgarten had referred to Bismarck's lack of 'moral gravity' (cited by Faber, 'Realpolitik als Ideologie' [see p. 31, n. 7], p. 12).

. . . All political forces in Germany of any consequence were solidly ranged against Bismarck's policy; but, scarcely hampered either by these innumerable opponents or by the mistrust of the European powers, he pursued it steadily and confidently. Two important facts were therefore established in the autumn of 1864: the war in Schleswig-Holstein had inflicted a serious defeat on German liberalism and at the same time had brought the German nation a victory of great potential importance. Condemned by German patriots Count Bismarck had obtained the first significant extension of the German frontier for centuries. . . . Prussia was once more recognized as a European Power, and only prejudice could deny to Count Bismarck his eminent personal contribution to this glorious ascent, followed by the institution which attracted the next closest attention of the Opposition group, the reorganized army. . . .

I remember, about 1859 and 1860, hearing many liberals in Prussia admit that we would make no progress until the Prussian sword brought recalcitrant kings to reason and cut through the net of Austrian intrigues. Well, now this sword had at long last been unsheathed, it was glittering splendidly in the sunshine of victory, a man of rare power was guiding it. . . . Was this not the time to postpone all internal dissensions? Fate was smiling on Prussian power while Prussian freedom was battling against adverse currents; was it sensible nevertheless to pursue only the latter and renounce the former? How long had liberals been longing for a man who would at last lead Prussia boldly forward! Well, now he was not only there, but he was at his post and had made considerable progress already. Admittedly he looked different from the liberal image. But as against that he was ascending the path to victory with a power far beyond liberal fantasies. . . .

We should accept this lesson with difficulty if it were linked with misfortune. But we have had the almost unprecedented experience that our victory would have brought us misery, whereas our defeat has meant our supreme salvation. . . . Now it is a joy to work in the public interest. Up to now it has been a hard and mournful service, performed only as a duty; now . . . we have really only One Task [sic], namely to overcome certain prejudices, to discard certain weaknesses that we have picked up in our unhappy past. As soon as German liberalism ceases to be diverted by misgivings of secondary importance and wholeheartedly takes up the cause of the events whose greatness it acknowledges there can be no doubt that the next century will see the appearance of the German state that has become a compelling need as much for our scholarship, art, and morals as for our political development and national power position. We alone can obstruct this beneficent process, we alone could pitch ourselves back into our former miserable condition. . . .

10. A. L. v. Rochau, *Right and Might* (1866): from *Recht und Macht*, Oct. 1866. Rochau, August Ludwig von (1810–73), historian and publicist, editor of the *Wochen-Blatt des National-vereins;* coined the word *Realpolitik*. (See also Doc. 16.)

Bismarck's Bill of Indemnity was passed by the Prussian Diet on 8 Sept.

Kassel and Wiesbaden were the capitals respectively of Electoral Hesse and the duchy of Nassau which, together with Hanover, were annexed by Prussia in 1866.

. . . Examples are . . . not lacking of the conversion, in the course of time, of the most flagrant wrong into indubitable right. This applies, above all, to territorial relationships created by conquest. . . . Even half of present-day Switzerland consists of conquered territory, not liberated but subjugated by conquest. . . . [But] nobody says that the Swiss Confederacy [*Eidgenossenschaft*] 'conquered' the Separatists

[*Sonderbund*], or the North American Union the southern states. . . . German liberalism never raised the slightest protest against the violence done to the Separatists or to the American South. . . . On the contrary, liberal public opinion rejoiced in the victory of the Confederacy and of the Union because it found it to its advantage; there was no mention of right.

It is therefore easy to deduce the significance of the storm of righteous protest from the radicals against the wrong that is supposed to have triumphed in the German war. If a German Garibaldi had overthrown the governments in Hanover, Kassel, and Wiesbaden and carried out a violent political upheaval at the head of an army of volunteers, they would regard this as quite in order. . . .

Herr v. Bismarck is admittedly no Garibaldi, and it is true that the expansion of Prussia carried out under his auspices is not likely to be so directly advantageous to liberalism as Garibaldi's annexation of Sicily and Naples. But there is another and equally important cause that is enormously advanced by the Prussian victories and their exploitation, the cause of the political unity of the German nation. . . .

In this situation it is a serious error of Prussian policy to insist on the right of conquest, the invocation of which, as superfluous as it is inapplicable, makes its own task harder and . . . gratuitously agitates public opinion in the annexed territories and in Germany generally. The overriding interest of the Prussian state and, coincident with it, the basic needs of the German nation provide Prussian policy with a better, juster and, above all, nobler claim to all its demands than it can ever find in odious formulations of an obsolete legalistic theory. The ultimate confirmation of this claim can in any case be obtained as little from rational argument as from a victory of arms; it is solely a matter of success. In the event of success, Prussia will have rendered an immeasurable service to the national cause and created a new and unshakable foundation for European public law; without success, Prussia will have gravely sinned against the present and the future. . . . For success is the verdict of history, . . . the highest court, from which in human affairs there is no appeal.

11. Letters and writings of Heinrich von Treitschke, 1862–66: from MAX VON CORNICELIUS, ed. *Heinrich von Treitschkes Briefe*, II, pp. 238–9, 421, 476–7, 481; Treitschke, *Zehn Jahre deutscher Kämpfe*, pp. 96–7, 99, 102–3, 105–8, 114, 130, 132, 134. Treitschke, Heinrich von (1834–96), noted historian and publicist, editor of the *Preussische Jahrbücher*. (See also Docs. 18 and 46).

Count Schmerling was prime minister of Austria.

Dresden and Munich were the capitals of the kingdoms of Saxony and Bavaria respectively.

(*To Wilhelm Nokk, 29 September, 1862.*) . . . You know how passionately I love Prussia; but when I hear a shallow *Junker* like Bismarck boast about the 'iron and blood' with which he hopes to subjugate Germany it seems to me even more ridiculous than vulgar. I have no doubt that the amazing determination of the Prussian people will win out in a few years. Unfortunately, however, a few years' delay can have the most serious consequences in this instance—especially since Germany's most dangerous enemy, the cunning Schmerling, is using all his ingenuity. . . . The fog of words that the Austrians know so well how to create confuses the good-natured Germans, and people will once more get used to thinking that the national task has been accomplished with a few sonorous speeches. . . .

(*To Louise Brockhaus, 1 October, 1865.*) . . . I have just been deeply moved by a good letter from Freytag. My poor friend, noble and sensitive as he is, cannot come to terms at all with Count Bismarck's insincere and intriguing policy. I confess I am made of stronger stuff. I agree with everything that Freytag says about the dishonesty of Prussian politics. But when I look at the other side and see the intrigues of the courts of Dresden and Munich, reminiscent of the Confederation of the Rhine, the unscrupulous demagogues who are corrupting an honest people on behalf of the duke of Augustenburg, and the stupid nonentities of the *Nationalverein*, intoxicated with words,—then I confess that compared with such adversaries Bismarck's policy seems to me not only reasonable but also moral. It aims at what we need, it aims to take a step forward in the direction of Germany unity. . . . The great words 'justice and self-determination' have always been abused by evil and artful men. . . . The just cause will prevail, the heirs of Frederick the Great will rule in Schleswig-Holstein, and before long the nation will be ashamed of its present folly. . . .

(*To Bismarck, 7 June, 1866.*) . . . The course which His Majesty's [i.e. the Prussian] government has so far adopted does not allow me to hope that I might enter its service, and so far I cannot look with any firm expectation of success to the project for reforming the German Confederation. . . . In my opinion, unconditional recognition of the budget powers of the [House of] Representatives is an unavoidable necessity; no device in the world will ever produce a Prussian Diet that would forgo this right.

Please allow me to remark that this question of right and liberty could easily become a question of power for Prussia. The Berlin Cabinet will have no illusions about the despicable intentions of several South German courts. The only thing that prevents these courts from going over with banners flying into the Austrian camp is the lack of realism characteristic of small states and the uncertainty about the mood of their own people which is even today still vacillating between its hatred of Prussia and its vague longing for parliamentary government. Supposing—which I do not believe but which, on the other hand, I do not rule out—that the first battle turned out to be unfavourable to us and if at that time the conflict in Prussia has not been settled then the malice of the small courts, of Red radicalism and of the strong Austrian party in the south will probably be more powerful than all the countervailing efforts of well-meaning patriots, and the south will join with Austria.

In my opinion it is terrible that the most capable minister of foreign affairs that Prussia has had for decades should at the same time be the best-hated man in Germany. I find it sadder still that the soundest proposals for reform of the Confederation that a Prussian government has ever submitted should be greeted by the nation with such scorn. But this fanaticism of the liberal party orientation exists, it is a power that must be reckoned with. Creation of the budget power and the inspiring force of war—these are in my opinion the only means by which confused public opinion can be brought back to its senses. Even after a victory for our army, if the domestic conflict has not been settled the insuperable suspicion of the liberals will still create great difficulties for plans for reform of the Confederation. Your Excellency has been preserved for our country almost miraculously by the grace of heaven. May you also succeed in establishing domestic peace which is so necessary for the success of your magnificently conceived national plan.

So long as I live outside Prussia my journalistic task is easy. As soon as I were to enter into any relationship with His Majesty's government I should have to assume my part of the responsibility for its internal policy; and this is impossible for me so long as the legal basis of the constitution has not been established. . . .

(*To Bismarck, 14 June, 1866.*) . . . Unfortunately the nation's mistrust of the Prussian government knows no bounds; there is only one way to soften it, and that is to establish the constitutional rights of the Diet. If this means is not available (and I know only too well that the infatuation of the Progressive Party makes a reconciliation infinitely difficult), then even a fine and well-written manifesto will find no echo among the masses of the nation. The number of genuinely political men who are capable of rising above a partisan point of view is vanishingly small in Germany. In these circumstances words are powerless, and the mood of the nation can be changed only by victorious battles. . . .

(*10 July, 1866.*) ... If, as a result of successful military operations, it becomes feasible for Prussia to integrate the small states of the south into a great national community, the south will never again offer such a repulsive spectacle of political immorality and indiscipline; the noble qualities of its people, in some respects superior to those of the north, will at last serve national purposes again.

The conviction is growing that this war, which originated in the tranquillity of government offices, is a national war, which will result in the rejuvenation of our fatherland. The accusation is already being heard in the small states of the north that Prussia alone is spilling her blood for Germany's highest aspirations. Even more widespread is the realization of the moral bankruptcy of our petty princelings. . . .

Unforgettable events have demonstrated that Prussia and the small states stand in a relationship of power and impotence, of state and non-state. This knowledge, and the exclusion of Austria from the smaller federation, afford the possibility of a serious national policy. . . . Prussia has proved herself as the only organized purely German Power. The task now is to attach the soft mass of the small states to the hard core of Prussia as she is, with all her rude greatness, her hardness and roughness, for the time being in a sort of federative connection. . . .

[This] constitution . . . will hardly last longer than a generation. It will, to be sure, be called a federation, since the liberals have fallen in love with this expression. . . . [But] serious politicians will recognize that from the current struggles will emerge a stronger Prussia, connected with several more or less dependent satellite states. Such a situation does not give promise of any permanence. It is hard to see how in the long run a German and a Prussian parliament can exist side by side. . . . But to recognize that the present crisis does not yet represent the final settlement of the German revolution is not to rejoice less in the blessings of the last few weeks. Liberation from Austrian foreign domination provides the basis for a national political life. . . .

Anyone who is not so blinded by doctrinaire prejudices that he can no longer learn from the facts must at last realize how meagre the actual achievements of German liberalism and of our constitutional development have been. . . . The glorious recent successes have been won—not, to be sure, as the reactionary zealots assert, by the Conservative Party, but by the devotion of all parties, by the people in arms—but not by liberal means either, but rather by the monarchical discipline of the army. The agitation of the *National-verein* has been entirely wasted; this party managed to delude itself into doing exactly the opposite of what reason and the pressure of events imperiously demanded; the more the Prussian state proved itself to be the only effective political force of the German nation, the farther this party moved away from it.... This does not mean that we should give up our struggle for a parliamentary system. The new Germany cannot maintain itself without an orderly participation of the nation in the government of the state; the solution of the problem of unification will also benefit the cause of freedom. But the liberals must at long last recognize the modest scope of their power, they must reduce their demands to the limits of what is attainable and stop imagining that this Prussia, in whose political development the Crown, the army, and the self-government of the communities are the strongest pillars, can without further ado be converted into something else, on an English-Belgian model....

At such an hour even a less gifted statesman than Count Bismarck must resist the temptation to exploit the nation's victory for the benefit of a party.... In the long run it is impossible to pursue a reactionary domestic policy and, in a great and noble sense, a revolutionary foreign policy. Ideal political goals are not attainable without the help of the power of ideas.... The only concession that we require immediately is the establishment of the constitutional budget power of the Diet; but on this we must insist....

(*30 July, 1866.*) ... There was a time when the ideas of French democracy dominated Germany and when those sudden and successful street battles in the capital city of a centralized state which decided the fate of a country served as models of glorious revolutions. The last decade has taught us that the great political upheavals of civilized peoples as a rule take place by other means, through the agency of orderly military forces. ... The German revolution, too, ... received its first impetus from above, from the Crown. ...

The elimination of the petty thrones represents no more than an act of historical necessity. Anyone who has not learned from the past of all the nations of Europe that small states have no place among the mature and civilized peoples and that the trend of history points to the conglomeration of great national masses must have had his eyes opened by the experiences of these eventful weeks....

Liberalism played no part in the launching of the German war. According to the laws of historical logic, this party will therefore not come to power in the near future; we must be content if the imminent Conservative government does not degenerate into a purely partisan régime. The position to be occupied by the liberals will depend on the zeal which they devote to the work, not begun by them, of unifying Germany....

If the nation's political judgment had kept pace with the growing power of the Prussian state, the first cannon shot of this war would have produced a loud demand throughout the north for union with

Prussia. The nation has missed its great opportunity, it must be content, for the time being, with an unfinished political edifice which is half federative and half unitary. . . .

(*10 August, 1866.*) . . . Now it is up to the nation to complete, in peacetime, the task begun by Prussian arms, and . . . to win over European opinion for our great national cause. . . . We too [like Italy] can succeed, by a serious and persevering pursuit of our national policy, in persuading our neighbours in the near future to accept our complete unification as an unavoidable natural occurrence. . . .

c. The immovable opposition to Bismarck in 1866

12. A South German retort to Treitschke, 1866: from VENEDEY, *An Prof. Heinrich v. Treitschke*, pp. 4–5, 8–9, 12, 14–15, 17, 21–2, 25. Venedey, Jakob (1805–71), publicist and democratic politician.

... Your pamphlet 'The Solution to the Schleswig-Holstein Question' [1865] is a worthy forerunner to your latest one: 'The Future of the Middle States of North Germany.' Just as one can discern the future fruit in the bud, so the latter work is contained in the former ... : the same grotesque effrontery, the same cynical distortion of facts, the same insolent contempt for the customary decencies in an honest struggle; the same lies and the same arrogance characterize both pamphlets. ...

One thing, in particular, completely disgusted me about the [first] pamphlet. It begins with the admission that less than a year earlier, in July 1864, the professor had taught what a year later, in 1865, he found it necessary to condemn. ...

In 1864 he had taught that he regarded the 'incorporation' of Schleswig-Holstein into the Prussian state as not feasible; in 1865 he wrote a pamphlet in defence of the 'annexation.' ...

In 1864 Treitschke taught that right must remain right; in 1865 he said: ... 'nothing remains but a political decision.' ...

It is your example, Herr Professor Heinrich von Treitschke, that has served as model for the insolent and impudent turncoats and deserters who are today throughout Germany claiming a special merit for their own infamy. ...

It is not only in the 'last decade' but throughout history that 'orderly military forces' have caused 'great political upheavals': but at all times and among all peoples where such 'military revolutions' have taken place ... they have always been the result of something rotten in national life. Only the future can show whether the 'revolution' that Herr von Treitschke preaches and that Count Bismarck is bringing down on Germany with 'orderly military forces' will be better than its predecessors. But history teaches that all abiding, formative political upheavals that have created something new and great had their origins in other soil than that of 'orderly military forces,' of 'military revolutions,' whether these were produced by a victorious general such as Bonaparte, an intriguing courtier as in Spain, a child of fortune and of chance such as Napoleon III, or even by a king and his minister.

Only the future can show where this 'revolution in the good sense,' this 'revolution from above,' this 'revolution carried out with orderly military forces,' will lead.

But Herr Treitschke shows us that even today it is cutting every legal ground from under the feet of all existing dynasties in Germany. He has drawn up a pretty complete list of indictments against the dynasties expelled from their thrones. . . .

But is there not a sort of cosmic irony, a real mockery, in the fact that Herr von Treitschke believes that on these grounds he can justify the expulsion of three dynasties for the benefit of Prussia, and is rewarded for it by Prussia with a professorship? . . .

If he measured all dynasties by the same yardstick the matter would be arguable. But his yardstick is different for Prussia than for Saxony, Hanover, and Hesse. . . .

Prussia was and is dominated by a political orientation that could not and cannot lead to German unity. If this policy, which has found its archetype in Count Bismarck, conquered Germany tomorrow and unified it by force, then even this conquest of all of Germany would not lead to German unity. A conquest of Germany by a Prussia that is not ruled in a German spirit would be merely a bare fact that would last until it was superseded by another fact. The unity of Germany must be founded on something beyond the 'majestic thundering of cannon,' . . . it must be rooted in German respect for law, German love of freedom, German popular honour and popular self-government if it is to last. . . .

The unity of Germany can be realized only by and with the German people, not by a 'Crown' with the help of a party that scorns German law and German nationality. A parliament of the whole German people is the natural bond among all the German peoples. In 1848 the nation was launched in the right direction, and if Prussia, the Prussian 'Crown,' had at that time accepted the national constitution and the imperial crown then it would have been legitimate to fight against Austria and the enemies of the nation and the emperor. But the Prussian 'Crown' did not want to accept the 'Crown' of Germany from the hands of the German people. . . .

13. E. L. von Gerlach: from *The Annexations and the North German Confederation* (1866), pp. 3–5, 7, 11, 15–16, 18–20, 25–8, 38. Gerlach, Ernst Ludwig von (1795–1877), judge, conservative politician and publicist.

. . .The author expressed his views on the situation in May of this year in three essays published in the *Kreuzzeitung*. He took as his point of departure the premise that God's law has its place, not beside, still less below, but above the spheres of diplomacy, politics, and war, and comprehends these fields, like those of private life, with sovereign authority, so that it constitutes their supreme guideline too. He warned of the erroneous notion according to which statesmen had no higher law than patriotic egoism.

'National needs and demands'—'world-historical moments and world-historical mission'—'providential calling and providential goals'—these and all similar ideas must find their place far below the holy majesty of God's commands, the same commands that the village child learns in school, but whose profundity and grandeur no human mind is capable of comprehending.

The French Revolution of 1789 and the execution of the king were certainly 'world-historical moments.' The 'great French nation' achieved an impressive 'marshalling and expansion of power' by amazing accomplishments in battle. It believed itself, in its thirst for military fame and domination, to be incapable of breathing without such an expansion. 'Providence' had to attain 'great goals' and attained them by way of Napoleon's 'historical mission.' ... But Moscow, Leipzig, Elba, and Waterloo were no less 'world-historical moments.' The victorious allies had a 'world historical mission' and 'providential goals' just as much on their side. . . .

We should be better advised to abstain from high-sounding words and, if we have to judge, to submit the ultimate verdict on all human deeds, even world-historical ones, humbly to the Last Judgment, the judgment whose ultimate criteria will be, not the great ideas of men, but God's commands. Justice and truth are the wisest policy; and the best patriotism is the one that says: 'What does it profit my country to gain the whole world and lose its own soul?'

'Realpolitik,' a policy based on facts that ignores God's commands —that is to say, the source of all law and the root of the state—is a policy without spirit in the proper sense of the term. . . .

The special object of those three essays was to contribute to the maintenance of peace in Germany. They were designed to show that Austria's general attitude and mobilization were of a defensive character. . . . [In 1863] Prussia rightly rejected the Austrian proposal [for reform of the Confederation]; now [in 1866] Austria did not accept the Prussian one. Probably Austria took exception to the idea of a parliament elected by universal suffrage. By this rejection Austria did not abandon its defensive and conservative posture. . . .

Prussia is at the moment of the opinion—and this is also the opinion of the author of this essay—that the hereditary prince [of Augustenburg] has no right of inheritance in the duchies [of Schleswig and Holstein]. For his father, who is still living, has formally and solemnly given up any rights of inheritance, for himself and his family, in exchange for an equivalent. If Prussia and Austria had clung to this disclaimer and to the Treaty of London and had not cast doubts on the latter, the whole complication would not have arisen. . . .

According to the articles of the Confederation, agreed by treaty, the Confederation was indissoluble and no member of the Confederation had a right to secede. If, therefore, the Confederation had by a majority, taken decisions in violation of the Confederation, the loyal minority would admittedly, in certain conditions, have had not only the right but the duty to resist those decisions, if necessary by force of arms. But such a war could always, according to the law of the Confederation, have as its object only the maintenance of the Confederation within its constitutional limits, not the dissolution of the Confederation. . . .

If, as Prussia maintained, the old Confederation was dissolved, the three states [Saxony, Hanover, and Electoral Hesse] were, in international law, foreign states with respect to Prussia. And nobody will assert that every stronger state has the right to impose alliances on all its weaker neighbours—for example Holland, Belgium, or Switzerland—as it sees fit. . . .

The Confederation, like all creations of the year 1815, had as its basis a noble idea, . . . the idea of law and of freedom, to some extent also of Christianity and of the Christian Church, the holy idea 'from above' in contrast to the unholy 'from below' and the revolution and tyranny defeated in 1815. . . . To cleave to this idea, to develop it in spirit and to vindicate it in all practical applications, especially in the holy struggle against all the godless and lawless acts of the revolutionaries, was the high task of the German princes after 1815, above all of the German Great Powers and of the entire German nation, the same task which is still to be heard in the Prussian note to Austria of 26 January, 1866, where it speaks of 'the common struggle against revolution.' . . . This 'common struggle against revolution' could have formed the living principle for Austro-Prussian fraternity, relegating their disputes into the background and preparing the unity of all Germany. . . .

Annexations—taking possession of foreign territories that have not been ceded—have not taken place in Germany . . . since 1813. . . . Reference has been made to the right of conquest. But this right depends on the cause and nature of the war which preceded the conquest. The concept of right itself implies that right cannot be founded on force alone. . . .

Loyalty and honesty are the ancient sources of German nationality, not empty phrases about 'a realistic policy based on facts,' or 'world-historical necessities,' or the 'fulfilment of destinies,' and so on. . . .

It has been said, with respect to the annexations, that it is a matter for the populations, that dynasties exist for the sake of peoples, not peoples for the sake of dynasties. The truth is that God has created both dynasties and peoples, both fathers and children, for His glory. ... The notion referred to above is a half-truth which tears asunder what belongs together, so that even what is true in it becomes an untruth. At the base of this untruth lies the erroneous revolutionary doctrine that the masses create authority and that authority must obey the masses—a doctrine that would overthrow no state more surely than Prussia, profoundly monarchical as it is. . . .

Next to the monarchy, with which it is intimately bound up, the army is not only the most popular but also the most fundamental Prussian institution. . . . Let us not forget that the monarchical army presupposes a monarchically organized country and is a monarchical people in arms only on that condition, and that democratic electoral procedures form no basis on which loyalty to the king and the monarchical spirit of the army can firmly rest.

B. Foreign and domestic problems between 1866 and 1871

14. Adolf Schmidt, *Prussia's German Policy*, 1867: from *Preussens deutsche Politik*, pp. iii–iv, 215–6, 279, 281–3, 287–8. Schmidt, Adolf (1812–87), historian and publicist.

... Last year, justifiably and in character, I desired peace to be maintained so long as I judged it possible. But as early as April the decisive struggle seemed to me hardly avoidable, by May I regarded it as necessary in principle and from the beginning of June as demanded by the situation. The possibility of such rapid and magnificent successes as actually occurred was not within my capacity to estimate, since I was neither familiar with the Prussian means and forces nor, as a layman, able to evaluate them. But I never for a moment doubted Prussia's ultimate victory since it seemed to me to be a postulate of history, in other words, because I had always regarded the way of German national unification by Prussia as the only possible way and the one ordained by history....

We know that the recent experiences of 1866 were in fact of a quite different nature from those of the past and therefore evoked quite different interpretations. But this metamorphosis was clearly not, at any rate among intelligent, enlightened, and politically educated men, a matter of 'adulation of success,' a phrase currently much abused; it is, rather, a matter of recognizing an actual reversal of Prussia's German policy, of acknowledging its energetic alignment with the great tendencies of history.... So long as there is history, success will, must, and should determine historical judgment, as it has done through the centuries. But only he can be counted great in history who consciously wills and carries out the will of history. And historical greatness consists not in a temporary but in an enduring success, not in the achievement as such but in sustaining and building on what has been achieved....

Every future historian of the German nation will proclaim the events of the year 1866 as a tremendous step forward in the progress of world history; he will at the same time acknowledge the year of Prussia's independent action in its German policy as the year of the most magnificent and momentous upheaval that German history has ever known; he will, we hope, be able to prize it as the year in which German unity and freedom were born. In this year Count Bismarck entered upon the fourth phase of his activity and his transformation,

the one most filled with actions and expectations. . . . It will serve
to scatter or to lighten even the darkest shadows that lie over all his
earlier phases if it continues with unshakable determination to be
directed toward the further united and free development of Germany.
For both form part of the will of history, and only that statesman is
great who wills the will of history. . . .

The most urgent need is for us all to cease our grumbling and complaining and indignation at the catastrophe of 'blood and iron.' We
have all been saying to each other, over and over again, especially
since 1849, . . . that things would never get better or move forward
in Germany except by way of 'force' or 'revolution' or 'war and civil
war.' . . . Now that the prophecy has been fulfilled have we any reason
to recoil in moral indignation at the reality of what has been regarded
as inevitable by so many people, including ourselves?

To be sure, it is not proper for anyone, whoever he may be, to
value war or revolution as such. But it is proper for everyone, without exception, to judge the outcome of great and momentous events
objectively. And this means that we must have regard not only to
the undermining or destruction of edifices of the past, but above all
to their effects in creating or laying the foundations for the future.

Time and time again we hear the accusation: might has taken
precedence over right! The law has been violated by force! So it
has, but through its own fault. . . . Law is nothing but past history,
finished and immobilized; but history is law eternally becoming,
eternally flowing. . . . Whenever the special rights of tribes and princes
or of particular states or corporations are sacrificed to general national
needs or demands, interests, and purposes, it is never a matter of
violation of right by wrong, or of an overthrow of morality by immorality, but rather of a replacement of a lower by a higher right, of
a lower by a higher morality. . . . In fact, the moral power of history
is so undeniably the highest moral law as well that for this very reason
the proverb is universally accepted that 'the world's history is the
world's court.'

. . . The preservation of the thrones of Hanover, Electoral Hesse,
and Nassau depended . . . on their occupants. . . . By arrogantly rejecting what would have maintained them on their thrones and in
their rights and privileges they dispensed Prussia from any legal and
moral responsibility and brought their own downfall on themselves
alone. This is their tragic guilt. We acknowledge the rights that
existed before the fateful development of the consequences of this
guilt; but we can never concede that they continue to exist after
history has delivered its verdict. . . .

Truly, I do not underestimate freedom. I also value it more than
life itself; but I value the consciousness of being a member of a great

national entity more than the enjoyment of a momentary freedom.
. . . In case of extreme need I would not hesitate to sacrifice even the
last spark of freedom temporarily for the sake, not of a completed
unity, but of the completion of unity. . . . As a former member of the
Frankfurt Parliament I should have liked to see the constitution of
1849 form the basis of the new German order. . . . But parliamentary
action itself is more important than fulfilment of that desire. The
nation will be served not by long-winded controversies about possible
foundations or by fruitless party wrangles, but only by actions which
will bring the work of unity and freedom to completion as soon as
possible. The motto of the North German *Reichstag* should be:
'Little talk and quick action.' . . .

15. Ludwig Bamberger: from *Herr von Bismarck*, 1868, pp.
xvii–xix, xxxi–xxxiv, xxxix–xl, xliii–xlvi, 7, 25, 27, 108, 128.
Bamberger, Ludwig (1823–99), banker, liberal politician, in exile
1849–66, later National Liberal, Secessionist, and Progressive
Reichstag deputy. (See also Doc. 54.)

[*From the Introduction: 'Germany, France, and the Revolution'*] . . .
The essence of any free movement had for generations and for good
reasons been concentrated, on the European continent, in the
symbol of revolution; adherence to this symbol is naturally connected
with its first and most powerful expression, the great upheaval of the
end of the last century. Once the theme had been found that Prussia
went to war only to combat the principle and the legacy of the
revolution, first in Germany and then in the rest of Europe, it could
by dint of some imagination be applied to all sorts of instances. . . .
It must be admitted that, more than anyone else, Herr von Bismarck
had offered materials for this game . . ., since in the recent past he
had on a number of occasions made frequent use of slogans which,
in providing justifiable bases for revolutionary fanaticism, also per-
petuate fanatical hostility to the revolutionary tradition. . . . Moreover, proof was easily to hand to show that he was entirely serious in
such utterances. The whole long period of conflict between 1862
and 1866 had everywhere been understood in this sense alone; and,
in view of the general inclination to think in this way, the assertion
could easily gain currency that the only purpose had been to suppress
any aspiration to freedom and to introduce a system of absolutism
for which militarism . . . was both a means and an end. This, incidentally, proved at the same time that the Prussian government regarded
its work as only half done, and therefore not secure, so long as revolutionary forces in France had not been exterminated. . . .
     The war that eventually broke out against Austria, which for

Germany immediately became the turning-point in interpretations of the experiences of past years and of current events, appeared to foreign theorists, on the contrary, as the most flagrant confirmation of everything evil that had always been said about Prussian *raison d'état*. . . . It therefore became important, after we ourselves had been converted to different views, to demonstrate to the French that the Prussian campaign against Austria and her allies was not an instrument of reaction, of counter-revolution, either in its deeper historical origins or in its personal motivations, but that in its visible and predictable consequences it was precisely the contrary. . . .

A clarification of the position for Germans, too, is desirable as well as profitable. . . . The high moral esteem that the great French Revolution had attained in the whole cultured world was, after all, as justified in Germany as anywhere else. . . . Accepting this historically unassailable validity, . . . most educated men had stayed close to the course of French ideas . . ., appropriating to themselves all the slogans of the . . . revolutionary catechism. What the German mind lacked in natural aptitude for rigid formulas and authorities it easily made up in its stronger inclination toward pure abstraction, which tends to carry a given theory to its most extreme consequences, in sovereign contempt for all practical obstacles.

So it came about that, despite different mental habits, roughly the same result occurred in both countries. It became a moral duty in political activity to cling not only to the content but to a specified form. By regarding the brief period that had made use of this form as a lost ideal to be recaptured, men aspiring to higher things ran the risk of falling into a retrogressive movement, of copying all the mistakes of reactionary ideas, losing sight of what has happened and is happening and becoming romantically infatuated with the restoration of past conditions. . . .

The revolution dates from the rebellion of the American colonies against the mother country. . . . A century has elapsed . . . between this great turning-point and the present day. . . . Should we not therefore at last accept that the problems are no longer at the same point and cannot therefore be solved by the same methods as three generations ago? . . . Sensible progress in the great civic affairs of Germany now depends on the rulers no longer regarding revolution as a spectre . . . and the ruled no longer regarding it as a saviour. . . . If we can succeed . . ., both above and below, in giving prominence to freer cultural forces that can confront each other without prejudices, then politics will be on the path on which science has preceded it long since. For science has burst out of the confines of Aristotelian scholasticism and studies life instead of preconceived concepts of nature. . . .

What is at stake is to grasp that the great innovation which was introduced into society a hundred years ago is to be neither extirpated nor repeated, but continued; that it advances every day of its own accord; that almost any useful activity contributes toward completing the programme of revolution, even if it is by other means and with other results than those conceived by the authors of the Rights of Man. If we could once succeed in distinguishing between the legal content and the mere procedure of revolution we should have gone a considerable way toward clarification. . . . If we can get used to finding our programme for world conditions, not in the original Creation or in the pure blue sky of abstract thought, but in the study of the advances which can be achieved in life from day to day, then we shall have placed politics on the same basis as modern science. . . .

This does not mean abolishing the supremacy of principles, still less their hold on the mind of the masses. The latter, on the contrary, occurs when doctrinaires try to hang on to conceptual formulas that have long been overtaken by events. . . . Principles, too, are not eternal in all their elements. After the displacement of the cultural epoch of humanism by that of nationalism we can even now see the latter taken to extremes which give clear indications of the limit having been reached. Principles are not invented, but derived and put together from the needs and experiences of mankind. . . .

[From the text.] Politics is not a science; at most it is an art. Consequently one of the greatest dangers to which it is exposed is that of falling into rigid, traditional formulas. The incalculable boon that was the French Revolution could not have left the world with nothing but benefits. Human affairs are not as absolute as that. . . . [But] the succeeding generations believed . . . that they could solve a problem in real life by looking at it under the aspect of a single alternative: either revolution or counter-revolution. Herr von Bismarck shared this error in his early political career. He has expiated it to a considerable extent since he ceased subscribing to it; for those who see salvation only in a strict application of revolutionary formulas are now the most implacable enemies of him who once knew no goal other than counter-revolution. . . .

The idea of a rehabilitation of the German nation by elevating Prussia is not to be seen as a tradition clung to by the royal house; it is of nobler ancestry. . . . The idea which Herr von Bismarck undertook to convert into reality sprang from the free and noble urgings of the great national spirit and not from selfish dynastic greed. . . . Only causes which persist are great causes; but they persist only if they correspond to a general need, a higher necessity: this is the difference between a statesman and an adventurer. . . . Whatever errors or mistakes he may have committed, in this sense Herr von Bismarck undeniably has the right to be called a statesman. . . . It is not possible to doubt for a moment that he is a born revolutionary. . . . The revolutionary consciousness is one which believes itself to be in possession of a heroic means of attaining the highest end. . . .

[*From the Epilogue.*] In his capacity as a revolutionary, who in a great crisis succeeded in overcoming all legal misgivings, Herr von Bismarck has settled into an antipathy against anything that looks like a pedantic intervention of judicial authority and so exposes himself to the same danger as his most extreme opponents: of pursuing a revolution as a permanent institution. . . .

16. A. L. v. Rochau, *Principles of 'Realpolitik'*, 1869: from *Grundsätze der Realpolitik*, II, i, vii–ix, 7, 26–7.

Fifteen years ago I published the work of which this is the second part. . . . From its very title that work established its dissent from political idealism as well as from politics based on fantasy and sentiment by whose dark impulses the German people has all too long been led astray. . . .

The state is by nature a realistic politician, if only by virtue of the conditions of its existence, and has therefore always had to suffer being treated as a criminal by political idealists and visionaries. . . . In contrast to the politics of the state, the politics of the people is most susceptible to idealism and fantastication. The causes of this difference are obvious. On the one hand we have the school of political life and the consciousness of responsibility, on the other hand inexperience and yielding to intellectual or emotional whim with little or no thought for the consequences. . . .

For the state, in contrast to the individual, self-preservation is the supreme law. The state must survive at any price; it cannot go into the poorhouse, it cannot beg, it cannot commit suicide; in short, it must take wherever it can find the essentials of life.

Politics, in so far as they are not in the hands of the community, are a mandate which carries responsibility toward the constituency as well as toward the moral law, two responsibilities which need to be weighed against one another.

The right of the politician to sacrifice the welfare of the state to his personal scruples of conscience may be undeniable in simple matters or those of secondary significance, but it may be extremely doubtful in difficult and important cases.

The clash of duties, which the individual can as a rule easily avoid, occurs so often, so unavoidably, and so fatefully in the life of the state that politics is often a matter of a choice between two moral evils.

Finally, there occur historic necessities and political acts of nature [*Naturereignisse*] before which the state and the people resign themselves irresistibly and passively, for which responsibility can be attributed to nobody, and to which, therefore, the ethical criterion of human conduct is quite inapplicable. . . .

The drive toward German unity is not a fiction but a palpable fact of the history of the last few decades. The trouble is that both the source and the nature of this fact have usually been misunderstood. The German drive toward unity does not . . . derive from a spiritual sympathy but from a more or less legitimate selfishness; and it aims not at satisfying national emotional needs but at securing this or that common interest. The most important of these interests is none other than that of self-preservation, rightly or wrongly understood, an interest which hitherto, as everyone knew or suspected, Germany was in no position to guarantee even for a day. In short, unity is at bottom purely a business proposition for the Germans, for which nobody is willing to make sacrifices but from which, by contrast, everyone wishes to gain as much as possible for himself—reduced taxes, lighter military burdens, public liberties, guarantees of internal legal order and of external peace. . . .

17. Letters of Franz von Roggenbach to Heinrich von Treitschke, 6 and 12 February, 1870: from HEYDERHOFF, pp. 449–53, 457–9.

Roggenbach, Franz von (1825–1907), liberal politician, foreign minister of Baden 1861–65. (See also Doc. 57.) Karlsruhe was the capital of the grand-duchy of Baden. Stuttgart was the capital of the kingdom of Württemberg. Emile Ollivier was the reforming prime minister of France in the last years of the Second Empire.

. . . The question [of admitting Baden to the North German Confederation] can be examined from a number of angles.

One could consider whether . . . [it] is possible at all, or more possible than in the last three years.

Or again, whether its entry would be useful in the interests of Germany, whether to work for it is patriotic or unpatriotic with reference to its encouraging or discouraging effect on the power position of Germany and its internal consolidation. All this, in turn, could be regarded from a north German or south German, a unitary or a particularist point of view. You will see that it is not easy to give a comprehensive answer, the less so since public opinion on both sides of the Main and in all camps is not formed on the basis of thorough, historically precise knowledge and examination of the political situation. . . .

You know that, in my personal opinion, there has rarely been a more shallow, unclear, and pernicious position that that taken up by National Liberals on both sides of the Main with the slogan 'Entry into the North German Confederation.' ... No north or south German patriot ... can at the moment desire the entry of a small or large part of south Germany into the North German Confederation as at present constituted.

Let us look at the possibility, and to begin with in a European context. It is clear that the German nation would, despite its internal racial and religious divisions, be able at any time to defend its independent political development against a hostile Europe so long as in Prussia the Crown and the leading statesmen are high-minded and courageous. It is no less clear that even they would be enabled to do so only if the proper use of military and material means for the assertion of power is supported by the united heroism, moral force, and willingness to make sacrifices on the part of the nation itself. These were present in 1866 among the victors in Bohemia and could have been awakened in south Germany too if the enterprise started at that time had been continued on a grand scale. . . .

But at the moment conditions are not so favourable. Disintegration and factionalism of all kinds have extinguished the last traces of the movement for national unity and have left the field for some time to centrifugal forces. Today an attempt by Prussia to unite Germany would find far less support and would be able to command the moral power to resist external interference only in the event of an unjustified attack, certainly not if Prussia were spontaneously to attempt unification and thereby provoked a conflict with Europe. So long as things remain like this Prussia would be well advised not to risk such a dangerous game. . . . Even granted that France is very preoccupied with domestic matters and Austria helpless and weak, this does not compensate for the unfavourable internal conditions, where a foreign enemy would find traitorous parties in Germany only too willing to offer him aid and comfort.

In circumstances like these, to embark in the immediate future on a venturesome policy and to pursue the aim of unification steadfastly despite all the difficulties would require courage greater than that displayed by the present Prussian policy-makers in 1866 and 1867; even braver men than Count Bismarck would need to be convinced that great decisions would lead to great national achievements. Whether this is the case can easily be judged from a consideration of the possible results. Only in one respect do conditions indicate a more favourable opportunity than during the last three years. If in Bavaria the prospect of having at least one reliable ally in the Munich government should definitely disappear, then the temptation to convert into reality Baden's desire to enter might gain the upper hand in Berlin over the reluctance felt up to now to offend Bavaria by such a yielding to Baden's wishes. The main criterion by which the decision will be taken in Berlin, the possibility of danger from abroad, is of course only moderately affected by this change of detail.

The question, therefore, remains the same: are the expected results so important as to justify dangerous and uncertain risks?

The first point to clarify is whose interest is paramount and in whose interest results are to be gained and secured.

If Prussia and the North German Confederation is [sic] to take action then surely it is only its interest that is under discussion, since it is the one that is above all taking the risks.

We cannot accept that the interests of Germany as a whole, as distinct from Prussia, are decisive, since this Germany, precisely, does not yet exist as a decision-making entity and is still to be created as a factor in Europe capable of action and having interests and a will of its own. Equally, the interests of Baden or of any other individual state are not under discussion. Since all of us, even if we are, for example, citizens of Baden, owe our first duty to our nation and fatherland, we could in any event impose our particular desires on the great whole, the paramount factor of German greatness and the German future, only by neglecting our duty. . . . This would, as stated above, be unpatriotic in the highest degree and almost amount to a crime against the nation. It is therefore clear that the only criterion according to which the advisability of a policy involving new initiatives in this matter can be decided is whether it will yield results useful for the North German Confederation and for Prussia and whether it justifies the assumption of grave risks on Prussia's part. At the moment I have no doubt that the answer to this question is in the negative.

The initiative demanded of Prussia, in the face of all these dangers, is the admission of Baden to the North German Confederation. . . . The certain advantages are listed as follows:

1. Strengthening of our moral position in that the notorious tripartite division of Germany will be on the way to being healed, that the line of the Main will have been crossed.

2. Favourable effects on Württemberg and Bavaria.

We need not concern ourselves with the egotistical motives dominating the dynastic self-interest of the Court of Karlsruhe or with the government's timidity. From the Prussian point of view which, as already stated, should also be that of all good patriots and therefore of the National Liberal party everywhere, these two meagre advantages are outweighed by an infinite series of disadvantages.

To begin with, the expected favourable effect on Württemberg and

Bavaria at the same time runs a very grave risk of turning into a danger. Let us suppose that the goal has been attained and that Baden's entry sooner or later forces Bavaria and Württemberg into the North German Confederation as well. Would it not amount essentially to abolishing the North German Confederation, which consists in the hegemony of Prussia over weak states and in the diplomatic *entente cordiale* with Saxony, to introduce into the Federal Council a state of five million inhabitants imbued with a particularist spirit and with racial jealousy, which will immediately convert the laboriously constructed will to rule into a voting mechanism according to the mode of the Frankfurt Assembly and put Prussia in a minority?

Let us imagine about seventy deputies from Bavaria alone (not to mention the Swabians), all sworn ememies of the north German state, members of the *Reichstag* with the opportunity to discuss and to ruin there very few Bavarian but very many north German vital interests. . . .

Let us imagine this unreliable, treacherous state, always ready for betrayal, as a perpetual ally and protected with our blood and material, while, of course, the door would be closed on all further development of the federal constitution.

The possibility must also be weighed in Berlin that this hoped-for and dreamed-about admission of Bavaria, which is actually to be feared and to be avoided at any price, might *not* take place and the entry of Baden would remain isolated. Certainly this would not be a matter of indifference for her two neighbours and they would regard it as an attempt to push them along the same road and to prepare their own entry. But this is abominated by the existing, politically relevant organized forces in these two countries, the dynasty and the government, and no less so for the fact that its effect would be more damaging to Prussia than to themselves. In place of the fairly reliable, externally secure alliance based on treaties among princes there would be instead a situation of extreme suspicion and utter unreliability in the event of danger. . . .

The mistrust felt in Munich and Stuttgart, which implies a weakening, would, however, also be transmitted to Vienna, with whose government it is a cardinal principle of Count Bismarck's policy to be on good terms, and rightly so. Since Austria has retained her power even after 1866 it is obvious that a friendly relationship between the two governments is all the more desirable for the fact that we can no longer expect any reliable friendship from Russia.

For all these reasons it is completely inadvisable to make any exception for Baden and to allow her unilateral entry. This is the more true for the fact that it would involve giving up the attempt to create a federative tie with the southern states (between north Germany and the southern states), which is what we should strive for if common cause is to be made *vis-à-vis* the outside world, especially as regards military preparations. That such a league would represent an institution essentially different from the North German Confederation requires no demonstration. . . .

Certainly I agree with your sentence: 'we are dealing with an active monarchy that has converted wandering jurists and mercenaries into a civil service and a national army and still looks to them for support.' I also agree that the simple formula of the rule of varying parliamentary majorities is not likely to prove very practical for a political organism such as Prussia dressed in the ornamental garment of the North German Confederation. Finally, I am as convinced as anyone that states and peoples can be welded together in a common political outlook and national spirit only in the fire of common actions purified by exalted devotion.

In all these respects our liberals have sinned grievously and have almost constantly misunderstood the historical and moral foundations of our past. . . .

Nevertheless, I cannot share to the same extent your optimistic hope that German liberalism will now give up its false ideals. We must not be under any illusions about the material with which we have to work. There are no parties in Germany, except for the Ultramontanes and the remnants of the north German Conservatives, that are well enough organized for any decisive influence to be exerted on their conduct. We have to deal with two groups of differently oriented people, one of them with a stronger sense for the state, the other more concerned with social and individual independence. These two groups are exploited by two coteries, the National Liberal and the particularist-*grossdeutsch*-democratic. Both are absolutely impervious to any idea that is not in harmony with their favourite notions and their special coterie interests. . . . The National Liberal coterie is at the moment politically thoroughly confused. Suckled on the milk of English parliamentary principles, it has only very vague notions of the real nature of English political life but is too self-satisfied to accept any instruction (as shown by Gneist's fate) or to take into consideration the undeniably unpleasant consequences for recent political development in England. These gentlemen have absolutely no understanding of the fact that from the given bases, namely the Prussian monarchy, the existing vested interest of the army, and the internationally guaranteed and fixed constitution of the North German Confederation, there is no way of reaching an English parliamentary development. They do not even see that there is an enormous difference between the National Liberal party in the *Reichstag* and the House of Representatives and an English ruling party. The victory of Ollivier and of allegedly English-style parliamentarism strengthens the leaders in their assumption that a similar development cannot fail to take place in Germany too, perhaps even now, certainly when the crown prince comes to power. The inadequacy, the obstinacy, the bad mistakes of the present administration in almost all departments, even the chaotic nature of Bismarck's occasional interventions, must confirm them in their assumption. . . .

Against all these dangers we can be protected only by a great monarch and an intelligent government. . . . Only in this way, against the prevailing current toward the falsest kind of parliamentarism but rather as a living development from the given premises, can a constitution be evolved which will be in harmony with the historic elements of the Prussian state and of the North German Confederation and will stimulate them to new and fruitful activity. So long as the Crown remains neutral and passive in the most important areas of political life and the ministers display a childish incompetence it will be impossible to stem the tendency to move the centre of gravity of political decisions toward a legislative majority patched together by artificial intrigue. . . .

18. The political writings of Heinrich von Treitschke: from *Zehn Jahre deutscher Kämpfe*, pp. 349, 356–8. (See Doc. 11.)

(*7 December, 1870.*) . . . We have never had any illusions that the inclusion of the south at the present moment would be anything but the greatest sacrifice that the north has ever made for the German cause. . . . But such a cornucopia of particularistic concessions as are contained in the treaty with Bavaria exceeds our worst fears. . . .

It cost me a bitter struggle before I recognized that in spite of all this the *Reichstag* has no mandate to reject the Bavarian treaty. Our justified resentment must yield to a higher duty, to the faith that we must keep with our south German compatriots. . . . Those who do not accept such a sentimental policy will perhaps be persuaded by the sober consideration that the *Reichstag* does not even have the power to eliminate the treaty. There are no two ways about it: anyone who rejects this treaty does not have the nation behind him. The people know and care nothing about three-quarters majorities or the foreign affairs committee or the other anxieties that cast a shadow over the joy of these last days for those of us who are politicians. The people wish and expect that German unity will come about. . . .

But above all other considerations we must have regard to the fact that the paragraphs of a constitution mean little by the side of real political power and the patriotic spirit of a nation in the ascendant. . . . If the noble ideas of this war prevail in peacetime too, the German state can exist and grow despite its loose institutions. . . .

C. The Franco-Prussian War

a. Bismarck and the Hohenzollern candidature

19. Bismarck to the king of Prussia, 9 March, 1870: from
BONNIN, pp. 68–73.
Isabella II, Queen of Spain (1833–68), deposed in the latter
year.
The Carlist claimant to the Spanish throne was descended
from a younger line of the Spanish Bourbon dynasty. Henri de
Rochefort was a republican publicist opposed to the régime of
Napoleon III.

Your Majesty,

Will, I trust, graciously permit me with my humble duty to
summarize in writing the motives which in my modest opinion
speak in favour of an acceptance of the Spanish Crown by His Serene
Highness, the Hereditary Prince of Hohenzollern, now that I have
already respectfully intimated them by word of mouth.

I am of the opinion that it would serve Prussian and German state
interests and bring indirect advantages if the acceptance takes place,
and also that in the opposite case disadvantages and dangers are to
be feared.

Acceptance of the Spanish Royal Crown by a Prince of Your
Majesty's illustrious House would strengthen existing sympathies between two nations, which, exceptionally, are in the happy position of
having no conflicting interests, not being neighbours, and whose
friendly relations seem capable of considerable development.[1] The
Spaniards would have a feeling of gratitude[2] towards Germany, if
they are rescued from the state of anarchy into which a people predominantly monarchist in sentiment threatens to sink because it lacks
a king.

For Germany it is desirable to have on the other side of France a
country on whose sympathies[3] we can rely and with whose feelings
France is obliged to reckon. If during a war between Germany and France conditions prevail such as those under Queen

[1] King of Prussia's marginal note: 'Agreed.'

[2] King of Prussia's marginal note: 'This feeling, this sympathy, on the part
of a nation which for the last forty years has wantonly proceeded from one
revolution to another, seems to me highly problematic.'

[3] King of Prussia's marginal note: 'How long would these sympathies last?'

Isabella when there was a prospect of an alliance of the Latin Catholic Powers, and if on the other hand in such an eventuality one conceives of a Government in Spain sympathetic to Germany, the difference between the two situations in terms of the armed forces that France could put in the field against Germany may be estimated at not less than one to two French army corps.[4] In the former case it would even become possible for French forces to be relieved by Spanish and thus made available for use, in the latter case it would be necessary to keep at least one French Corps stationed on the Spanish frontier. French peaceableness towards Germany will always wax or wane in proportion to the dangers of war with Germany. We have in the long run to look for the preservation of peace not to the good will of France but to the impression created by our position of strength.[5]

The prosperity of Spain and German trade with her would receive a powerful impetus under Hohenzollern rule. If even in Rumania the Germany dynasty has given a remarkable stimulus to trade relations between that landlocked country and Germany, it is to be assumed in all probability that the renewal of friendly feelings towards Germany in Spain with her long coastline would provide new openings for the once so prosperous German trade there.[6] It should not be forgotten that the political attitude of Prussia towards Spain after the events of 1833 turned out disastrously for our trade, particularly for the Silesian linen industry; the opposite effect may be expected from a revival of our mutual political sympathies.[7] The repute of the Hohenzollern dynasty, the justifiable pride with which not only Prussia regards its Royal House but Germany too, tends more and more to glory in that name as a common national possession, a symbol of German fame and German prestige abroad; all this forms an important element in political self-confidence, the fostering and strengthening of which would be of benefit to national feeling in general and to monarchist sentiment in particular. It is therefore to Germany's political interest that the House of Hohenzollern should gain an esteem and an exalted position in the world such as does not find its analogy in the past record of the Hapsburgs since Charles V. This element of pride in the dynasty is not to be estimated lightly as a force operating in favour of the contentment of our people and the consolidation of conditions. Just as in Spain scant respect for the ruling house has paralysed the forces of the nation for centuries, so

[4] King of Prussia's marginal note: 'What potentate in Spain would be in a position to *guarantee* such a policy?'

[5] King of Prussia's marginal note: 'Agreed.'

[6] King of Prussia's marginal note: 'I daresay that is possible.'

[7] King of Prussia's marginal note: 'Are great sympathies for Spain noticeable or existent in Prussia?'

with us pride in an illustrious Dynasty has been a powerful moral impetus to the development of Prussia's power in Germany.[8] This impetus will make strong growth if the hitherto so imperfectly satisfied need of the Germans for recognition by other countries receives the incentive of a dynasty occupying an incomparable position in the world.

A rejection of the proffered crown would probably have undesirable consequences. It could not but highly offend the Spaniards[9] if a crown which in the past always occupied a high rank should not meet with acceptance and if a nation of 16 million souls, begging to be rescued from the anarchy into which it feels itself to be sinking, should suffer the rebuff of being refused the King of its choice.[10]

In the event of a rejection, the wishes of the Spaniards would probably turn to Bavaria. If Prince Adalbert's line or the Ducal line there accepted the offer, Spain would have a ruling house which looked for support to France and Rome, maintaining contact with antinational elements in Germany and affording them a secure if remote rallying point. The same tendency to enter into relations with Rome, France and Austria[11] with the approval of native ultramontane reactionaries would take place in Spain under Carlist rule. We should then consistently have to regard her as belonging to the ranks of our adversaries.

Failing the Bavarian and the Carlist possibilities Spain would in the first instance probably lapse into a republic. The repercussions of a Spanish republic would most immediately make themselves felt in France and Italy. How easily revolutionary movements spread from Spain to Italy is in our memories since the beginning of the twenties. In France the now repressed party of Rochefort and Co. would draw fresh strength from a Spanish Republic[12] and whether then the increased dangers of a republic in France would impel the Emperor to a breach of the peace is a possibility which at least cannot be ruled

[8] King of Prussia's marginal note: 'This appreciation of Prussian conditions, spirited, highly creditable and true, would however be profoundly shaken and damaged if the Hohenzollern Dynasty in Spain were to meet *the same* fate as the dynasty which reigned there for over a century.'

[9] King of Prussia's marginal note: 'The rejection of the Spanish crown by the House of Savoy has caused no offence, although after all *these same* arguments must have appealed to Florence too.'

[10] King of Prussia's marginal note: 'Would this choice be any more certain than three months ago? when the Cortes rejected the Cabinet's proposal of the Italian prince?'

[11] King of Prussia's marginal note: 'These hypotheses are possible, but equally possible is their non-occurrence.'

[12] King of Prussia's marginal note: 'These *possibilities* cannot be denied, but the pros and cons seem to be equally balanced.'

out. For all lack of concord in Spain, for all the dangers with which a Spanish republic would threaten Europe, public opinion in Germany—since the present proceedings can scarcely remain secret in the long run—would hold those responsible from whom emanated the rejection of the Spanish crown.[13]

Acceptance would lead to a development of the Spanish question free from hazard.[14] For France it would be of great value if both the Orleanist candidature and the republic in Spain were to seem definitely eliminated.[15]

According to information given, the election of the Hereditary Prince would result by a majority of over $\frac{3}{4}$ of all the votes.[16] For centuries it has only happened twice in history that a great nation like the Spanish has appointed its ruler by such a majority bordering on unanimity: in England at the election of the present ruling house in place of the expelled Stuarts, and in Russia at the election of the Romanov dynasty. The legitimacy of the right by which these dynasties rule in England and Russia is uncontested. The same can hardly be maintained of the rights of the Bourbons in Spain, since this dynasty was forced upon the country by foreign arms at the beginning of last century to the prejudice of the hereditary Hapsburg dynasty, and since 1808 a succession of revolutions and outrages have called every claim to the throne in question.

A reappearance of Queen Isabella on the throne would seem to me a danger to all monarchic interests in the whole of Europe.[17] The English would never have tolerated even for a year a Queen of such habits of conduct. It says much for the rigorously monarchical feeling of the Spaniards that after all the upheavals since 1808 and all the misgovernments of the last hundred years they have borne the rule of Queens Christina and Isabella for 35 years.

No danger to the person of the Hereditary Prince need be anticipated. In all the revolutions which have convulsed Spain the idea of

[13] King of Prussia's marginal note: 'The responsibility whether for *rejection* or for *acceptance* of the Spanish crown by a foreign prince seems to me equally great, as would be the resultant sequelae and consequences, which after all can be only of a purely hypothetical nature.'

[14] King of Prussia's marginal note: 'A development free from hazard is hardly to be anticipated when there exist more candidates with valid claims to the throne than those in France.'

[15] King of Prussia's marginal note: 'True.'

[16] King of Prussia's marginal note: 'The same proportion of votes was promised to the candidature of the Prince of Savoy but was reversed at the ballot. So who can now undertake to guarantee that things will not go again in the same way? Could one wish the Hohenzollerns a result like this?—Is it permissible to expose that House to such an affront?'

[17] King of Prussia's marginal note: 'Undoubtedly.'

an outrage against the person of the Monarch has never arisen, no threat has ever been uttered.[18] The forces of the present Spanish army have displayed great valour and extraordinary devotion to the monarchic principle[19] in fighting the republican insurgents in the towns; they will provide a reliable support[20] to the future Monarch whose rewarding task it will be to develop anew the rich resources of the country by benevolent rule.

I can therefore only respectfully commend to Your Royal Majesty that You should graciously prevent the rejection of the Spanish crown unless there exists invincible repugnance on the part of the Hereditary Prince.

In view of the need for absolute secrecy in regard to all the relevant negotiations I do not venture to recommend a discussion of them by the Ministry of State,[21] but I venture the respectful proposal to admit the Minister for War, von Roon, the General of Infantry, von Moltke, and perhaps also the Minister Delbrück, into the secret,[22] and, at a full discussion of the matter in the presence of His Royal Highness the Crown Prince, who is against acceptance, and of His Royal Highness the Prince of Hohenzollern, to be graciously willing to hear the advice of these loyal and judicious servants of Your Royal Majesty. If I am not mistaken they know Spain from personal experience; this is also the case with the Minister, Major-General von Schweinitz, whose inclusion in this important discussion would likewise seem to me open to no objection.[23]

I feel a personal need to make it plain by the present humble memorandum that if the outcome is a refusal the responsibility will not lie at my door, especially if in a near or more remote future historians and public opinion were to investigate into the grounds which have led to a rejection.[24]   V. BISMARCK[25]

[18] King of Prussia's marginal note: 'But the *expulsion of the dynasty* did take place.'
[19] King of Prussia's marginal note: 'It seems to be not so much monarchic principle for which the troops fight well as for the preservation of the rulers whom they support in a revolutionary spirit in order to get into power.'
[20] King of Prussia's marginal note: 'Reliable support from an army which has made all the revolutions for the last 40 years is hardly to be expected!'
[21] King of Prussia's marginal note: 'Agreed.'
[22] King of Prussia's marginal note: 'and Minister von Schleinitz; and State Secretary von Thile. W.'
[23] King of Prussia's marginal note: 'Do not recall. W.'
[24] King of Prussia's marginal note: 'The above marginal notes make it clear that I have strong scruples against the acceptance of the Spanish crown by the Hereditary Prince of Hohenzollern and would only consent to his acceptance of it if his own conviction told him it was his duty to mount the Spanish throne, in other words, that he regarded this act as a definite vocation. In these circumstances I am unable to advise the Hereditary Prince to such an act. William.'
[25] King of Prussia's marginal note: 'At the discussion which took place

20. Bismarck to Prince Karl Anton of Hohenzollern, 28 May, 1870: from BONNIN, p. 158.

On my return to affairs I learned of the latest negotiations about the candidature for the Spanish throne and cannot resist the impression that in them German interests have not received their due. The reports coming in in the interval show that the interim rulers have endeavoured, not without success, to create order in the finances, the army and the general administration, and that this nation of 17 millions, depending like ourselves on the preservation of peace in Europe, is already capable in the event of European complications of casting a weight in the scales which would not be without practical importance to us. Today no less than before I feel no doubt that Germany has a vital interest here, and that at critical moments the pointer on the scales might well register differently according as we know Madrid to be a friend or an enemy. I have once more begged H.M. the King to reconsider the question in this light and received the answer that as soon as any Prince of the House of Hohenzollern showed any inclination to accept the crown he would raise no opposition whatever to this inclination. This I regard as the fullest reply which can be expected from H.M. in the present state of things, since the King will certainly never make a decision to *command* a member of the Royal House to undertake a mission the success of which lies predominantly in the sense of *vocation* personally felt by him who undertakes it. I believe that public opinion and the judgement of posterity will agree with this when the facts become known in detail. In my opinion H.M. the King cannot be expected to undertake a personal responsibility in a matter which does not involve his own decision but is a command to other members of the Royal House to undertake a responsibility.

I do not doubt that this view is fully shared by H.R.H. the Crown Prince. If His Serene Highness the Hereditary Prince or one of Your Royal Highness's younger sons were inclined to render service to *both* countries and earn the gratitude of Spain and Germany I think that a still unanswered telegram addressed to me by Marshal Prim

on . . . March in my presence and that of the Crown Prince, the Prince, and Hereditary Prince of Hohenzollern, the Minister-President Ct. Bismarck and the persons mentioned above . . . all reasons pro and contra were taken under consideration and the majority gave adherence to the view put forward by the Minister-President, namely to acceptance of the Spanish crown by the Hereditary P. of H.

Since however the latter upheld his verbal and written declaration that he could only decide on acceptance at my command and I from conviction am unable to give this command, the discussion was thereby brought to an end. William.'

K

after the latest refusal would afford a possibility for me to reopen the question. . . .

21. Bismarck to the President of the Spanish Council of Ministers, Marshal Prim, 1 June, 1870: from BONNIN, pp. 163–4 Salazar y Mazarredo, Spanish councillor of state, emissary between Madrid and Berlin.

Monsieur le Comte,

I am seizing the first moment of quietude to thank Your Excellency for the letter you were so kind as to write to me on 24 April. I only received it on my return from the country not yet quite recovered from a very serious indisposition which made it entirely impossible for me to attend to any business. I trust that in spite of so long a delay Your Excellency will not doubt my eagerness to give account to you of the steps I have taken with a view to the realization of plans so much in accord with the regard I have for you and for the welfare of your country.

Having come to the conviction that Prince Frederick must be entirely ruled out, I took up the thread of negotiations afresh and today I think that in spite of his previous refusal we have succeeded in proving both to the Prince and to his august father that the misgivings and anxieties with which they had at first regarded the plan and the state of affairs in Spain were ill-founded. But the general difficulties which I had the honour to mention to Y.E. in my letter of 11 April still stand in the way of a definite resolve. I have just received from H.R.H. the father the assurance that his son, the Hereditary Prince, no longer maintains his refusal on personal grounds. To this statement the father adds the promise that his eldest son would accept the result of the voting provided that by then an understanding could be reached on the conditions and the future position of the King in matters not regulated by the Constitution. Whether or not the Spanish Government is in a position to agree to such an arrangement is a question outside my competence. Still hoping that the presence of M. de Salazar might hasten the final solution I have requested him by telegraph to come to Berlin. Whatever turn the affair may take I beg Y.E. to be convinced that I have done and will do all in my power and that if I do not in time enough achieve the result desired by us both it is only because of the difficulty of bringing about an agreement between persons of that rank as quickly as would have been necessary. . . .

22. The Ems Telegram (original text): TELEGRAM from Councillor of Legation Heinrich Abeken in Ems to Bismarck, 13 July,

1870. Translation from Bismarck's *Reflections and Reminiscences*, II, 96n. Count Benedetti, French ambassador in Berlin.

His Majesty writes to me: 'Count Benedetti spoke to me on the promenade, in order to demand from me, finally in a very importunate manner, that I should authorise him to telegraph at once that I bound myself for all future time never again to give my consent if the Hohenzollerns should renew their candidature. I refused at last somewhat sternly, as it is neither right nor possible to undertake engagements of this kind *à tout jamais*. Naturally I told him that I had as yet received no news, and as he was earlier informed about Paris and Madrid than myself, he could clearly see that my government once more had no hand in the matter.' His Majesty has since received a letter from the Prince. His Majesty having told Count Benedetti that he was awaiting news from the Prince, has decided, with reference to the above demand, upon the representation of Count Eulenburg and myself, not to receive Count Benedetti again, but only to let him be informed through an aide-de-camp: That his Majesty had now received from the Prince confirmation of the news which Benedetti had already received from Paris, and had nothing further to say to the ambassador. His Majesty leaves it to your Excellency whether Benedetti's fresh demand and its rejection should not be at once communicated both to our ambassadors and to the press.

b. The conduct of the war: Bismarck and the military

23. The secret war diary of Lieutenant-Colonel Paul Bronsart von Schellendorff, 1870–71: from PAUL BRONSART VON SCHELLENDORFF, *Geheimes Kriegstagebuch 1870–71*, pp. 174, 212–3, 233–7, 279–80, 309–10, 315–17, 415, 427–8.

Bronsart von Schellendorff, Paul (1832–91), chief of operations in the General Staff of the Prussian army 1870–71, later minister of war. General Theophil von Podbielski, chief of staff. Jules Favre, French republican statesman, foreign minister of the provisional government in 1871.

(*10 November, 1870.*) ... A report from the command of Third Army declares that it is hoped to begin firing on Paris on December 4. We completed the siege of Paris on September 19. So the artillery needs over ten weeks! It was a great mistake to launch this operation, since we shall never get to the point of firing. Either Paris, with the help of the provinces, will break out of the siege, or it will be starved into submission before. The fall of Metz ensures that the latter alternative will occur. . . .

(*Dec, 7, 1870*) Count Bismarck is really beginning to be fit for a lunatic asylum. He has complained bitterly to the king that General Moltke has written to General Trochu and maintains that, being a negotiation with a foreign government, this should fall into his own sphere of competence. But General Moltke, as a spokesman of the High Command, has written to the Governor of Paris; the matter is therefore a purely military one. Since Count Bismarck asserts further that he had stated to me that he regarded the letter as dubious whereas the contrary is the case, I have immediately reported to General Moltke that the chancellor's statement is not true and have asked to be relieved in future of oral missions to him. The king, to whom General Moltke spoke about this matter, of course finds the whole thing very disagreeable, and the war minister said, very naively, that we ought not to pursue the matter too far, since in view of the diametrically opposed statements of my report and of Count Bismarck the only conclusion would be that one of us had been lying. General Moltke can hardly be in any doubt which one of us this was.

It is lamentable how inefficient our ministry of war is. . . . General Roon is lazy. . . . I have . . . shown that we must and can do more. . . .

In the evening a telegram arrived from Under-Secretary von Thile in Berlin in which he reports to Count Bismarck that diplomatic circles in Berlin are convinced that the government in Paris is only awaiting the beginning of the bombardment to offer capitulation. This is possible but not likely! It is more plausible that Count Bismarck ordered this telegram in order to lend more weight to his requests for bombardment. . . .

(*Dec. 18, 1870.*) A hard day! The hardest of the campaign so far for me, but one on which perhaps I performed the most successful service for my country.

The king had written to General Moltke asking him to inform Count Bismarck of the results of yesterday's Military Council at which he had not been present; Count Bismarck had already stressed several times that he must always be kept informed of the course of military events in order to conduct his diplomatic activity accordingly. This demand is justified to the extent that he must be informed of *faits accomplis* and of the overall situation of the army. But if he is informed of intentions, then on the one hand this will invite criticism from a man who is striving after supreme power, including military power; on the other hand it incurs the risk that he will embark on a diplomatic exploitation of a plan of operations that ought still to be kept completely secret, an exploitation that may seem desirable to him but would be highly dangerous to the course of operations itself. Since the man imagines that he understands everything we are no longer secure against indiscretions that he might commit out of a defective appreciation. . . . The first point, however, is by far the more important. It is contrary to all well-founded usage to discuss operations under way or intended with persons who lack the necessary understanding. . . . But Count Bismarck regards himself as qualified and has already made several attempts to acquire an influence on military operations.

Recently he has tried to begin a premature and hasty bombardment of Paris. Earlier, after the battle of Sedan, he asked General Moltke if it was not possible to leave France entirely to herself now and to take up a defensive position in Alsace and Lorraine in which we could await a French attack.

These, to be sure, were merely private conversations with General Moltke. . . . So long as everything was going without a hitch he was content to offer his expert advice to General Moltke.

But the apparent halt in operations brought about by the resistance of Paris and Metz gradually caused him to approach the king as well. The latter does not like arguments with this irritable man, seeks all possible ways of avoiding them, and relies on the self-denying General Moltke always to yield. It is in such reflections or sentiments that the request to General Moltke to inform Count Bismarck of the results of a Military Council to which he had not been invited has its origin.

As a matter of fact this Council, after the purely technical members had been dismissed . . ., determined the basic lines of our operations for the immediate future. . . . The main points of this were to be communicated only to the army commands, not as a rule to other commands; and we are supposed to tell a diplomat what in this respect we do not tell our commanding generals! The king's order, three pages long, positively demanded it. General Moltke was annoyed, General Podbielski was also displeased, but they did not feel the need to offer complete resistance. I was ordered by General Podbielski to draft a missive to Count Bismarck telling him as little as possible but still telling him something; this draft was to be taken to the king and his consent obtained to this somewhat limited report. I expressed to General von Podbielski my misgivings about this, stressing that it was high time to offer resistance in principle if the . . . element of a unified command was not to be lost, as it would inevitably be if Count Bismarck was to participate, directly or indirectly, in military councils. So far the king has stood fast against other influences and in the end always approved General Moltke's proposals; but if a man of Count Bismarck's ambition and lust for power were involved this could no longer be counted on. I reminded General von Podbielski of the efforts of Count Bismarck in the last years of peace to gain an undue influence over military matters, of the successes he had achieved in view of General Roon's complete failure to resist, etc.

General von Podbielski admitted all this but thought that a favourable outcome could be expected only if General Moltke confronted the king with the stark alternative of dismissing him or Count Bismarck; but General Moltke would never do this; therefore I should draft the missive.

I thought for about ten minutes; the usual obedience to orders had led me to the point of writing the address, then it gave out and the sense of a duty to refuse obedience even to the king, and even at the sacrifice of my own person, gained the upper hand. I went in to General von Podbielski and declared to him privately that I would not lend myself to the proposed solution of the problem. Since, moreover, it was not desired that either General Moltke or Count Bismarck should leave the king's service at the moment, I was prepared to offer myself. The destruction of my military career might make the king see that he could not go any farther down the proposed road. . . .

General Podbielski gave in; he promised to tell General Moltke, who was in church with the king, of my views before his audience with the king and to add that he himself also regarded any report to Count Bismarck as absolutely out of the question. And so it came about. After his report to the king General Moltke asked for a private audience which resulted in the royal order being revoked. . . .

(*Jan. 7, 1871.*) Privy Councillor Keudell came to me in an effort to prevent further conflicts between us and Count Bismarck. The latter is most annoyed that he has had no response yet to his memorandum to the king on the use of the railways and railway equipment. I told Keudell that the matter had nothing to do with me, but that Count Bismarck was, as usual, in the wrong with these most recent manoeuvres, both in his premises and in his conclusions. . . .

There is no denying that in such a war the military and diplomatic leadership must go hand in hand. But Count Bismarck interprets this one-sidedly: he wants to conduct politics without listening to General Moltke but wants to have his say in the conduct of operations. The best solution might be for Count Bismarck and General Moltke always to report to the king together. But this requires two characters, like General Moltke's, who do not strive to invade someone else's sphere of activity. If Count Bismarck were a different kind of person this sort of reciprocal arrangement would work. . . .

(*25 January, 1871.*) . . . General Moltke received a command in the king's own handwriting to inform Count Bismarck at once of the military situation in detail, since in his negotiations with Favre he had to know how things stood. Now, in fact, Count Bismarck receives all reports coming in to us so quickly that he even finds it possible to let the news from the battlefield that he turns over to Reuters in London reach the home country first via this source; they arrive there earlier than our official telegrams, which he has probably ordered to be delayed on the state's wires. Recently, moreover, he has been ordering corrections in telegrams signed by General von Podbielski, a procedure which, so far as I know, is liable to be punished by imprisonment. But petty thieves are hanged and big ones are allowed to go free!

. . . [Bismarck,] I understand, is negotiating the capitulation of Paris with Favre on a militarily quite new and unexpected basis, without General Moltke's opinion being asked beforehand. In view of the lack of military knowledge characteristic of this civilian in a cavalry officer's coat we could therefore easily find ourselves suddenly confronted with a '*fait accompli*' which is not militarily feasible. But even if we should be lucky enough to escape this contingency it is almost impossible for us, in view of the enormous dimensions of the task before us, to issue orders to the army commands suitably and at the right time.

While Count Bismarck is in this way leaving the Commander-in-Chief entirely out of the picture in a matter of a purely military character he has laid with the king an accusation against [Moltke] for continued interference in his sphere as well as for insufficient information on the military situation. . . . But General Moltke has only conducted military negotiations with the Governor of Paris. . . .

(*28 January, 1871.*) . . . General Moltke made a rather long speech to us in which he discussed the pros and cons of the proposed agreement with the conclusion that on the whole the convention was favourable for us. . . . On behalf of the three heads of sections I said that we regarded the agreement as unsatisfactory in every way since we were now in a position simply to prescribe conditions to the enemy. General Moltke objected first that the situation was not yet so clear. . . . Finally General Moltke declared that he was sorry to differ from us, that he also would have regarded a more significant military result as very desirable, but that he must limit himself in the light of political considerations which above all required maintenance of the present governing power [in France] if we were to have peace at all. Thereupon I asked him at least to insist that the text of the agreement should refer specifically to the *capitulation* of the city and fortress of Paris, and he promised to use his influence in this sense.

Count Bismarck, however, did not obtain even this when Favre declared that in that event he would not sign; this very refusal on the part of the French made clear the importance that the presence of this word in the text of the treaty had for us too; but we were weak enough to give in on this as well. . . .

(*June, 1871.*) . . . The total incompetence and exhaustion of General Roon is generally known, but nobody dares to tell the emperor the truth. . . . Prince Bismarck is certainly the man who is most content with this situation; he could find no more amenable Prussian minister of war than General Roon and in view of his megalomania this is all he needs for the time being. He has no understanding of the fact that this must lead to the total disintegration of the instrument to which alone he owes all his successes. He is also trying to attract able military men into the diplomatic service in order to make himself more and more independent of the military authorities at home. . . .

(*July 1871.*) . . . Prince Bismarck is assiduously trying to perform the duties of [an imperial minister of war], at times with decided skill and success. . . .

D. The Bismarckian Empire

a. Two views of the federal problem

24. Bismarck's report to William I on the nomenclature of the Federal Council, 29 March, 1871: from PUTTKAMER, pp. 150–1.

... The constitutional position of the Federal Council [*Bundesrat*] in the North German Confederation as well as in the German Empire derives its peculiar character from the fact that its members are bound by the instructions issued to them by their governments and therefore do not, like the deputies to the *Reichstag*, represent the whole but only the state which nominated them. ...

This constitutional position is properly indicated by the term 'Federal Council' since the assembly of representatives of the federal states bound by their instructions is the organ in which the federative aspect of the Empire is manifested. The term 'Imperial Council' [*Reichsrat*] would not correctly indicate the position of the Federal Council, both by reason of its relationship with the 'Reichstag' of the imperial constitution and because of the constitutional meaning given to the appellation in Austria and Bavaria and therefore in constitutional terminology generally; it would provide grounds for the assumption that the German *Reichsrat*, like the German *Reichstag* and the Austrian and Bavarian *Reichsrat*, contained representatives of the whole and not of individual states.

For this reason the Federal Council [of the North German Confederation], in its decision on the draft imperial constitution, retained the appellation 'Bundesrat' in the draft, and for the same reason, in my respectful submission, its replacement by the term 'Reichsrat' is not feasible. ...

25. Constantin Frantz's critique of the Bismarckian Empire, 1875: from PUTTKAMER, pp. 151–2. Frantz, Gustav Adolph Constantin (1817–91), political publicist.

... It is clear that a country containing as many different elements as Germany does, a country entwined with its neighbours on all sides and bordering on six different nationalities, a country, moreover, that has experienced a history comparable to no other in respect both of the variety of political forms created and the intrinsic importance of its events—that such a country must necessarily have achieved a constitution peculiar to itself. If this constitution was to be amended or improved, how could the appropriate forms be found except by deriving them from existing conditions? Instead an attempt was made to borrow these forms from various foreign constitutions and by means of such a compounded copy to produce a German national constitution, while at the same time proclaiming the principle of nationality which ought rather to have excluded anything foreign. What a strange contradiction!

Those involved in this attempt did not even understand the fact that Germany was not and will never be a *state* in the proper meaning of the word. It was, rather, a *Confederation,* and before that it was an *Empire* in the specific sense of the word in which it signifies something different and higher than a state. The main difference then becomes apparent, namely that in an empire constitutional relations are connected with international relations, in that political life merges into national life, the empire thus providing the link between the two.... It was Germany's special privilege and special calling to constitute this living connection between state law and international law in the development of Europe. From this follows the peculiarity of German conditions, which it is therefore from the beginning impossible to understand if they are seen only from the point of view of the state, as is the case at present. Clearly people want to turn Germany into a state; the National Liberals are always talking precisely about the 'German *state*.' This is the goal of everything that has happened since 1866; it is descended solely from the idea of the state.... The clearest indication of this is the current attempt to make *legislation* omnipotent, whereas in a true empire *treaties* take their place beside laws and impose appropriate limits on legislation. One cannot simply issue decrees, one must make agreements. This is the way it always was in the old Empire. And because the Empire itself had an international character it could comprise various nationalities. It could contain members which belonged to the Empire only in part and in part reached beyond it, and members which depended on the Empire only in some respects and were independent in other respects. In this way a great variety of elements could coexist, and also a great variety of relationships in which these elements stood to each other and to the Empire. The Empire was the framework which comprehended and protected them all.

It is only on the basis of this flexible idea of the Empire, of which the old Confederation was also only a metamorphosis, that forms could have been found wide and elastic enough to accommodate Austria as well as Prussia and even to leave open the possibility of admitting other members later. In this way different means and different degrees of connection would have been feasible, and nationality difficulties would have been avoided from the beginning. It would have been possible to meet all contingencies....

b. Two Reactions to the Founding and Nature of the Empire

---

26. Friedrich Nietzsche on the cultural consequences of Prussia's victory in 1871: from 'David Strauss, der Bekenner und der Schriftsteller' (1873), in Nietzsche's *Werke*, II, 27–32. Nietzsche, Friedrich Wilhelm (1844–1900), eminent German philosopher.

Public opinion in Germany seems almost to forbid any discussion of the evil and dangerous consequences of war, especially of a victorious war. . . . Nevertheless, it must be said; a great victory is a great danger. Human nature finds it harder to bear than a defeat; it seems easier, paradoxically, to attain such a victory than to behave in such a way that it does not turn into a heavy defeat. Of all the evil consequences following in the wake of the recent war against France the worst, perhaps, is a . . . general error: the error of public opinion and of all those who air their opinions in public to the effect that German culture also won a victory in that conflict and therefore deserves to be decorated with the laurels appropriate to such extraordinary events and successes. This delusion is highly pernicious: not at all because it is a delusion—for some errors are most salutary and beneficial—, but rather because it is capable of converting our victory into a complete defeat: the defeat, even the death of German culture for the benefit of the 'German Empire.'

On the one hand, even assuming that two cultures were in conflict, the standard by which the worth of the victorious culture is to be judged would still be very relative and would in some circumstances by no means justify any celebration or glorification of the victory. For we should need to know the worth of the defeated culture; perhaps very little; in which case victory, even the most splendid military successes, would not call for jubilation by the triumphant culture either. On the other hand, in our case, there can be no question of any victory for German culture, for the simple reason that French culture continues to exist as before, and we continue to be dependent on it as before. German culture did not even contribute to the military successes. Strict discipline, natural bravery and endurance, superior leadership, unity and obedience among the rank-and-file—elements, in other words, that have nothing to do with culture—helped us to victory over an enemy lacking in the most important of these elements; what is surprising is that what passes for 'culture' in Germany proved no serious obstacle to these military requirements for a great success, perhaps only because this self-styled culture regarded it as expedient in its own interests to be of service on this occasion. If it is allowed to grow and to proliferate, if it is flattered into the illusion that it was victorious, then it will have, as I said, the power to kill the German mind—and it is doubtful whether the body will be of any use without it.

If it should prove possible to mobilize against the internal enemy, against that highly ambiguous and certainly un-national 'cultivation' ['*Gebildetheit*'] that at the moment misleadingly goes under the name of culture in Germany, the calm and steady courage that the Germans showed in the face of the sudden and impetuous violence of the French, then there would still be hope for a real, genuine German culture [*Bildung*], the opposite of that cultivation; for the Germans have never lacked imaginative and bold leaders and generals—it is only that the Germans have often failed them. But I doubt increasingly whether it is possible to turn German courage in this new direction, and since the war it seems to me less likely every day; for I can see how everyone is convinced that there is no struggle left for which such courage is needed, that, on the contrary, almost everything is in the best possible order and that in any case all that is necessary has long ago been found and done—in short, that the finest cultural crop has either been planted or is sprouting or is even blooming luxuriantly here and there. In this respect people are not merely contented: they are joyful and ecstatic. . . . One might expect that the more thoughtful and informed members of the educated class would recognize the dangers of this sort of abuse of success, or would at least feel embarrassed by the spectacle. . . . But this class are content to let things take their course and are too occupied with themselves to bother about the German mind. Indeed, they are quite certain that their own culture is the ripest and finest fruit not only of this age but of all ages and have no understanding for any concern about German culture in general. . . .

The assertion [that German culture defeated France] therefore appears quite incomprehensible. It is precisely in the wider knowledge of German officers, in the better instruction of the German troops, in the more scientific conduct of the war that all impartial observers and even the French themselves saw the decisive advantage. But in what sense can the victory be said to have been that of German education as distinct from German proficiency [*Belehrtheit*]? In no sense: for the moral qualities of stricter discipline and steadier obedience have nothing to do with education. . . . Any talk of a victory for German education and culture bespeaks a confusion derived from the fact that the pure concept of culture has been lost in Germany.

Culture is above all unity of artistic style in all the manifestations of a people's life. But to have learned and to know a great deal is neither a means to culture nor a sign of it and could if necessary quite easily consist with the opposite of culture, barbarism: that is, absence of style or chaotic mixture of all styles.

But such a chaotic mixture is characteristic of this country today; and it is a serious problem how Germans, despite all the information at their disposal, can possibly not notice this and can even heartily rejoice in their present 'culture'. . . . This sort of 'culture', which is really nothing but a phlegmatic insensitivity to all culture, cannot be used to defeat enemies, least of all those who, like the French, have a genuine and productive culture, no matter of what quality, and whom we have imitated in everything, mostly without any skill.

Even if we had stopped imitating them we should still not have defeated them but only liberated ourselves from them. Only if we had imposed an original German culture on them could we speak of a triumph of German culture. Meanwhile we see that in all matters of style we are as dependent on Paris as before—inevitably, since we still have no original German culture. . . .

27. Otto Gierke on Natural Law, 1880: from GIERKE'S *Johannes Althusius*, in his *Natural Law and the Theory of Society, 1500–1800* pp. 223–6. Gierke, Otto (1841–1921), jurist and legal historian.

. . . The development of natural-law ideas in regard to the relation of the State to Law attained its culmination at the end of the eighteenth century. After that time we can begin to trace a process of collapse and disintegration in the whole of the natural-law system of thought.

In Germany the theory of Natural Law disappears before the new world of ideas introduced by the Historical School. It was the achievement of that School to transcend, at last, the old dichotomy of Law into Natural and Positive. Regarding Law as a unity, and conceiving it as the positive result and living expression of the common consciousness of an organic community, the thinkers of the Historical School refused to content themselves with merely continuing to emphasize one or the other side of the old antithesis: they sought and achieved a synthesis of both in a higher unity. The factors which determined their conception of the relation of the State to Law were factors equally derived from the Natural and the Positive Law of the older doctrine. In the new view which they attained, Law ceased to be regarded as partly anterior and superior to the State, and partly produced by and inferior to it. Law and the State were held to be so intertwined that they were regarded as coeval with one another; as intended to supplement one another; as dependent upon one another. The philosophical elaboration of this idea has not yet been fully achieved. Meanwhile there has been an abundance of criticism, from all sorts of quarters, some of it devoted to discovering the errors of the Historical School, and some of it even to calling in question again the very foundations of the historical view of Law. So far as the problem of the relation between Law and the State is concerned, we can detect in the chaos of modern opinion two particular currents of thought, opposed to one another, but united together in opposition to the historic-organic idea of Law. On the one hand, there has been a period during which conceptions of an abstract Law of Nature pressed once more to the front, and menaced the very idea of the State. On the other hand, there is now a current of thought, which is gradually gaining volume in Germany, that threatens to undermine all the foundations of Law. It recurs to the old ideas of Positive Law, but it abandons the notion of Natural Law which used to be the complement of those ideas. In this last and newest way of approach, the idea of Law ultimately vanishes altogether. So far as its content or substance goes, it is engulfed in the idea of Utility; so far as its power or efficacy is concerned, it is engulfed in the idea of Force. If this way of approach should prove victorious, the only merit of the Historical School will have been its rejection of Natural Law; and the ideas of Natural Law, reduced to an idle play of the human imagination, will have pursued in vain their many centuries of evolution.

But if there is to be a true Law in the future—a Law which is not a mere *décor* of traditional well-sounding names, but the genuine expression of a specific, unique and intrinsically valuable idea of the mind of man—a different historical perspective reveals itself to our eyes. In that perspective, we can see that the idea of Law has won real and permanent conquests from the development of Natural Law; we can see that the Historical point of view, far from surrendering those conquests, has only generalized and diffused them; and we may confidently believe that these conquests will never be lost in the future, whatever changes or improvements may be made in men's conceptions of Law. On such a view the sovereign independence of the idea of Justice, secured before by the old conception of Natural Law, will still continue to be firmly secured by our new conception of Law as something thoroughly positive—no matter whether the idea which opposes that conception be the idea of social utility, or the idea of collective power.

If Natural and Positive Law thus coincide in their essence, the relation of Law and the State will no longer be conceived in two opposite ways, as it was in the older theory; and the ideas which found expression in opposite points of view may now be united in one. We shall no longer ask whether the State is prior to Law, or Law is prior to the State. We shall regard them both as inherent functions of the common life which is inseparable from the idea of man. They will both be primordial facts: they will both have been given, as seeds or germs, coevally with man himself: they will both appear, as developed fruits, simultaneously with one another and in virtue of one another. We shall regard the State, and all other organised forms of collective power, as no mere product of Law; but we shall hold that every form of power, from the lowest to the highest, can only enjoy a sanction, and receive its consummation, when it is stamped and confirmed by Law as being a legal power. Conversely, we shall regard all Law as needing the sanction and consummation of power; but we shall not count the State, nor any other human power, as the maker and creator of Law.

Law, which is, in its essence, a body of external standards for the action of *free* wills, cannot itself be made of the substance of will; for if will is made the standard for wills, the logically inevitable result must always be that will turns itself into power. If there is to be an obligatory external standard for the action of will *in general,* and not merely for the action of this or that *particular* will, such a standard must be rooted and grounded in a spiritual force which confronts the will as something independent. That force is Reason. It follows that Law is not a common will that a thing shall be, but a common conviction that it is. Law is the conviction of a human community, either manifested directly by usage or declared by a common organ appointed for that purpose, that there exist in that community external standards of will—in other words, limitations of liberty which are externally obligatory, and therefore, by their very nature, enforceable.

It is true that the State, in its capacity of legislator, not only shows itself active, over a large and important field, as the 'bearer' and the corroborator of this conviction of Right (or Law), but also consummates every development of such conviction (1) by the issue of a command and (2) by the use of compulsion. But (1) the action of the common will in commanding obedience to what *is* Law is not an action which *creates* Law: it is only an action which sanctions Law. Similarly, (2) the fact that a supreme power is needed, in order to realise fully the compulsoriness demanded by the nature of Law, does not prevent Law from still being Law even though, in a particular case, compulsion is lacking, or can only be imperfectly applied, or is altogether impossible for want of a higher power which is capable of using it—provided only there really is a common conviction that compulsion would be right if it were possible, or if a competent authority were in existence.

On this basis, we may, indeed, hold that the State is more than a legal institution, and exists for more than the purpose of Law; but we shall also hold that the purpose of Law is pre-eminent among all the purposes of the State's existence—just because the full consummation of Law requires the presence of a sovereign power—and we shall therefore regard the legal purpose of the State as its essential purpose, which cannot for a moment be abstracted from our idea of its nature. Conversely, we may, indeed, regard Law as intended primarily to serve the purposes of the State's life; but we shall also consider its objects as far from being exhausted by, or limited to, such service. There is indeed one admission which we shall have to make on such a view. If we place the State neither above Law. nor outside it, but *in* it, thus confining the liberty of the State within the bounds of the system of Law: if, again, we set Law neither above the State, nor outside it, but *in* it, thus allowing the formal omnipotence of the sovereign authority to assert itself even against Law—then there will be a possibility of contradiction between the Matter and the Form of Law, the actual and the ideal. But to deny the possibility of such a contradiction is to deny the very idea of Law.

A deep element in the spiritual nature of man longs for the union of Law and Power—of Right and Might. Division between them is always felt to be something wrong. This feeling is the best evidence that Law may exist without Power, and Power may exist without Law. But it is also the source of a healing and reconciling influence, which is always tending to bring us back to a unity of Right and Might. The human conscience cannot permanently endure the separation of the two. Right which cannot establish itself vanishes at last from the common conscience, and thereby ceases to be Right. Might which exists without Right, if it succeeds in maintaining itself, is felt at last by the general conscience to exist as of right, and is thus transformed into Right. . . .

I still live to-day in the conviction that our legal theory and our legal life can only thrive on one condition—that 'positivism' should somehow learn to preserve for the idea of Law that original and independent title to existence which was vindicated for it by the School of Natural Law. I regard as mistaken all the attempts to resuscitate Natural Law into a bodily existence, which can only be the existence of a simulacrum. But the undying spirit of that Law can never be extinguished. If it is denied entry into the body of positive law, it flutters about the room like a ghost, and threatens to turn into a vampire which sucks the blood from the body of Law. We have to accept together both the external experience which testifies that all valid Law is positive, and the internal experience which affirms that the living force of Law is derived from an idea of Right which is innate in humanity; and when we have done that, we have to blend the two experiences in one generic conception of the essential nature of Law. . . .

E. The Kulturkampf

28. Prussian Minister of Public Worship and Education, Heinrich von Mühler, to King William I, 21 November, 1870: from CONSTABEL, pp. 53–5. Mühler, Heinrich von (1813–74), Prussian minister of public worship and education, 1862–72.

I beg to report to Your Royal Majesty on the movements instigated at the University of Bonn by the decisions of the Vatican Council on the primacy and infallibility of the pope. . . .

The first official agitation of the matter came from the desire of several members of the Catholic theological faculty . . . to be officially requested to state their position with respect to the majority decision of the Council. I declined this . . . and remarked that the government for the moment regards the decision of the Council on papal infallibility as an entirely internal matter of the Catholic Church and does not intend to start a theoretical discussion of its possible consequences. Only if the Church authorities should draw practical consequences from it which were liable to damage the right or interest of the state would the state intervene. . . .

In handling this matter I have adhered strictly to the principles established by the government with respect to the decision of the Vatican Council. In particular I have carefully avoided any discussion of the question of dogma and anything that might be interpreted as taking sides for or against the new dogma. . . .

It is highly likely that the future development of the matter will have far-reaching consequences for the Catholic theological faculty in Bonn. But this is not something that can be prevented by any measures taken by the state, since the effectiveness of Catholic theological faculties in Prussia in general depends on a moderate and tactful attitude not only on the part of the state but also on the part of the Church authorities. . . .

29. From the minutes of a meeting of the Prussian Council of Ministers, 11 January, 1871: from CONSTABEL, p. 165.

. . . With reference to his . . . desire to restore to the Education Bill two paragraphs concerning [compulsory] religious instruction in the grammar schools which were struck out at the previous meeting, the Minister of Public Worship and Education was referred to the appropriate procedure of a written motion to be submitted to the Council of Ministers.

30. Mühler to the Prussian Council of Ministers, 5 June, 1871: from CONSTABEL, pp. 97–100.

... I take it for granted that states in general, and a state which maintains parity among religions, as Prussia does, in particular, have every reason to adhere, if possible, to the strictest neutrality with respect to the decisions of the Vatican Council on papal infallibility. From this assumption it follows, in the sphere of educational policy, that the state itself has no interest in whether instruction includes the dogma of papal infallibility or not. ...

(Marginal note of Councillor Hahn in the Ministry of the Interior dated 22 June, 1871: 'In my opinion ... the question cannot be settled by the state merely remaining "neutral." ')

31. The king to the Prussian Council of Ministers, 17 July, 1871: from CONSTABEL, pp. 115–6.

... I have reservations ... about appointing as head of an institution for the training of future primary-school teachers an adherent of a new dogma of the Catholic Church which manifests dubious consequences in its effect on the political situation. ... I request of the Council of Ministers an opinion on the general question whether it is not necessary or at any rate advisable to take measures for the security of the state in general, and in its relations with the Old Catholics in particular, in view of the already actually evident undesirable consequences of the dogma of infallibility.

32. Mühler to the Prussian Council of Ministers, 9 October, 1871: from CONSTABEL, pp. 126–7.

... It remains ... to arrive at a decision on the general question raised in the royal decree [of July 17]. ... The government has so far confined itself to resisting any repercussions of the dogma of infallibility on political matters. It has never provoked conflict, but it has not evaded it either. ... I regard this attitude as the correct one in the present circumstances. Any step beyond this would have very far-reaching consequences. Any aggressive step by the state on account of the new dogma could be justified only on the assumption that the Catholic Church and all its official organs has ceased to be that Catholic Church which is mentioned in agreements made with the Papacy and in the Prussian constitution. ... Any half-measures in this field would do more harm than good. ...

33. Mühler to Bismarck, 14 October, 1871: from CONSTABEL, pp. 131–2.

I beg to submit to Your Highness in brief compass a programme of those legislative and administrative measures which are necessary in the field of education and ecclesiastical administration and in respect of which I desire energetic action.

I. I regard as of paramount importance a clarification of the relations between state and Church and emancipation of political and civil interests from subordination to the Church.
This heading includes:

(1) Full freedom of secession from the Church and exemption for those who secede from duties and contributions to their former Church. Legislation drafted by me on this subject was submitted to the ministers of justice and the interior several weeks ago.

(2) Regulation of civil matters, in particular with regard to civil marriage. On this subject also my draft has been before the ministers of justice and the interior for a fortnight. ... In principle I am in favour of compulsory civil marriage, but implementation of this will require important practical measures and provision of ecclesiastical equivalents, comprising a thoroughgoing revision, on the state's initiative, of the system of contributions to the Church and establishment of an orderly ecclesiastical discipline. ...

(3) Abolition of supervision of schools by organs of the Church and unconditional subjection of schools to agencies of the state. ... This idea will be implemented in the next few days in a new draft of the Education Bill. At the same time it will also find expression in a special law connected with determinations on the language question. ...

II. These points concerning relations between state and Church in general lead to two measures directed specifically at excesses of the Catholic Church, namely:

(4) A decree requiring state censorship of pastoral letters and similar publications of Church authorities in so far as these concern political subjects, and punishment of evasion of this censorship.

(5) Banning of the Jesuit Order throughout Germany. ...

III. It is not sufficient, however, merely to combat a party that has become too powerful within the Catholic Church it is indispensable, at the same time, to promote the interests of the Protestant Church on a large scale. It is the positive aspect of the duties of the Prussian Minister of Public Worship and Education to take on this task. ...

34. From the minutes of a meeting of the Prussian Council of Ministers, 1 November, 1871: from CONSTABEL, pp. 136–41.

... [The] rapporteur of the Ministry of Public Worship and Education reported on the draft of a Bill ... concerning the direction and inspection of the system of education and instruction. ... The purpose of the draft was to clarify the position of schools as a state institution and to assert the right of the state to appoint district inspectors of schools. ...

The President of the Council of Ministers agreed with the tendency of the draft to submit schools to the sole direction of the state, but wished the state's scope to include not only district inspectors but local inspectors of schools, the local clergy. ... The extension of the German language in the Polish parts of the country deserved special attention. ... The influence of the local clergy impeded the use of the German language, since Slavs and Latins, in league with Ultramontanism, sought to preserve crudity and ignorance and to combat German culture, which sought to spread enlightenment, throughout Europe. He was bound to describe as a shortcoming of the administration of schools the failure so far to combat more energetically the polonizing influence of the clergy in the schools, and he expressly requested discussion of this matter today or at the next meeting. ... He was unable to determine whether the present Bill gave the state the power to remove a school inspector and to replace him with another person of its choice. In any case it appeared useful to him that this power should be clearly stated in the new law. ...

The Minister of Public Worship and Education said that he ... fully recognized the importance of local school inspectors but had reservations about doing too much all at once. ... The existing law was adequate for exceptional cases. ...

The President of the Council of Ministers then put the following questions:

(a) whether the state's power to appoint different inspectors of schools should be legally established?

This was accepted without dissent. ...

The Minister of Public Worship and Education said that ... in the public schools the state had the power to control instruction, whereas in the private schools it had only a general power of inspection to prevent occurrences damaging to public order. ...

The President of the Council of Ministers replied that the state had merely so far customarily refrained from determining the curriculum in private schools.

Councillor Wehrmann begged to remark ... that the state also had the right of inspection of religious instruction directed by religious societies.

The President of the Council of Ministers supported this view; in a military analogy one might regard the inspecting authority as a division and the offices in charge of external relations, religious instruction, and other instruction as brigades which must obey the divisional command. . . .

35. Falk and Eulenburg to the king (5 March, 1872): from CONSTABEL, pp. 187–9.

Falk, Adalbert (1827–1900), Prussian minister of public worship and education 1872–79. Eulenburg, Count Friedrich (1815–81), Prussian minister of the interior 1862–78.

. . . It is notorious that the successful national agitation in the province [of Posnania] derives its chief support from the public and secret activities of the Jesuit Order, and the governors of the province have repeatedly emphasized the necessity of depriving the Order of its spearhead by expelling its foreign members. . . .

Since the Polish-Catholic agitation in the province of Posnania has in the course of time become more and more intense and important, and particularly since, during the war with France and more recently, it has manifested itself with increasing virulence, the matter must be looked at in a new light. This reconsideration has led to the conviction that the government would relinquish an indispensable means of defending itself if . . . it continued its policy of nonintervention in the settlement and activities of the Jesuits in the province of Posnania. . . .

We beg humbly to remark that steps similar to those against the members of the Jesuit Order should be taken against foreign members of other Orders and foreign secular clergy, and that the procedure outlined above should also be applied to the Polish districts of the provinces of Prussia and Silesia to the extent that conditions there require it. . . .

36. Falk to the Prussian Council of Ministers, 25 March, 1872: from CONSTABEL, pp. 204, 219–20, 223–4, 196–7.

The greater (as distinct from the lesser) excommunication not only deprived a person of the right to administer or receive the Sacraments but also prohibited all intercourse with Christians.

. . . The state employs the teacher of religion. The state alone can dismiss him. Whether there are grounds for this is exclusively a matter for its decision, as is also the question to what extent the withdrawal of an ecclesiastical mission involves a disability of the person concerned to continue to hold the office conferred on him by the state. The state is not only entitled to make such a decision but in the nature of the case obliged to do so, having regard to the protection it owes to its subjects against arbitrary treatment or deprivation of their rights as citizens. Moreover, such a decision does not represent any encroachment on the part of the state, since it is relevant only to the state office in question and does not claim to have any effect on the internal life of the Church. . . .

Since the greater excommunication is not a purely ecclesiastical punishment but, because of its civil consequences, a mixed matter, . . . the unilateral imposition of the ban by an ecclesiastical superior involves an invasion of the jurisdiction of the state which it is entitled to resist merely on the basis of its sovereign right, even if explicit laws prohibiting it are lacking. This resistance can be purely negative, where the state would declare the ban imposed without its permission to be non-existent for its purposes, would reject the demands of the ecclesiastical authorities based upon it, and would refuse it any effectiveness in the field of civil law. But it can also, without requiring any special legislative regulation, be extended to withholding the funds provided by the state for ecclesiastical administration, and in case of necessity intensified by withdrawing state recognition from all actions on the part of the Church authority in question and of his officials.

Such repressive action is

(1) required by the situation in the case in question. For the action of the ecclesiastical authority involves an open violation of the law which no state can accept without surrendering itself—an injury to citizens in their honour, their social position, their economic situation, all of them disadvantages against the arbitrary imposition of which they are entitled to claim the protection of the law—a danger, finally, which is capable of seriously threatening the state's own interests. Even the excommunication of a single official has placed in jeopardy the whole system of state education and, as things are now, there is no guarantee that as the conflict goes on the state will not be driven to measures obedience to which will subject all of its Catholic officials to excommunication, which in turn would involve repercussions likely to impede public administration to a degree varying from locality to locality. In the face of such encroachments the state cannot fold its arms and take the position that the consequences of the punishment in question do not exist for it, that the proscription of one of its subjects has no civil effect, that disruption of its institutions has no legal validity.

Such repressive action is, moreover,

(2) not only appropriate to the situation, ... but also in principle the only correct way to avoid a collision of state and Church by constitutional means. Instead of interfering with the Church's autonomy it is based on full respect for the Church as an independent sphere of life, attached to the state but not incorporated in it. Even at its highest intensity the recommended action on the part of the state remains essentially negative. By revoking its recognition of Church administration it is merely ... dissolving the present connection and thereby removing the conflict from the disagreeable area of police action to one where autonomous living forces confront each other. . . .

The further consequences of the situation thus created will depend on the powers of resistance and material resources of the episcopate, on the scope of the conflict in time and space ..., and above all on the attitude of the affected Church communities and the lower clergy. The interpretation by the courts of the legal questions involved will also have some influence.

These factors cannot be estimated in advance with any certainty. But one point can be emphasized even now: the Catholic Church performs not only its own spiritual functions but political ones at the same time. Throughout most of the country there is no special state form or secular registration for Catholic marriages. In both respects Catholics are dependent on ecclesiastical officials. But since these functions may be legitimately exercised only by clergy who are properly qualified so far as both state and Church are concerned, and since this category does not include those clergy whose appointment has been made by superiors whom the state does not recognize, to paralyse diocesan authority is tantamount, through its repercussions on parochial law, to imposing an absolute prohibition on the relations mentioned above which affect civil life. Whether it will be advisable to take these consequences into account in every case is a question of expediency which can be left open for the time being. But ... there can be no dispute that it may be necessary to employ extraordinary measures to maintain the authority of the state, to protect religious freedom, and to satisfy the civil needs of the Catholic population.

... [These] extraordinary measures do not furnish an actual solution to the problem, but at best can only provide temporary relief from the most immediate inconveniences. If the government is to be in a position to deal energetically in the long run with an ecclesiastical conflict that seems to be breaking out in several places at once, comprehensive legislation will be required. . . .

37. Bismarck to Falk, 11 August, 1872: from CONSTABEL, pp. 302–3.

... I should like to ask Your Excellency to reconsider whether it is really unavoidable to extend the prohibition on civil functions to all the priests of the diocese. Confining it to the person of the bishop would have the immediate advantage of inclining His Majesty the Emperor ... toward the proposed measure which, if His Majesty persists in his ... reservation, would be delayed indefinitely. Moreover, such an extension of the interdict appears to me to be open to a number of objections. ... From a strategic point of view I do not think it is useful for the state to involve the population in an emergency measure which would affect family life. We ought, as far as possible, to isolate Bishop Krementz and not to increase the number of our adversaries unless and until it is unavoidable. The whole population of the diocese would be subjected to inconveniences which would be resented even by Catholics who are not favourably disposed toward the priesthood. Furthermore, it is possible that other bishops might associate themselves with Krementz's declaration and thereby force the government to suspend all ecclesiastical functions which enter into the field of civil law. This national calamity would be represented as one brought on by the government and one which the government could arbitrarily prolong or end. It seems to me, therefore, that the consequences flowing from the extinguishing of the bishop's powers should be drawn by the bishop himself and not by the government. ...

38. Bismarck in the Prussian Upper House, 10 March, 1873: from ROTHFELD, pp. 236–7.
    The last representative of the Hohenstaufen line of Holy Roman Emperors, Conradin, was beheaded in 1268 with at least the tacit approval of Pope Clement IV who was in league with Charles of Anjou, brother of Louis IX of France.

... The question before us is, in my opinion, distorted, and the light in which we see it is a false one, if we regard it as a religious ecclesiastical question. It is essentially a political question. It is not, as our Catholic citizens are being persuaded, a matter of a struggle of a Protestant dynasty against the Catholic Church, it is not a matter of a struggle between belief and unbelief, it is a matter of the conflict, which is as old as the human race, between monarchy and priesthood, a conflict that goes back even beyond the appearance of our Saviour in this world, ... the conflict which under the name of the struggle between the popes and the emperors occupied German medieval history to the point of the disintegration of the German Empire and which found its conclusion in the death on the scaffold of the last representative of the exalted Swabian line of emperors under the axe of the French conqueror and with that French conqueror in alliance with the pope. Allowing for the different manners of our day we have been close to an analogous solution of this situation. If the French war of conquest whose outbreak coincided with the publication of the Vatican decrees had been successful, then I do not know what stories would have been told so far as the Church in Germany is concerned about the *gestis Dei per Francos*. . . .

The struggle of priesthood against monarchy, in this case the struggle of the pope and the German emperor, which we have already seen in the Middle Ages, is to be judged like any other conflict: it has its alliances, it has its peace treaties, it has it suspensions, it has its armistices. There have been peace-loving popes and there have been belligerent and conquering popes. There has even been a peace-loving king of France, although even Louis XVI found himself in the position where he was conducting wars. . . . Even in the conflicts in which the power of the papacy was involved it has not always been the case that only Catholic powers have been the pope's allies, and the priests have not always aligned themselves with the pope either. We have had cardinals as ministers of great Powers at a time when these great Powers were conducting a strongly anti-papal policy even to the point of using force. . . . This kind of conflict therefore, takes place under the same conditions as any other political conflict, and it is a distortion of the problem which is designed to impress people who are incapable of an independent judgment if it is depicted as turning on the oppression of the Church. What is at stake is the defence of the state, it is a matter of delimiting the scope of domination of priests and of kings, and this delimitation must be drawn so that the state can maintain itself, for in the realm of this world the state has the paramount power. . . .

Where conditions are favourable it is possible to have a dualistic constitution in a country; the Austro-Hungarian state is an illustration of this. But no confessional dualism is to be found there; but here what is at issue is the establishment of two confessional states that would necessarily find themselves in a position of dualistic conflict, one of which would have as its sovereign ruler a foreign ecclesiastical prince whose seat is in Rome, a prince who because of the recent changes in the constitution of the Catholic Church is more powerful than he used to be. If this programme had been realized we would therefore have had, instead of the unitary Prussian state, instead of the German Empire which was in the course of development, two political organisms running in parallel: one with its general staff in the Centre Party, the other with its general staff in the government and person of His Majesty the Emperor. This situation was a totally unacceptable one for the government; and it was its duty to defend the state against this danger. . . .

39. Heinrich von Sybel on the Church and German unification (1874): from *Kleine historische Schriften*, III, 444, 446–51, 453–4. (See Doc. 4.)

. . . As is well known, the war of 1866 ended in a total triumph of the national over the clerical forces. . . . All over Europe the clerical press continued in its attacks on Prussia; no one in France was more eager than this party to demand war against the hated *parvenu*, and we can all remember how this same party in Bavaria mustered all its resources on the occasion of the impending French attack to prevent south Germany from coming to the aid of the North German Confederation against the national enemy. At the same moment the Vatican Council announced the infallibility of the pope. But for the second time and to an even more glorious extent victory in the war which the clerical party had helped to launch went to the defenders of the national interests; the Italians entered Rome, and Germany completed its unification.

We can see that if ever a state has rebelled against clerical pretensions from sheer necessity, from the duty of self-preservation, it is our state. At a time when the Prussian government in no way limited the autocracy of the bishops, when with a population two-thirds Protestant it contributed a third more to Catholic Church funds than to Protestant ones, at a time when the government was doing everything to subject a third of its citizens to a spiritually fatal dependence on the clergy: it was in such circumstances that the clerical party all over Europe went over to the offensive against us, certainly not because Prussia was threatening religion but because it was striving for the unity of Germany. Wherever at that time an opponent of Prussia appeared the clerical party eagerly ranged itself at his side without the papal curia expressing a word of disapproval at these hostile activities. . . . A party with branches all over Europe, strongly disciplined and unconditionally subject to the orders of the pope, has been doing everything it can for six years to prevent the advance of Prussia and the unity of Germany. Immediately after the German victory the German members of this party constituted themselves into a parliamentary party in order, as their manifestos openly proclaimed, to defend the interests of the pope, this same pope whose servants and agents everywhere are fighting with passionate bitterness against the German cause. . . . It was perhaps politically wise to take little notice of this clerical hostility before the French army was defeated; but after France had been overwhelmed it was an urgent duty of the state to render the internal enemy of our national cause harmless. There has never been a juster defensive struggle. . . .

Wherever the clerical party speaks of the freedom and security of the Church it always has in mind a power situation in which on the one hand it is subject to no kind of limitation in the exercise of ecclesiastical discipline, in the education of the growing generation, and in the accumulation of property and wealth, and in which on the other hand it deprives all dissenting opinions of the slightest possibility of any disturbing influence, that is to say it persecutes and exterminates them by all possible means. . . . If a government adopts an attitude of independence towards it, . . . the party gives a splendid virtuoso performance of revolutionary demagoguery, as we have seen in Ireland, in Belgium, and from time to time in Prussia. In those conditions it demands in the name of freedom . . . the inalienable rights of man, eternal fundamental rights, freedom of the press and assembly, independence of the individual from the state, dissolution and dissipation of the state's power. Then it employs all the arts of radicalism and socialism until victory has been won, and the state lies broken or crushed at its feet. Having got this far the advocate of human rights suddenly turns again into the toughest defender of authority, and the short-sighted libertarians who, up to that point, have been helping her in her fight against the kingdom have an opportunity to consider what they have gained by this exchange of rulers. . . .

The essential objectives in the struggle against the clerical system are to be attained only by a positive exercise of the power of the state, and a merely negative attitude, a supension of state support, does not affect the decisive issues at all. The slogan which is frequently heard: separation of Church and state, is a hollow phrase for the clerical system. . . . A further point which is no less clear from all the events of the last sixty years is that it is entirely useless and vain to enter into diplomatic negotiations and agreements with the clerical system. . . .

If the liberal party should lack the necessary insight and self-control, if it suffered an internal split or quarrelled with the government the certain result would be not a parliamentary development in a radical sense but a change in the direction of a conservative clerical régime. . . .

For Germany, as we all know, these things are the more serious since our country is not only confronted with the clerical party as an internal adversary but is at the same time threatened from outside by the thirst for revenge of a France becoming daily stronger. . . . The clericals and the French pursue the same goal for very different reasons, namely, the dissolution of the young empire of the German nation. This makes the problem simpler and the responsibility of every German patriot clearer. Anyone who promotes the wishes of the clerical party in any important matter is also opening the frontiers to the foreign enemy of the empire. . . .

F. The Social Problem

40. A speech by Ferdinand Lassalle, 12 April, 1862: from HOHLFELD, pp. 115–24. Lassalle, Ferdinand (1825–64), socialist politician.

On February 24, 1848, the first dawn of a new historical period appeared. On this day, in France, in the country in whose mighty inner struggles the victories as well as the defeats of freedom amount to victories and defeats for all mankind, a revolution broke out which brought a worker into the provisional government, which declared the purpose of the state to be the improvement of the lot of the working classes, and which proclaimed universal and direct suffrage, whereby every citizen who had reached his twenty-first year, without regard to his property situation, received an equal part in control over the state, in determining the will and purpose of the state.

You see, gentlemen, if the revolution of 1789 was the revolution of the Third Estate, this time it is the Fourth Estate . . . that proposes to make its principle into the dominating principle of society and of all its institutions.

But with this supremacy of the Fourth Estate we find the immense difference that the Fourth Estate is the last, the disinherited estate of society, which makes and which can make no exclusive conditions either in law or in fact, whether nobility or landowning or property, which it might shape into a new privilege and cause to penetrate all the institutions of society.

We are all workers, in so far as we have the will to make ourselves useful to human society in any way.

The Fourth Estate, which contains no germ of any new privileges, is, for that very reason, identical with the whole human race. Its cause is, therefore, in truth, the cause of all mankind. Its freedom is the freedom of all mankind. Its rule means the rule of all.

If, therefore, we make the idea of the working class into the dominating principle of society, in the sense in which I have just explained it, we are not uttering a cry which separates and splits the classes of society; we are uttering a cry, rather, of reconciliation, a cry which comprehends all of society. We are expressing a desire for resolution of all the contradictions in society, a desire for unity in which all those should join who oppose privilege and who oppose suppression of the people by privileged classes. We are uttering a cry of love which will always remain the true cry of the people, and which will remain a cry of love because of its content, even when it rings out as the battle cry of the people.

We will now examine the principle of the working class as the dominating principle of society in three respects: one, in respect of the means by which it can be realized; two, in respect of its moral content, and three, in respect of the political conception of the purpose of the state which it implies. . . .

The formal means by which this principle will be realised is universal and direct suffrage. I insist that it must be universal and direct suffrage, gentlemen, not merely universal suffrage, such as we experienced in 1848. . . .

Admittedly even universal and direct suffrage will not be a magic wand which will protect you, gentlemen, from temporary abuses.

In France, in 1848 and 1849, we saw two bad elections succeed one another. But universal and direct suffrage is the only means which, in the long run, will cancel out the abuses to which its temporarily mistaken use can lead. . . . In the long run universal and direct suffrage must produce a situation where the elected body is the exact and true likeness of the people that elected it.

The people must therefore always regard universal and direct suffrage as the indispensable means for its political struggles, as the most fundamental and most important of all its demands.

I turn now to the moral content of the social principle which we are considering.

Perhaps the idea of making the principle of the lowest classes of society into the ruling principle of the state and of society may appear as a very dangerous and immoral one, as an idea which exposes morality and culture to the threat of decline into a 'modern barbarism.'

And it would not be surprising if this idea appeared in this light nowadays, for public opinion as well, gentlemen, is being moulded, by means of the press, by capitalism and by the privileged upper bourgeoisie.

Nevertheless, this fear is merely a prejudice, and it can on the contrary be proved that this idea represents the greatest advance and triumph of morality that human history has yet known.

This view, as I say, is a prejudice. It is in fact only the prejudice of our own day still dominated by privilege.

At another time, in the days of the First French Republic in 1793 . . ., the opposite prejudice in fact prevailed. At that time it was accepted as an axiom that all higher classes were immoral and perverted, that only the common people was good and moral. . . .

This view, gentlemen, has, in fact, some basis in truth, but a truth which appears only in an untrue and perverted form. Now there is nothing more dangerous than a truth which appears in an untrue and perverted form, for whatever attitude one may adopt toward it one will be equally badly off.   If you adopt that truth in its untrue, perverted form, then sometimes this will lead to the most terrible destruction, as was the case with Sansculottism. If, because of the untrue, perverted form, you reject the whole proposition as untrue, you are even worse off. For in that case you have rejected a truth, and in this instance one whose acceptance is indispensable to any healthy measures in modern political life.

So there is no alternative to trying to overcome the untrue and perverted form of that proposition and to be clear about its true content. . . .

The problem arises at once whether selfishness does not prevail among the lower classes as well, or why it does so less there. Indeed, at first glance it must appear as a surprising paradox that less selfishness should be alleged to prevail among the lower classes than among the upper, who are considerably more advanced in culture and education, elements acknowledged as conducing to morality.

The real basis and the solution of this contradiction . . . is the following:

For a long time now, as we have seen, the development of peoples, the whole direction of history is tending toward an increasing abolition of the privileges which guarantee to the upper classes their very position as upper and ruling classes. The wish to preserve them, in other words personal interest, therefore from the beginning puts every member of the upper classes who has not had the vision to rise above his whole personal existence—and you will appreciate, gentlemen, that this can never be more than a few exceptions—into a position in principle hostile to the development of the people, to the spread of education and knowledge, to the progress of culture, to every breath and victory of historical life.

It is this contrast of the personal interest of the upper classes and the cultural development of the nation that leads to the great and inevitable immorality of the upper classes. It is a life whose everyday demands, as you can well imagine, must lead to a profound inner degeneration. To have to resist, day in and day out, everything great and good, to have to deplore its success and applaud its failure, to prevent its further advance, to reverse or condemn those already made. It is a continual life, as it were, in enemy territory. . . .

This is a life, gentlemen, which of necessity leads to entire contempt for all ideal striving, to a pitying smile at every mention of the great word idea, to a profound insensitivity and resistance to everything beautiful and great, to a complete submergence of all moral elements in our nature under the single passion for selfish advantage and pleasure.

It is this contrast between personal interest and the cultural development of the nation, gentlemen, which is fortunately absent from the lower classes of society.

Admittedly there is still a lot of selfishness among the lower classes, too, much more, unfortunately, than there should be. But here selfishness, where it is present, is the fault of individuals and not the unavoidable fault of the class.

It does not take a very powerful instinct to tell the members of the lower classes that if each of them thinks only of himself he cannot hope for much improvement in his lot.

But to the extent that the lower classes of society strive after the improvement of their lot as a class, to the improvement of their class lot, to that extent their personal interest, instead of resisting the movement of history and therefore being condemned to immorality, runs entirely in the same direction as the development of the whole people, as the victory of ideas, the progress of culture, the life principle of history itself, which is none other than the development of freedom. In other words, as we have already seen, its cause is the cause of all mankind. . . .

You are therefore in the happy position that your true personal interest is identical with the pulse beat of history, with the driving life-principle of moral development. You can therefore dedicate yourselves with personal passion to the development of history, and you can be assured that the more ardent and consuming your passion, in the pure sense explained here, the more moral you will be.

These, gentlemen, are the reasons why the rule of the Fourth Estate over the state must lead to a flowering of morality, of culture, and of knowledge unprecedented in history.

But there is another reason for this too, which is intimately connected with and forms the coping-stone for all our preceding observations.

The Fourth Estate has not only a different formal political principle from the bourgeoisie, namely universal direct suffrage instead of the property qualification of the bourgeoisie. It has not only, because of its economic conditions, a different relationship to moral potentialities from that of the upper classes, it has also—partly as a result—a quite different conception of the ethical purpose of the state from the bourgeoisie.

The moral idea of the bourgeoisie is that nothing should be guaranteed to each individual except the unhindered activation of his own powers.

If we were all equally strong, equally clever, equally educated and equally rich, then this idea might be regarded as adequate and moral.

But as we are not, and as we cannot be, this idea is not adequate and, therefore, necessarily leads to profoundly immoral consequences,

M

for it leads to a situation where the stronger, the cleverer, the richer, exploits the weaker, and puts him in his pocket.

The moral idea of the working class, on the contrary, is that unhindered and free activation of individual powers by the individual is not adequate, but that in a morally ordered community something else must be added to it: the solidarity of interests, community and reciprocity in development.

In accordance with this difference the bourgeoisie has the following conception of the ethical purpose of the state: that it consists exclusively in protecting the personal freedom and property of the individual.

This, gentlemen, is a night-watchman theory, because it conceives the state only in the form of a night-watchman whose sole function consists in preventing robbery and burglary. Unfortunately this night-watchman theory is to be found not only among liberals properly speaking but even among many ostensible democrats. . . . If the bourgeoisie were to take its idea to its logical conclusion it would have to admit that if there were no robbers and thieves the state would be superfluous.

The Fourth Estate, gentlemen, has a quite different conception of the purpose of the state, a conception which corresponds to its true nature.

History, gentlemen, is a struggle against nature, against misery, against ignorance, against poverty, against powerlessness and therefore against absence of freedom of all sorts. . . . The development of freedom in which history consists means the progressive overcoming of this powerlessness.

We should have been able to take no step forward in this struggle, and should be able to take no step in the future, if we each took it by himself alone as an individual.

It is the state that has the function of completing this development of freedom, this evolution of the human race toward freedom.

The state is the unity of individuals in a moral whole, a unity which increases the powers of all the individuals comprising it a millionfold.

The purpose of the state, therefore, is not to protect the individual's personal freedom and property with which, according to the idea of the bourgeoisie, he entered into the state; the purpose of the state, rather, is to enable individuals to attain such purposes, to reach such a level of existence as individually they would never be able to reach, to enable them to acquire an amount of education, of power, and of freedom which would be entirely unattainable to them as individuals.

The purpose of the state, in other words, is to bring human beings to a position of positive development and progressive evolution, to make a reality of human destiny—that is to say, the culture of which the human race is capable; the purpose of the state is the education and development of the human race to freedom.

This, gentlemen, is the real moral nature of the state, its true and higher task. . . .

The working classes, gentlemen, the lower classes of society in general, because of the helpless position in which their members find themselves as individuals, feel instinctively that this is, and must be, the purpose of the state: to enable the individual to attain a level of development which he could not reach by himself by uniting them all.

A state, therefore, which is ruled by the idea of the working class would no longer, as has been the case with all states up to now, be driven unconsciously, and often even against its will, by the nature of things and by the compulsion of circumstances, but would make this moral nature of the state into its task with the greatest clarity and with full consciousness. . . .

Everything that I have said so far demands a new attitude from the working class.

Nothing is more apt to give to a class a dignified and profoundly moral attitude than the consciousness that it is destined to be the ruling class, that it is called to elevate the principle of its class into the principle of the whole age, to make of its idea the leading idea of all society, and thereby to create society in its own image. . . .

The more exclusively you immerse yourself in the moral seriousness of this idea, the more undividedly you devote yourselves to its ardour, the more, you may be sure, you will hasten the day on which the task of our present period of history will be fulfilled. . . .

41. From Hermann Schulze-Delitzsch's *Worker's Catechism* (1863): from *Kapitel zu einem deutschen Arbeiterkatechismus,* in SCHRAEPLER, I, 178–82. Schulze-Delitzsch, Franz Hermann (1808–23), economist, Liberal deputy in the Prussian House of Representatives.

First of all we must be clear about this: that the state cannot solve the problem of the workers by its intervention, that its activities can do no more than make our solution of it easier or harder. The problem is not a political but an economic one. An evil of an economic nature can be combated only by economic means, not political ones. . . . An illness in any organism, in this case the economic one, can never be healed from without by some magical means but only by stimulating and strengthening the inner powers of the organism itself.

Now the constituent elements of this economic organism are individual live people. . . . Everything moves around and through them, the whole operation is put into motion through them. It is a matter of the physical necessities of life, of physical existence, and nature knows no other existence in this connection but the individual one. Needs are felt by individual people differently in each case, differently in direction and strength as determined by the individuality that distinguishes each man from every other. And it is the same with the forces whose activation alone can satisfy the needs. These also have been placed by nature in the individual separately and differently and unequally. People, therefore, can never be lumped together in an undifferentiated mass for the purpose of providing them with their necessities of life, and neither the needs of each individual nor his performance can be determined by any general average. We are not mere quantities, mere numbers which can be added together in some arbitrary sums and then arbitrarily divided to make new arbitrary quantities. It is the case that nature has placed both needs and means of satisfying them in the lives of individuals, and nature has, therefore, placed the vicissitudes of life with ourselves, has thrown each of us on his own resources, and has left him to draw up the balance sheet of his own life. It is impossible to take this act of balancing away from the individual, every attempt to do so is an infringement of individuality, of the basic form of our life, an impairment of the natural drives and powers of individuals which are the only ones in the world available to tackle the problem at all.

There is no other way of solving this problem, then, but to begin with individuals, with developing and perfecting in individuals all those things on which success in economic matters, in gaining one's livelihood, depends. The only proper goal here is and remains to educate men to help themselves. It is a matter, above all, of developing mental, moral, and physical faculties, the teaching of useful knowledge and skills, training in thrift, diligence, and a sound way of life. If we are to improve our circumstances and our situation we must first of all begin with ourselves. It would be difficult to find anything defective in our circumstances that could not be traced back to some defect in ourselves, and the world will not become better until men become better in insight and willpower, in serious aspirations and morality. . . .

Economic relations among men are regulated in the same manner as all other relationships given in nature, by certain eternal laws based in their innermost existence. Any success in making one's living and in managing one's life depends on knowing these necessities of nature, on complying with them and taking advantage of them, just as the farmer must know the changes in the seasons, the influence of weather . . . and so forth if he is to succeed in agriculture. In the same way the industrialist and the worker must know the laws governing production and consumption, exchange and value, capital and credit and so on.

To regulate one's activities according to this knowledge, to use the forces on which success in this field depends instead of combating them, not to dissipate one's energies in vain attempts to frustrate these forces or to alter the nature of things, these should be our aims in our attempts to improve the economic situation of the working classes.

Since, as we have ample reason to know, the conditions of economic prosperity are not arbitrarily to be discovered, but are necessarily based on man's essential nature and on his position in the world, . . . our problem can only be formulated as follows: 'to find a means of generalising those conditions of success which are only rarely to be found in the case of individual workers and which will make accessible to those of average talents things which otherwise would be attained only by those of exceptional talents.'

These means, however, we already have in the free industrial and economic association as it has developed for over thirty years in those countries where industrial work is most advanced. Taking as its point of departure the age-old proposition of the association of forces, it has even in its earliest stages produced such important results that we are justified in looking to it for that source of reconciliation by means of which general industrial progress with its undeniable blessings for the community as a whole need not be bought at the price of sacrificing industrial prosperity for numerous classes of society. 'What you cannot do yourself obtain by combining with others who want the same thing,' and: 'several small forces combined form a great force'; these are the simple truths that associations are striving to bring about in the economic field, and in fact they have already proved themselves. . . .

I have said earlier that guilds have no further function nowadays and that on the contrary it is now a matter of eliminating the last vestiges of privilege belonging to selected classes and of merging the old state based on Estates entirely in the state based on law with equality before the law. It is for this reason that unity has been transferred from the political to the economic field where the problem of the working class is at the moment to be found, and here we welcome unity in the form of an association of workers which has got rid of the compulsions, the restrictions, and the exclusiveness that were inherent in the political character of the old guilds and in the legal customs of the Middle Ages, an association that has focused on the freedom of the changing interests of its participants to group themselves differently as the guiding principle that has made it into such a valuable member of the economic organism. . . .

Neither the guildsmen in league with feudal reaction nor the socialists who are, in an equally remarkable manner, attracting the sympathies of our so-called conservatives shall ever tempt German workers in this fatal direction. Anyone who claims the right to help from someone else, even if it be the state, immediately yields up to him authority and supervision over himself and gives up his independence. But this amounts to giving up oneself, to despairing of one's own power, which is the more wrong and the more unnecessary since associations prove that the workers can very well help themselves if they go about it the right way, that they are not in need of help from anyone else. . . . The spirit of self-help, this truly German spirit shall manifest itself in you. . . .

42. From John Prince-Smith, *The Pseudo-Problem of the Working Class* (1864):from SCHRAEPLER, I, 173–7. Prince-Smith, John (1809–74), economist, leading advocate of free trade.

The so-called 'question of the workers' is again occupying many minds, or rather emotions. . . . The heavy demand for solutions of this 'question of the workers' naturally produces a corresponding supply of projects. But in the sense in which this question is put it can not only not be answered; it cannot even be asked. The 'question of the workers' is understood to mean the following: 'how can the economic situation of the wage earner be suddenly improved independently from the general raising of the standard of living for which we do not want to wait?'

The economist will see at once that such a problem is insoluble. . . .

Custom determines whether a given wage or amount of satisfactions of other sorts allows a working population to feel contented and to multiply or whether, on the contrary, it feels discontented and dwindles. A wage on which the ragged Irish are highly delighted to see their naked offspring multiply together with those of the family pig in the filth in front of their mud huts would cause the English working population which is used to better things to feel deprived. It is custom, therefore, that determines what wage the employers must offer in order to obtain the number of workers necessary to make use of their capital. If they do not offer a wage which meets what the workers are used to sufficiently for them to multiply at the same pace as the growth of capital then in due course there will be a shortage of labour which will compel a raising of wages. The natural impulse to procreate has, to be sure, a tendency to increase the number of those among whom the total amount of available wages is to be divided, a tendency, that is to say, to make each individual's share smaller, his wage lower. But custom . . . will inhibit procreation as soon as the shares become too small to provide that measure of satisfaction which has become indispensable to the workers. Up to the limit of this measure of satisfaction which has become indispensable through custom, wages will, however, in fact in the long run be depressed because of the competition of increasing numbers of people seeking work. But this measure of satisfaction can be a relatively considerable one. There is therefore only one way to increase the average wage permanently: that is by raising the habits of the workers. The economic situation of the workers can be improved only by the workers improving themselves economically, by becoming used to better things, becoming more economical. . . .

Such a raising of customs, although difficult and slow, has, nevertheless, always taken place wherever one class of wage-earners found themselves in a relatively better situation than another. . . . Instead of that alleged 'iron law' which is supposed to depress the workers into utter misery we suggest the true 'golden law' whose effect is to raise them up into an ever more comfortable way of life.

For sometimes events occur which lead to an unusually rapid increase in capital. . . . Such an accelerated increase in capital cannot be followed immediately by a corresponding increase in the work force. In such a case the demand for work grows faster than the supply. Wages rise and the workers live better than before. They can marry more easily and, most important, they can have more children which will survive the dangers of the first years of life. . . . But it takes about twenty years before a worker is grown up and trained. This is how long it takes before the impulse toward a growth in population given by a rise in wages leads to a higher number of persons seeking work on the labour market, which in turn then once more depresses the wage rate. During this interval of higher wages the general standard of living of workers normally rises. The young generation becomes accustomed to more spacious and cleaner accommodation, more comfortable furniture, more adequate equipment, a greater quantity of food, better clothing, also certain cultural pleasures and a better social life. When in the end the time comes when the new larger generation of workers begins to depress wages again the generation which has become accustomed to better things begins to feel very uncomfortable; it makes unusual efforts to raise its wages; it postpones marriages and children; it resists with all its moral energy any tendency to return to its earlier lower standard of living. And if its improved way of life is tolerably firmly established then it is in a better position to make its improved situation into a permanent one, since as a result of better physical, mental, and moral training it is capable of a higher performance and therefore able to attract higher wages permanently. . . .

It is, however, scarcely permissible to speak of those without capital and who must work for wages indiscriminately in terms of a working class, since there are very important differences among them on which their economic situation as well as its improvement of necessity depends. First of all we must distinguish those who occupy a place in capitalistic industry, whose labour is completely divided and supported by machines, tools, and other capitalistic aids. Among this group poverty is to be found only in exceptional cases. Most of them can live tolerably, many can even live well. Steady progress towards better things is in their case evident and secure. They are used to regular activity and to receiving regular income. They have admittedly a limited but nevertheless relatively secure existence, and no need acquires a more powerful hold on men than the need to maintain security from total deprivation once it has been won. It impels him to be careful and to be active. It makes him thrifty, it prevents him from taking actions which might endanger his future standard of living. Such workers do not marry without having laid the foundations for an adequate home; they do not produce children whom they are not tolerably capable of raising. Such workers have already acquired that economic sense which we have defined as the basic condition for raising economic conditions generally, whether it be of the wage-earning classes or of any other class of people. . . .

The class of workers among whom misery is to be found consists for the most part of those who have not yet been able to be absorbed into capitalist industry, whose labour, still not much helped by capitalist resources, is still rather unproductive. For the most part they do occasional work which requires little training and only simple tools. . . . The kind of work which is easiest to learn or scarcely needs to be learnt and for which even the poorest man can equip himself will always attract an excessive labour force and will always pay mere subsistence wages, so long as there are so many people without help and without resources; and in the case of such people it is very difficult to limit their rate of reproduction and to prevent them from sinking into even deeper misery, for they know nothing but the most elementary meeting of physical needs, no satisfactions of life, no pleasures; they simply vegetate along without acquiring any habits which could serve them as means to elevate their dull existence. . . . They take no thought for the morrow because their condition is already too bad to be made any worse by carelessness. And if they are still used to receiving a wage, be it ever so little, from regular work this does nevertheless constitute a possible means to correct their miserable condition. . . .

If now we ask ourselves on what economic culture is based, why it is that an industrial people can attain so immeasurably more means of satisfaction than a people which is still in the first stages of economic development, the answer is simple: it is based on accumulated capital. It is therefore natural as well as just that among an industrial people those who have accumulated the capital and who administer and maintain it should receive a major portion of the surplus which they have achieved by means of their capital, and it is wrong as well as inappropriate to demand that those without capital ... should enjoy benefits which can flow only from possession of reserves. Nevertheless those without capital derive a great benefit from the capital accumulated by others; for as wages for their work they receive, admittedly not very many, but still many more means of satisfying their demands than they could produce themselves without the help of capital; for if a densely populated industrial country were suddenly to lose all its capital it would necessarily become a thinly populated country. ...

If in general the too slow rate of growth of capital and the too small increase in demand for labour are the reasons for the low wages which are the subject of complaint, then self-evidently we must not reduce the gain in capital which is the basis for the ability to invest capital as well as for the incentive to do so. If the present allegedly too high profits for the industrialists allow capitalisation to proceed too slowly for the good of the worker what would be the position if profits were lower? High profits for the employer rapidly benefit the workers; for the greater the profits in a business the more rapidly can new capital be created; and the earlier the amount of capital is likely to increase the greater will be the incentive for present abstinence, saving, and investment; and investment means higher wages.

43. Bishop W. E. v. Ketteler, *Christianity and the Problem of the Workers* (1864): from *Die Arbeiterfrage und das Christentum*, in SCHRAEPLER, I, 146–8. Ketteler, Wilhelm Emanuel v. (1811–77), from 1850 Bishop of Mainz.

The so-called problem of the working class is essentially the problem of the workers' subsistence. It is therefore on the one hand as important as subsistence itself, i.e. procuring the barest necessities of life, food, clothing, shelter. On the other hand it is as important as the number of workers in proportion to all other classes.[1] As regards its subject, therefore, it concerns the most essential needs of man; as regards its scope, it includes by far the majority of the whole human race.

The problem of the working class therefore has a significance quite different from that of any so-called political problem. Anyone who listens to legislative debates or reads the press might think that political questions are the things that matter most to men; that they concern the most important and most essential interests of mankind. But that is a great illusion. Political questions often have real significance only

[1] (Note of Ketteler's:) We mean by workers not only the workers properly speaking, the hired labourers, but also those who run their own business with so little capital that they are in fact in the same condition as the hired labourers, e.g. the small artisan or tradesman, and also small householders or landowners who live chiefly from hiring out their labour.

for a small section of the population, those who work with their pens, those who talk and write most and therefore dominate the platform and the press. ... But all these things that are treated at great length in these legislative debates and newspaper reports hardly touch on the life of the working class who have to earn their living by the sweat of their brow. What the mass of the people, the workers and their families, think, say, and feel all day, what they are really concerned about, what improves or worsens their lot and their essential needs, is hardly touched on in discussions of current affairs. Exceptions occur only when the workers are brought into political movements by the political parties as means to their ends. ... When the political goal has been attained they are allowed once more to follow their accustomed ways, and their situation remains unchanged. This has happened many times in the last hundred years. The parties have always pretended that all the true interests of the people were connected with their activities; under this pretext they have always called on the people at the hour of decision; the people had to help the party to victory with its blood; and every time, when the victory has been won, the people's condition has remained the same. ... The people is in fact deceived by the political parties, especially by the dominant party of liberalism. ... They endeavour, by using their supremacy in the chambers and in the papers, to convince the people of the entirely mistaken notion that the people's real interests are contained in political questions, and then by ceaselessly exploiting this illusion they give themselves out to be the people's best friend in engaging in this writing and talking. Many celebrated names of the liberal party owe their entire reputation in Germany to this illusion, while their owners have done nothing for the people's true welfare.

44. A memorandum for Bismarck by Hermann Wagener on social problems (1872): from SCHRAEPLER, II, 47–9. Wagener, Hermann (1815–89), landowner, conservative politician; deputy in the Prussian house of Representatives 1856, ministerial councillor, 1866, member of the *Reichstag* of the North German Confederation 1867.

Since, in my humble opinion, the manner in which social problems are being handled is wrong, I take the liberty of respectfully submitting to Your Highness a short summary of what, on the contrary, appears necessary to me. ...

It seems to me ... to be an exceedingly dangerous undertaking to wish to combat the Ultramontane and the Socialist parties at the same time and thereby to drive the Socialists even more and irrevocably into the clerical camp. Even though it may be justified and necessary to enforce existing laws energetically, on all sides, and thereby to keep away from the Socialist movement foreign elements and any other elements who are pursuing anti-national goals, nevertheless I regard it as definitely a political mistake to subject the Socialist leaders to exceptional laws solely on account of their social aspirations, particularly if one does not, at the same time, do anything substantial to satisfy the justified demands of their supporters.

The most recent reports on developments within the International leave no doubt that in its English and German sections not only has the national element won the day but they are even beginning to go back on their previous injection of social aspirations into politics, and that for this reason a complete split has appeared between the German and English sections on the one hand and the Russian and French sections on the other.

It would be very unfortunate if this development were not put to use by the German government, in order to remove the Socialist movement from susceptibility to anti-national agitation. . . .

Recent reliable reports from England and America show that in England, for example, the nine-hour day is hardly any longer regarded as a question of legislation, but that the trade unions already feel themselves strong enough to enforce it by themselves, and the American Congress has, as we know, formed a committee to investigate the position of the working class as a basis for legislation. The fact that the latter is at the same time an election manoeuvre increases rather than decreases the significance of this step.

I respectfully submit that the German government should follow these examples and, in particular, that it should also begin by instituting a thorough inquiry which should be conducted with all possible publicity. It would also be necessary to select the persons who are to testify on a broader basis and to include people with a merited reputation as experts in this field. . . .

All history teaches that it is impossible to combat a vigorous idea with material means alone, and there is only one idea with which the currently very powerful Catholic-ecclesiastic idea can be confronted with any chance of political success, the social idea; in my considered opinion the next phase of European history will consist in the reciprocal relations of these two ideas.

My immediate practical suggestions would be as follows:
(1) Establishment of a committee on the American model to prepare and to introduce legislation in this field;
(2) Extension of the hearings of expert witnesses already under way in the ministery of commerce with all possible publicity;
(3) Practical steps to establish factory inspectors or—if this description is found more acceptable—labour offices.

The latter institution, particularly, could develop into an organization which in the political field might be not only a match for but even superior to the Catholic Church. The Social Emperor would be in an even stronger position in relation to the materialist tendencies of the day than the Social Pope. . . .

The masses of the population are at present uncertain which way to turn. International agitation has not yet gained a broad basis of support, although it seems at times as though they were looking for easy ways to get some martyrs.

But the way the masses turn will in the long run be of decisive significance not only in politics and in parliament but for the character of the army. The latter will be completely and permanently reliable only if the workers, who provide the main body of recruits, are attracted and bound to the idea of the German Empire by its achievements.

45. From Gustav Schmoller, *The Social Question and the Prussian State* (1874) from SCHRAEPLER, II, 62–6. Schmoller, Gustav (1838–1917), economist and historian.

. . . Our era is saddled with social classes that are deprived and neglected and have been abused for centuries. Suddenly left to themselves and exposed to the competitive struggle, these classes necessarily were left behind to the same extent as those who were better situated, the more educated and the propertied classes, advanced more quickly. Small industry could not compete with large. Modern technology was available only to large-scale capital. The enormous increase in production and in trade did not benefit all social classes equally but mainly a privileged minority. Until a few years ago wages in Germany lagged dangerously behind the general movement of prices. Even apart from this, the effects of big industry on living, education, and family conditions were in any case predominantly unfavourable. It was the working class, thousands of members of which were suddenly dismissed, who suffered the most from economic crises. The same worker who was daily receiving new political rights, who on all sides was being summoned into the political arena, who was assured every day that he was the real people—this same worker until not very long ago found himself, for the most part, worse off every day. The moment was bound to come when he would say to himself: it seems that in political life, in serving my country, I am to count for as much as the noblest and richest, but in economic and social life the gap is not only to continue but is to be widened.

It is on these premises that the current social question has arisen and was bound to arise. A social class-consciousness was bound to appear the moment that a single voice pointed out with sufficient emphasis and clarity that the propertyless working class had different interests than even the most radical section of the employing class. The cavalier dismissal of all complaints emanating from the Fourth Estate with the phrase that the new legislation had done everything that it was possible to do, that everyone who now could not advance himself was to blame for it himself, was bound to increase their bitterness the more rapidly the clearer it became that the propertied classes were dominated by reprehensible materialism and narrow egoism, the more obviously unscrupulous they became in using doubtful means for the sake of quick profits. The masses have enough feeling for elementary justice to accept any existing property system which seems, even remotely, to be in accord with the virtues, the knowledge, and the performance of individuals and of the different classes. On the other hand, however, every system of property and income, of which the world has known many, has in the course of time collapsed if it could no longer base itself on this conviction. The nail in the coffin of any existing distribution of property is a spreading conviction that morally reprehensible means of making profits are becoming prevalent without let or hindrance, that large fortunes are more likely to be made by dishonest than by honest means, that there is too unjust a discrepancy between the various actions of individuals and their economic results—that is to say their incomes. . . .

In my opinion Social Democracy represents merely the youthful exuberance of the great social movement which we are entering. Our Social Democracy is a little different but it is hardly worse than English Chartism was in its time, and I hope that like the latter it will prove to be merely a transitional phase of social development which will soon give place to more mature and clearer conceptions and attainable plans. Admittedly grave complaints may be made against it, particularly the one that some of its leaders appeal only to bad passions: to envy, to hatred, to unbridled appetites, but by the side of these passionate and dishonest leaders there are also others who are personally highly honourable. . . .

Public opinion in this country has not so far done much justice to the social question. Influenced mainly by those for whom the social movement signified in the first place disturbance of the ordinary comfortable course of business, it is for the most part prejudiced against the working class. . . . Unsavoury people are to be found everywhere. There is no lack of examples, and so people are able to talk incredible nonsense about the roughness and worthlessness of the working class and of the excellence of their opponents.

Certainly the whole working class is at the moment suffering from the fact that it has entered into new economic conditions for which the moral conceptions and relationships and the customs of former times are no longer suitable and for which it has not yet formed the appropriate new ones. The working classes are not sure what they can and should demand, what they are to do with their higher wages, what they can afford to do in their new situation. They find themselves on rather uncertain ground, but in this respect they are entirely similar to the upper classes. The moral spectacle afforded by many speculators who become rich overnight seems to me to be no different from that of many workers who spend their higher wages on drinking. . . .

The working classes are nowadays and have always been what they are made in their schools and in their homes, at their place of work and by their work, in their family life and in their environment, by the example of the upper classes, by the ideas and ideals and sins of the day.

Are the working classes by any chance alone to blame? Is the individual worker to blame that often he lives in holes that degrade him to the level of an animal or of a criminal? Is he to blame for the fact that child and female labour are increasingly dissolving family life; is he to blame for the fact that the division of labour and the mechanisation of work allow him to learn less than the apprentice and the journeyman used to learn in their workshops, that the moral influences of the large factory are much less favourable than those of the workshop; is he to blame for the fact that he can never become independent, that normally he has no hope for the future, and does not psychology teach that the absence of any hope for the future makes men slack and ill-tempered and inclined to revolt? Are the workers to blame for the fact that they have a school and technical education that is not adequate and that causes them so often to lose out in the competitive struggle?

If these simple truths were generally recognized by public opinion then social matters would be evaluated quite differently and we should be much closer to a relative solution of the problem.

The attitude of leading parliamentary and governmental circles toward the social question would in that case also probably be different, and this in my opinion would be highly desirable. It is true that nowadays in a parliamentary state, with a free press, with the right of free association and assembly, the monarchy cannot, as it could in the last century, directly take over the leadership of the lower classes vis-à-vis the property owners, the government must adopt a more neutral position; but it must then really be impartial among the economic classes; it must not regard every demand of the working class and all its aims which are entirely compatible with current legislation but which are inconvenient for the propertied classes as being directed against itself and against public order, and it must therefore not look on them with disfavour as appears from time to time to be the case, as is certainly the case with several agencies of the state. The government is abandoning all the traditions of Prussian politics if it looks at the social question exclusively from the point of view of the propertied classes and of the great entrepreneur, if it directs its enquiries only to the chambers of commerce which naturally stand for a one-sided selfish interest, if in its legislation it does not resist with the utmost energy the excessive influence that is today exercised in all public representative bodies as well as in a frequently corrupt press by the great private railways, by the great banks and companies, by the great industries with their paid and well-trained agents. . . .

The social dangers of the future can be averted by only one means: by the monarchy and the civil service, the most appropriate representatives of the idea of the state, the only neutral elements in the social class war, reconciling themselves to the idea of the liberal state, absorbing into their midst the best elements of parliamentary government, and taking a resolute and determined initiative toward a great venture in social-reform legislation and unwaveringly holding fast to this idea for one or two generations. . . .

46. From Heinrich von Treitschke, *Socialism and Its Sympathizers* (1874): from SCHRAEPLER, II, 66–73. This pamphlet was written in rebuttal of Schmoller's (Doc. 45).

Bourgeois society among a rich people is always an aristocracy, even under a democratic constitution. Or if we are to pronounce a hated but true phrase unvarnished: class rule, or better order by classes, follows as inevitably from the nature of society as the contrast between rulers and ruled follows from the nature of the state. Social Democracy admits by its very name that its aims are nonsense. . . .

It has to be admitted that this aristocratic constitution of society disfigures some talents. Nature is a munificent provider, it goes about its business generously. In the realm of animals and plants it produces every hour innumerable new germs which disappear before their time. Among men it equips its favourites so prodigally that we may say boldly: all the great men of history were greater than their works, none of them could develop every gift of his being. It is therefore certain that at any time there are individual great talents among the hard-working masses which are prevented by the social order alone from revealing their innate nobility. . . . But history deals with large numbers. If we turn from the tragic exceptions to finding a law then we must recognize that the human race is so meagrely equipped, the mere sustaining of life and the satisfaction of the most elementary needs take up such an enormous part of its strength, because only a small minority is ever capable of seeing the light of the idea with open eyes, while the masses receive only the broken ray. . . .

Our state nowhere grants a political right for which there is not a corresponding duty; it demands of all those who wish to take part in any way in the direction of public life that they must first earn this power through property and education; it is ceaselessly active on behalf of a wider and deeper spiritual life; it mitigates even the most general of its civic duties, the duty of bearing arms, in favour of these spiritual forces. . . . Universal suffrage goes clean against these basic ethical conceptions of the German state; it rewards ignorance and awakens pride in the stupid. Anyone who has taken the trouble to be born receives, after a few years and without limitations, in a state that gives unprecedented honour to culture, the highest political right of the citizen! It can be no surprise that the poor man who enjoys such a right comes to the conclusion that in society also birth is a valid pass-port to power without work for every man. There can be no doubt that universal suffrage has immeasurably encouraged the fantastic over-estimation of their own power and their own value among the masses. The irreconcilable contrast between the democratic equality of political suffrage and the necessary aristocratic structure of society proves to the dissatisfied little man with all possible clarity the social decadence of the present and makes him into a credulous victim of demagogues. In this state of noble culture universal suffrage means organized indiscipline, it amounts to a recognition of the revolt of sovereign ignorance, the revolt of the soldier against his officer, of the journeyman against his master, of the worker against his employer. But these destructive effects have already taken place to excess and are no longer to be eliminated; to abolish the right which has already been granted would only encourage all the more the arrogance of the uncivilised. All we can do, therefore, is at least to protect the founda-tions of our monarchical state, the administration of our localities and communities, from the invasion of republican principles and to protest against the assertion that the reward of ignorance is a result of enlightened social policy. . . .

German Social Democracy really is 'as black' as it is depicted in the majority of cultured journals. It merits attention as a symptom of serious social abuses but it does not offer us a single valid idea which would lend itself to discussion or which could be absorbed into our social order. Envy and greed are the two mighty forces that it employs to lift the old world from its hinges; it thrives on the destruction of all ideals. If those who sympathise with socialism value as a good sign the fact that the party undeniably has, in addition to its insidious agitators, its cheap demagogues, and its long line of adherents who have no ideas at all, many honestly unselfish apostles and even a few visionary poets in its ranks as well, this praise is only one more proof of the way in which the present time is inextricably caught in the bonds of its materialist conception of the world. . . .

The learned friends of socialism are in the habit of pointing out by way of mitigation that the Social Democratic worker is at least learning to think. In so doing they only prove that they themselves are unknowingly infected by the materialistic moral teachings of socialism, which sees in the development of reason, in the so-called Enlightenment, the roots of virtue. If the discontented little man who does not succeed in finding his way among the new forms of public economic life hears it announced day after day that the whole order of society is based on injustice, that force must destroy what force has created, if in addition the preachers of this doctrine can call in aid the historical constructions of moderate liberal professors—this sort of instruction may indeed enable the worker to accumulate some items of knowledge. But is it an accident that every prison contains a large group of devoted adherents of Social Democracy? Does a party which every day appeals to force not share the blame for the terrible increase of brutality among the masses, for the cowardly knifings which have become so common in the factory districts of the lower Rhine that no-one pays any attention to them anymore? The very foundation-stones of all community life are endangered by Social Democracy, those very simple concepts of discipline and shame which among civilized men are not even matters for discussion. The doctrine of the injustice of society destroys the firm instincts that the worker has about honour, so that fraud and bad and dishonest work are scarcely held to be held reprehensible any longer, and on the contrary encourages him to be chronically and suspiciously sensitive to justified criticism. . . .

Such a crudely materialist doctrine can know no fatherland, can know no respect for the personality of the national state. The idea of nationalism, the moving force of history in our century, remains inconceivable to socialism. Socialism is everywhere in league with unpatriotic cosmopolitanism and with a weakness of loyalty toward the state. . . .

The learned friends of socialism are in the habit of pointing to the English Chartists who also began with cosmopolitan dreams but nevertheless in the end learned to accommodate themselves to their country. This overlooks the fact that the English island people possessed in the age-old unity of their state and in their rough national pride powers of resistance which are lacking in our unfinished country open to all foreign influences. It also overlooks the fact that Chartism was in its origins English, whereas German Social Democracy is led from abroad by a mob of homeless conspirators. With every passing year Social Democracy has become more antagonistic toward the idea of the national state. . . .

M

Socialism, therefore, alienates its adherents from the state and from the fatherland and in place of this community of love and respect which it destroys it offers them the community of class hatred. The nature of the modern state tends to extinguish class differences. At all levels of society class feelings nowadays count for little by the side of consciousness of citizenship, of patriotism. Among the lowest classes alone powerful agitators seek to encourage a boastful class pride, and by what means! No Persian prince was ever so flattered and fawned upon as 'the real people' of Social Democracy. All the contemptible devices of French radicalism in the 1840s are called upon in order to awaken among the masses an arrogance that knows no bounds. . . .

Social Democracy, according to its leaders, can be, and wants to be, only a workers' party, and public opinion is bullied into accepting this declaration, whereas it is well known that the formation of a purely class party always disturbs the public peace and that a party which would accept only landlords or only industrialists would immediately be met with general indignation. The socialist trade unions also exclude employers as a matter of principle. But class hatred must be indoctrinated and strengthened by struggle; and it is this praiseworthy goal that is served by strikes. Certainly the worker who is really aggrieved has a right to stop working, . . . but equally certainly many strikes in our recent history are the result of inexperienced arrogance which, encouraged by a first success, dared to demand the impossible. Many others have been the work of unscrupulous agitators. Almost all sections of Social Democracy, as is well known, declare that in principle they reject cessation of work and yet their leaders are untiringly fomenting new strikes. It is a matter of inflaming class hatred to fury, of getting people unaccustomed to loyally doing their work, of confusing the masses in their adherence to the law by breaches of contract which occur in every case of cessation of work. . . .

It is an indispensable fundamental principle of the constitutional state that property and culture are necessary for a deputy. It will always be normal that the man who is elected will be above the average of those who elected him. If the socialist workers today on principle give their votes to half-educated men who are not equal to the duties of a deputy and who are not able to represent effectively in parliament the views of their constituents, such behaviour is by no means a sign of proud class-consciousness but an effect of sullen class hatred which refuses to believe that someone who is not a worker can look after the interests of workers with justice and intelligence. In the long run this procedure cannot even be logically followed. Even a workers' party requires educated leaders, almost all dangerous demagogues of history did not belong to the 'people' whom they flattered, and the leaders of German Social Democracy are themselves 'bourgeois.'

In short, it is clear that Social Democracy is a party of moral savagery, of political indiscipline, and of social unrest. . . .

And now, I ask, is this a party with which we can negotiate? It is a party which by its unsparing criticism has made us aware of many weaknesses in our social life and by its crude materialism has shown us where in the long run the eudaemonism which was formerly prevalent in political economy in the end leads. It has no merits beyond these two negative and involuntary ones. It looks to the supremacy of force and we look to the supremacy of culture. In every sense we are farther away from it than we are from the Ultramontanes. Just as we say to the latter: first you must recognize the sovereignty of the state and then we can come to an understanding about specific issues, in the same away, and even more decisively, we must say to the Social Democrats: first you must submit yourselves to the traditional order of society. To be sure, this demand means, first you must become the opposite of what you are today! . . .

It does not mean that we are insensitive to the sufferings of the people if we decline to exchange manifestations of love with the boastful leaders of a crude mob. It is also not necessary in considering social questions to talk all the time as though we were assailed by a fever, as if the emancipation of the Fourth Estate were the 'problem' of the century. This emancipation does not lie in the future, it has already taken place and requires only to be firmly established. . . .

A proper ordering of the state is always based on the necessary structure of society. Property, education and, closely connected with them, the carrying out of burdensome political duties, are always the recognized entitlements to political power. Direct popular rule can never be more than a fiction in civilised conditions; actual political leadership is always in the hands of the educated and the propertied. This is the case with the democratic cantons of Switzerland as much as with our monarchies. The masses have not the capacity to fulfil the serious duties of government or to occupy the higher offices of self-government. Even the modest problems of jury service are often inadequately solved because the education of our lower middle class is not sufficient, and no thinking person will wish to make up jury lists by going even lower down in the social scale. . . . Almost all great mass movements of history have had their roots in economic necessity or in religious feeling. Purely political party questions seldom affect the little man; his enthusiasm can be kindled only for the highest political good, for the existence of the fatherland.

A correct assessment of this character of the masses leads to the sober Aristotelian advice which has been followed in all well-ordered states, namely: social peace is preserved best if the higher classes do not allow the masses to become too powerful and do not do them any injustice. . . . If that advice is not followed, if the masses succeed in taking power directly for themselves, then the world is turned upside down, state and society are dissolved, and rule by force sets in, which put an end to a thousand years of Greek civilisation. . . .

However generously the state may provide the lower classes with political rights it will always be the case that they themselves cannot govern. They may be given the right to vote but in fact they are eligible to be elected themselves only in rare exceptional cases; and this is not to be regretted, for parliament should not represent class interests as such but should represent the corporations exercising self-government, which are bound together by the community of performing their duties and which include all classes. However humanitarian society may be in its concern for the welfare of the lower classes, the manual worker will still always at best live in a modest house and the landlord in a mansion. By raising up the lower levels of society we therefore never reach the goal of equalizing demands which, according to Aristotle's nice phrase, is more important than the equalizing of property.

There is another and surer way of mitigating class antagonisms: to remove the barriers which prevent those who are born in poverty from rising into the group of the propertied and educated. The state and society can never do enough in this direction. . . . If it is impossible to allow the great majority of people to participate in all the pleasures of culture, nevertheless every enterprising person must be able to hope to leave this majority. The state should not merely enable people to work and to give the poor man the right to lift himself up out of his class, it should also by means of good elementary schools and an easily accessible higher education make it possible for the genuinely talented really to exercise these rights. This is the only way to infuse fresh blood into the upper classes constantly. This is the only way to come close to that equalizing of demand. . . . Free competition among all for the benefits of civilisation which can only ever be attained in full measure by a minority—this is what I regard as sensible equality. . . .

47. A speech by Adolf Stoecker (1880): from SCHRAEPLER, II, 74–9. Stoecker, Adolf (1835–1909), court chaplain in Berlin and politician.

Of the stirring questions that are currently of general concern the social question is certainly the most stirring. . . . We in Germany have particular reason to pay attention to this movement and not to allow any of its phases to escape us. Nihilism in the east, the Commune in the west, the whole great revolutionary movement in Germany all show that we are in fact, as the phrase so often goes, on volcanic ground. . . .

With respect to Social Democracy two different kinds of erroneous conceptions are prevalent. One group of economists see Social Democracy as something quite harmless, as a system of social reforms aimed at achieving the welfare of one's neighbours. They forget the immoral tendencies connected with it and the war against Christianity that is bound up with it, and—attracted by the intellectual energy of the Social Democratic Party, by its dedication, and by its willingness to make sacrifices—they have almost nothing but good things to say of the movement. This conception is certainly wrong. Social Democracy is not just a movement for social reforms; as it portrays itself in Germany and as it has portrayed itself for decades in pamphlets, books, and assemblies it is a new conception of the world—a conception which once it has taken hold of people pries them away from Christianity, patriotism, and German morality, separates them from the ethical foundations of our life and directs them down a road which, in my opinion, can and will lead only to an abyss.

But on the other hand it is equally an error to say that Social Democracy is a product of idle heads, mean dispositions, and evil agitators. For it is not this either. To be sure, the easiest way of disposing of this deep-rooted popular movement would be to place the entire blame for it on a few ambitious, unpatriotic individuals. But in fact the affairs of mankind do not occur in this way. A movement that bites so deeply, that attracts such a large number of German men, and also German women, in such a short time, that operates so persistently that it has to be dealt with by legislation contrary to modern ideas, such a movement is a product neither of idle minds, nor of chance, nor of foolishness, such a movement must have a source which it is our task and our duty to discover. . . .

I begin with a sketch of the phenomenon 'Social Democracy' which is so much feared. Its parents are the *Zeitgeist* and poverty. It was born of ethical brutalisation, religious defections, economic injustice and misery. The last point must not be overlooked. There really is social injustice and poverty; it is to be found everywhere, we have it before us in Berlin. Injustice manifests itself in the indiscipline of the capitalists and in wages which are both meagre and insecure; over the last five years misery has made a frightful impact on the artisans and workers—and it is these who are predominant in the Social Democratic movement—and continues to agitate deeply among them. This point of view must be kept firmly in mind; without it is impossible to evaluate Social Democracy correctly. We should not be impressed either with single examples of high wages or of wastefulness among workers; these examples are valid but they prove nothing and cannot change the general and permanent state of affairs. . . . The wages of our workers in some regions of our country are exceedingly small. . . . Another aspect of our current crises is, however, occupying a place almost more important for the workers than insufficient wages. In the last few years I have frequently had the opportunity to hear the complaints and cries of distress of workers, particularly of right-minded workers who are still attached to the Church, to the ethical foundations of our national life, to their country; and one thing became very clear to me and that is the complete insecurity of their existence. For four or five years thousands, sometimes tens of thousands of workers have been unemployed for months at a time. No-one comes so close to the misery of the people as we clergy; I assure you that we have found countless families in Berlin who, during the period of unemployment, had pawned everything, who possessed nothing except a table, a couple of chairs, and perhaps a bed of straw on which to lie down. . . . Such conditions have to be faced squarely, their origins must be discovered, and they must be remedied. They are caused by the present form of business life, by large industry in combination with free competition, by the alternation of boom and bust which occur at ever shorter intervals and which harm no-one more than the working class. . . . If such conditions were really unavoidable, if all the misery among the workers and artisans were inevitable then we could in fact give no other advice to those who suffer from them than passive resignation. But this is not the situation. On the contrary, for the most part it is human and visible sins and follies which produce and increase the difficulties at the roots of our social conditions. It is true that one ought to be tolerant of sins against society too, to work calmly and steadily toward eliminating abuses instead of immediately rebelling. But there is only one power that prevents us from grumbling while at the same time inspiring us to action: and that is religion. Unfortunately, this power has been broken among our people. For decades the learned and the ignorant, newspapers and books, lectures and assemblies have vied with each other to deprive people of the Bible and to cast the clergy and the church into contempt. We must not be surprised if people say: there is no hope, no salvation, no comfort for us there; you have taken heaven from us, now give us the earth! The atmosphere in which our workers live is not an ideal atmosphere; I do not think that I exaggerate if I say that the *Zeitgeist* is saturated with materialistic ideas. . . . Materialism makes people selfish and bad. The poor workers, the small artisans nowadays are well aware of this. They are abandoned and lost; they confront nothing but selfishness, therefore they also give up ethical ideas, they become bitter and they turn into enemies of present society. And often their poverty must be contrasted with a senseless luxury on the part of the propertied classes, excessive wealth which has not always been acquired entirely honestly or honourably. We in Berlin have witnessed the worship of the golden calf at its most extreme. . . . Is it surprising, then, that in the hearts of the poor and in the minds of thoughtful workers the idea should appear: is property which has been won dishonestly holy property? Property carries with it heavy duties, wealth carries with it heavy responsibilities. If property abandons the foundations on which it rests; if it ignores the commands of God and the obligation to love one's neighbour, then it is itself conjuring up the dangers of revolt. I think that our whole social edifice is based on the respect that the propertyless and uneducated feel toward the upper classes, and this presupposes above all that property honestly acquired shall be used nobly, charitably and kindly, not only for one's own pleasure and advantage but also for the good of one's fellow men, for curing the ills of others, and for generous participation in all the great occasions of community life. There are many rich persons among our people who have no idea at all of this conception of wealth, and it is their ignorance, lack of conscience, and refusal to do their duty that is above all responsible for the social question. . . .

What is needed is a great conversion, a thoroughgoing re-establishment of the Christian conception of the world, of a lively respect for the ethical and religious foundations of our people, if the damage that has already been done is to be repaired. Specifically the Christian spirit must once again inspire the whole nation and not just the so-called 'lower classes.' What is needed is a general renaissance. I am frank to say that the opinion that moral laws and articles of religious faith are meant only for the lower classes is an opinion which has neither any chance of success nor any claim to respect. Religious truth is for everyone, for the philosopher at his lectern as much as for the artisan in his workshop; moral laws are valid for all, as much for those who dispose of millions as for the very poorest. First of all our people must be made to understand that everyone must accept the principles to which the German people owes its history, the principles of a clear, strong, Christian conception of the world. . . .

Socialism, however, has a very serious side to it; it is a very understandable contrast against exaggerated individualism. The liberal economic system has proclaimed the unlimited freedom of the individual. . . . In this way the chasm appears which separates the upper ten thousand from the great mass of impoverished and decaying people. The bridge that crosses this chasm is already narrow and fragile. If things go on as they are then the chasm will become ever deeper and the possibility of rising out of poverty to prosperity ever smaller. But that is perhaps one of the most important motives in the

Social Democratic movement, that those without property confront a future on earth which is often completely hopeless.

In the light of this the social conception has something to be said for it. For socialism does not mean only the idea of converting all private property into state property, but it contains as well the demand that business life should be made over into something social and organic. And it is my conviction that we shall overcome the dangers of the socialist system only if we come to grips with its justifiable elements, that we can deal with the socialist fantasy of abolishing private property only if we take up very seriously two ideas of socialism. One: to cast economic life once more in an organic form, and two: to narrow the gap between rich and poor. . . .

Let us therefore do what we can to meet the great dangers that lie in the social movement. I think that we must see Social Democracy as something that has emerged from the far-reaching destruction of our material, ethical, and religious life; we must see it as the scourge that God uses to bring us out of this worthless materialistic conception of the world which menaces our highest values, our German fatherland, and our German future. . . .

It is no longer enough to give the propertyless classes alms out of pity. We must help them out of love and justice to obtain everything that they have a right to ask, and we must do this in the living spirit of Christianity and of patriotism. It is this goal that has been before me in founding the Christian Social Workers' Party. I turn now to sketching for you briefly what I understand by this term. I know no other that is so suitable to indicate and to solve all the problems of the social question as this one. 'Christian' means belief in the Trinity, in a providential world order, in peace, and in joy in the Holy Ghost. It includes all the virtues that the people need in economic life and all the duties that both employers and employees must perform. 'Social' means fraternal and communal. It directs us to the slogan: one for all, and all for one; to the inner spirit it adds the external form of economic life that must be present if business life is to prosper. Both words taken together provide the internal and external conditions of fruitful human activity. . . .

48. Bismarck in the *Reichstag*, April 2, 1881: from ROTHFELS, pp. 353–8. The bill under debate inaugurated the social insurance programme. Eugen Richter (1833–1906) was leader of the Progressive Party.

. . . The field of legislation that is inaugurated by this bill, and of which the previous speaker is quite right in saying that it has various possibilities which may cause even moderate Social Democrats to judge the government less harshly—this field of legislation concerns a problem that will probably be with us for some time to come. We have been talking about a social question for fifty years. Ever since the passage of the Socialist Law I have been repeatedly reminded, both by persons in high official positions and by common people, that a promise had been given at that time that something positive would also be done to remove the causes of socialism to the extent that they were justified. . . . . I do not believe that even our children and grandchildren will be able to dispose of the social question . . . entirely. In fact, no political problem ever comes to a complete mathematical conclusion which would enable the books to be balanced; they appear, last their time, and are then submerged by other problems of history; that is the way organic development works. I regard it as my function to take up these questions without partisan animosity and without agitation—I regret that party considerations have been brought into play—because I do not know who can take them up successfully if the federal government does not. . . .

Deputy Richter has called attention to the state's responsibility for what it does in the field which it is entering today. Well, gentlemen, I think that the state can also be held responsible for what it omits to do. I do not believe that a policy of *laissez faire, laisser aller* . . . can be applied to the state, particularly to a monarchical state which is ruled paternalistically. On the contrary, I think that those who repudiate the intervention of the state by this means, for the protection of the weaker, expose themselves for their part to the suspicion that they wish to exploit the resources of which they dispose, whether these be capitalistic or rhetorical or other, for the purpose of gaining a following, of oppressing others, of laying the foundations for a party domination, and that they become annoyed as soon as they are disturbed in this enterprise by any government action. . . .

Laws such as this one are not created on the basis of a theoretical dogmatism that broods over what kind of a law one ought to make now, but they have their origins and their prehistory out of which they arise. The reason why we are today presenting only an accident insurance bill is that it is this aspect of the welfare of the poor and the weak that has been particularly actively pursued at earlier periods when I was not concerned with these matters at all. . . .

In my opinion the principle of compulsory insurance entails the state taking over the insurance. . . . I would not undertake to impose compulsion without offering something for it in return. . . . If this is communism, as the previous speaker said, and not socialism, then that is a matter of indifference to me. I call it practical Christianity in legislative action—but if it is communism then communism has been practiced to a high degree and for a long time in the communities and by compulsion on the part of the state.

49. From the minutes of a meeting of members of the commissions established to investigate conditions in the coal mines of the administrative district of Düsseldorf (13 July, 1889): from ADELMANN, pp. 221–5.

... Several complements of mineworkers requested that miners other than those who had been invited should be heard, usually on the ground that those who had testified no longer enjoyed the confidence of the crew. The members of the investigating commissions do not regard it as feasible to undertake a subsequent hearing of delegates suggested in this way, since it would only increase the imbalance in favour of the views of the striking majority and suppress entirely the opinion of the orderly minority, which is in any case finding too little outlet. . . .

Many workers brought written answers with them to the hearings. On many occasions there were discussions among the witnesses and with others immediately before the hearing. By and large it seems that as a result of the influence of the leaders only the opinions of the extremists got into the record.

At the same time it was ascertained that the so-called delegates who testified, even though for the most part they were among the leaders and agitators in the strike, belonged in every case in the category of the more efficient miners. . . .

We were agreed that wages, length of shifts, and overtime should be regarded as the principal areas of complaint. . . . The majority inclined to the view that the question of wages was the most important and the cause of the strike. . . .

(1) *The question of wages.*

The members of the investigating commissions consider it desirable that statistics on wages should be published, in such a way that net earnings and deductions are apparent. . . .

We consider the miners to be the best-paid industrial workers in the area, except for technically skilled workers who are really specialists (joiners, locksmiths, etc.). As a consequence of the rise in mining wages other plants and particularly municipal institutions (gas and water works) have been forced to raise the wages of their workers. . . .

(2) *Length of shifts.*

On the whole the present length of shifts is regarded as satisfactory. . . .

(3) *Overtime.*

The excessive amount of overtime is the best-founded complaint. . . . The workers in principle reject overtime imposed by the mine management. The employers declare that they cannot entirely do without it. . . . . Not only the workers but the members of the investigating commissions desire an official ruling that no worker may be kept below the surface longer than a certain number of hours.

Many workers prefer a double shift to the prolongation of a single shift by one, two, or four hours. In the interests of the mines, too, the possibility of double shifts must be kept open, since it is economically the most convenient for the whole organization of mining operations. It seems desirable, therefore, to fix the maximum number of hours per day at sixteen and to rule at the same time that only one double shift per week may be worked without, and a second one with, the explicit permission of the regional official. . . .

50. From the annual report of the Chamber of Commerce of Essen for 1889: from ADELMANN, pp. 230–1.

. . . Many people who are close to conditions and think objectively have expressed the opinion that the strike would not have become a general one if those who were concerned with removal of the differences, in particular certain agencies of the government, had adopted a different procedure. On various occasions and from the very beginning of the movement, as has become undeniably clear, the mistaken procedure was adopted, in negotiations with striking miners or with their representatives, of leaving out of account the fact that they stood in a certain contractually defined working relationship with a particular employer; they ought therefore to have been told in the first place and exclusively to seek an agreement with their employer, that is to say the administration of the mining company in question. Instead of this, all the mine workers consisting of the complements of the various mines were treated as a single united party with which negotiations were repeatedly opened. This undermined the awareness that every worker must in the first place settle the conditions of his contract with his employer and brought about an artificial separation of the workers from their employers. This is a regrettable consequence, all the more so since in view of the effects of social legislation everything ought to have been avoided that was calculated to loosen the personal and individual relationship between worker and employer. Such a loosening is already taking place in consequence of that legislation. Until now help in sickness, old age, disability, or in case of accidents was something for which the worker had to thank his employer either entirely or in great part. The employer's contributions, even though in many cases regulated and fixed by statutory provisions, nevertheless by and large had a voluntary character. The social legislation, on the other hand, establishes a legal liability for large-scale enterprises which leaves entirely out of account the individual relationship between the particular worker and his employer and assures to the worker the benefits of the legislation without any regard to his relationship with his employer. This separation of worker from employer has evidently been increased by the direction which this strike movement has taken, and this circumstance constitutes a lasting injury which it will require a considerable time of very intensive work by the participating parties to remove in order to re-establish the former relationship. So far as is known here, in the case of strikes occurring in other industries no official interference which directly affects the relationship of workers and employers has taken place. Officials have confined themselves to maintaining law and order and have left the matter of reaching agreement on the conditions of contract exclusively to bargaining between workers and employers. . . .

51. Speeches by Freiherr von Stumm-Halberg to his employees (1889–95): from SCHRAEPLER, II, 99–104. Stumm, Carl Ferdinand, Freiherr von (1836–1901), industrialist.

. . . I believe that we shall all continue to demonstrate, as we have done in the past, that in the 'Stumm kingdom,' as our enemies sarcastically call our community, only one will prevails and that is the will of His Majesty the king of Prussia. . . . Wherever we look authority is maintained, in case of need by penalties imposed on those who do not submit to necessary authority. I do not propose here to speak of the army at all. It is frequently maintained that there is no analogy between industrial concerns and the army. I maintain the contrary. . . . In both cases, if they are to be successful, discipline is a quite indispensable prerequisite. . . . If an industrial enterprise is to flourish it must be organized in a military, not in a parliamentary fashion. . . . Just as the military profession includes all the members of an army from the field marshal down to the youngest recruit and all take the field against the enemy united when their king calls them, so do the members of the Neunkirch factory stand together as one man when it is a matter of combating our competitors as well as the dark forces of revolution. If we win it is to the benefit of all of us; if we are defeated we all suffer from it and you certainly far more than I. But in order to gain victory the strict maintenance of discipline is just as indispensable with us as it is in the army and is in both cases not merely compatible with loyal comradeship but is in fact its basis. . . .

Any cessation of the authority of employers . . . appears to me to be the more dangerous since in the long run it will not confine itself to those sections of the population which are under discussion here. Once the worker has overthrown the authority of the employer, if he no longer submits to it, if he simply ridicules him when he intends to punish him . . . then authority in other fields, in state and Church, will follow very soon. . . . But if this happens, if authority is destroyed all along the line in all branches of business, . . . then it will not be long before it is undermined even there where it is most necessary, in the army. . . .

So far as I personally am concerned I should not remain at your head one moment longer if I were to have to replace my personal relationship with each of you by negotiation with an organization of workers under outside leadership. . . . Such a relationship with, as it were, a foreign power would violate my moral sense of duty and my Christian conviction. . . . If this should ever change and if I should in fact be prevented from supervising and correcting the worker in his behaviour even outside the factory then I should not remain at the head of this business for one day longer since then I should no longer be in a position to carry out those moral duties which are prescribed for me by my conscience before God and my fellow-men. An employer who is indifferent to how his workers behave outside his factory, in my opinion, is not living up to his most important duties. . . . I could name . . . a whole series of actions by workers outside the factory which I regard as the absolute duty of an employer fully conscious of his moral task to prevent, instead of retreating to the comfortable position of saying: I do not care what the worker does outside the factory, I am interested only in his productivity within the business. . . . I mention all this not in order to claim credit for it, for in doing so I do no more than my duty as a man, as a Christian, and as head of the great Neunkirch workers' family. . . . I think I can say with a good conscience that I am second to none of my fellow-employers in the matter of welfare provisions, certainly not in the effort to look after your material and spiritual welfare to the best of my knowledge and conscience and to apply that practical Christianity for which I feel myself to be responsible before God. In this way I hope to make sure far beyond my own lifetime that you will remain unreceptive to the lures of the Social Democrats and other false prophets, that is the best welfare provision that I can give and leave you. Always remain firm in your old unshakable loyalty to our noble monarch, remain firm in your Christian love of your neighbours and your fear of God whatever denomination you belong to, and then you will continue to flourish as much as it is given to men to do. . . .

Every master and worker must behave even outside his work in such a manner as to bring honour to the firm of the brothers Stumm;

they should be aware that their private life is constantly supervised by their superiors. . . .

So far as the prohibition of marriage is concerned, I have stated before . . . that in my rules of work there is as little mention of a prohibition of marriages as of a prohibition on lawsuits and complaints. What is prescribed is merely the following: the worker must give me prior notice of his intention so that I shall be in a position, if I see fit, to prevent unnecessary complaints, in other words, foolish marriages. If in some cases I go so far as to say: . . . I regard this marriage as very rash, for example, if a man of eighteen or nineteen who is sickly and not even fully grown, who is earning low wages and has saved nothing, wishes to marry a girl who has also saved nothing, in a case, in other words, where it is to be expected with certainty that it will be an unhappy marriage in which the people will not even be able to feed their children, if in such cases I say: If you do not follow my advice then I terminate the working relationship, with notice of course, —that requires no further explanation. . . .

It is of course a necessary corollary of such regulations that I, for my part, feel myself duty-bound, if people have married and through no fault of their own are not in a position to feed their children, to come to their aid, in other words to take the consequences of my own system and to say: if you follow my instructions and my advice then I will in turn also come to your aid. The one is connected with the other. But if I were in fact to permit my workers to enter upon such rash marriages that they ruined themselves then none would be able to ask of me that I should come to their aid; otherwise I should be placing a premium on frivolity, and this I am not prepared to do and I should not believe myself to be fulfilling a moral duty if I were to do so. . . .

An important means by which academic and pseudo-Christian socialism supports Social Democracy is the legend of the existence of a Fourth Estate which must protect itself in general against 'capital.' No one recognizes more clearly than I do that the wage-earner must be protected by government measures against possible exploitation. . . . This tendency to degrade you to a fourth estate is nothing less than an insult to the whole working class. The working population nowadays is fully equal to all other categories of citizens before the law, and I shall never concede that the worker is made of different material or has less value than a commercial counsellor or a minister. But that there is a great deal of want and misery among workers is something that no one will deny less than I do who am concerned daily to reduce it when it occurs among you. This, however, is not a characteristic of the so-called fourth estate; for many peasants and craftsmen, even many members of the so-called cultured classes, are far worse off than most factory workers just because capital, by reason of its increase in

Germany in the last decades, is in a position to care better for the factory worker than was the case in earlier years. . . . I cannot see at all how these learned gentlemen conceive of the fourth estate. There are a large number of intermediate steps between myself and the lowest wage earner: the director, the factory manager, the factory engineer, the master, the foreman—and I should like to know where the third estate ends and the fourth begins! No, my friends, we all belong to one estate and that is the old honourable estate of blacksmiths, and I have everywhere and always proudly regarded myself as a member of this estate. . . .

This fiction of the existence of a fourth estate in contrast to property is also the basis of the ominous attempt to organize the workers against their employers and to place them under the leadership of people who lack any knowledge of their conditions, such as wages, hours etc. It is one of the most difficult tasks of my profession to determine precisely whether one person's wages are in a correct relationship with another's, and none of you and no committee of workers either, which otherwise I am very pleased to consult, is in a position to relieve me of this task. . . . Theory, however, says: the single worker by himself can achieve nothing, he must join with his comrades if he is to fight. But this theory entirely overlooks the fact that in maintaining this it is in contradiction with another of its main theses, according to which the employer is always economically the stronger. If, therefore, the workers organize against the employers then the latter will perforce also have to organize themselves against the workers and then, to be sure, they will be in a position to do great damage to the working class. A worker worth his salt must stand on his own feet, and this is also the way in which he will get farthest with his employer, whereas by joining militant organizations, which sooner or later always fall into the hands of foreign agitators, he destroys his own independence and is put in conflict with his employer, which must destroy that personal relationship that is the best guarantee for the worker's welfare. . . .

52. A memoir on life in the artisan class about 1880: from the memoirs of Karl Scheffler, *Der junge Tobias* (Leipzig, 1927), in Fischer, ed., *Quellen zur Geschichte des deutschen Handwerks,* pp. 151–64.

Among artisans and small traders, too, the old security of life was shattered. The masters no longer attached any value to taking on their sons as apprentices because their own life had become uncertain, because it no longer paid to keep the business in the family. Competition became acute. Where formerly two or three master craftsmen had been able to make a comfortable living, now there appeared three or four new competitors who were attracted by the increase in building activity. They undercut each other and introduced business practices which had been unknown to craftsmen in the village before. The new tempo of business was too quick for the old master craftsmen and shop owners, and the means that were sought and used to create new business were too dubious for them. They fell behind in relation to the entrepreneur. The time came when simple shop windows no longer sufficed, when large-scale displays with handsome plate-glass windows were put on, and when beside the articles of everyday consumption foreign luxury articles appeared which were calculated more to stimulate than to satisfy demand. The shop was gradually converted into a bazaar, into a department store. Added to this were the temptations introduced by the rapid rise in the value of land. Almost every craftsman or businessman owned a small mortgage-free piece of land with a house on it, and now it turned out that this property was sufficient to live on. The owner had merely to decide to sell his house and his shop and to put the resulting capital with its interest into an apartment, or else he could pull down his old house himself and build a block of flats with the aid of bank loans and then use the rents to pay off the mortgage as well as to keep himself and his family. In this case he would retain his business but it would no longer be the same; he was more a landlord by profession than a master craftsman. In any event the business no longer had anything to it that would lead his sons to want to carry it on one day, the less so since so many more opportunities were available in the village and even more in the town. At the same time as the word peasant became a word of abuse the opinion gained currency that the working clothes of a craftsman had something inferior about them and that only an occupation for which one wore cuffs and a white collar were respectable. . . . This strange view was spread to no small extent by the principle of general and equal education which was in full swing at that time. Artisans and businessmen began to send their sons to school in the town. . . . When they left school . . . they had acquired enough modern education to look down upon the honourable ignorance of their parents. The boys went . . . either into a merchant's office in the town as apprentices or they entered service as scribes with a lawyer. . . . The foundations were laid for an ambitious but yet insecure petty bourgeoisie which was stuffed with semi-education and derived its knowledge from the daily papers. They all wanted to appear to be more than they were, they were all more or less victims of a vague ambition and striving for the top. The daughters of artisans no longer wanted to enter service. Formerly it had been the custom that these daughters served for a few years in an upper-class town house or in the country houses of city merchants in the village. There they were well kept, had to dress neatly, and learnt to understand the nature of a rich and secure household. When they returned from these positions to their parents in order to marry an artisan or tradesman there was something secure, solid, even refined in their demeanour. Often a good relationship to their former employers remained as well; the young housewife paid an annual visit, presented her children, and her husband received commissions and orders. All this was now given up as undignified. The daughters who could not idly sit around the house sought positions as saleswomen in the town shops or they became seamstresses, tailors, or teachers. The daughters of former farm workers went to work in factories. They all wanted to earn as much cash as possible and be free in the evenings. . . .

But there was also a genuine force, a living talent, that was pushing its way up in this way in a whole class of the population. The cases were not rare in which the sons of small artisans or simple workers attained important successes and positions in the course of a few decades. Even though in many respects disruptive forces were dominant, nevertheless it was also unprecedently an era of self-help. The name of many a man was known in the village who came from restricted family circumstances and who played a role in the business life of the town, who had expanded an artisan's trade into something resembling big business. . . .

John's family was a faithful illustration of this general restlessness. . . . His father had lost his parents and hardly every spoke about them. A maternal grandmother was still living; but John could never find out anything specific about her family, her husband, or her own parents. As with all simple people, John's family were reluctant to speak of their own ancestry. . . . It is as though people were silently ashamed to speak of their ancestors if they could not be proud of them. If in this class the living outgrew their parents and ancestors socially, or even if they only thought they had risen above them, then it was as though the family only began with them. There was no reason in John's family to be ashamed of their ancestors, they had all been industrious men and highly honourable women . . . ; but if the boy asked about them he was told to mind his own business. So it came about that he could see back as far as his grandparents but no farther. His grandmother was already an old woman when John came to consciousness. She lived in a small house near the church in the last of a long string of terrace houses with a footpath in front and a garden behind. There she carried on a modest trade in tobacco and cigars. She had five daughters and two sons.

She was mainly supported by her eldest son. He was the family's pride and joy, he had got farther than any of the rest and passed for a rich man. As a boy, after he had left elementary school, he had become

N

an apprentice to a master painter. From his early days he had been an industrious and conscientious man who had early felt the duty of caring for his widowed mother and as far as possible to replace his dead father, but beyond this he was moved by a strong drive for success, by the ambition to acquire middle-class status. Favoured by the conditions of the times and using them cleverly he had gradually approached his goal. Being undemanding himself he had been able to save. Then, still at a young age, he had married a girl who had served as a housekeeper in one of the houses in the village belonging to an aristocratic town family and in this position had also been able to save. . . . Such a couple could not fail at that time if they were industrious and shrewd. When this uncle Joachim, the young John's godfather, established a household of his own he founded a small painter's business. For this he cleverly chose a place on the main road between the village and the town but closer to the town, amongst the houses of wealthy merchants outside the city walls which were at that time rapidly being built. His was the first business to be set in among an upper-class wealthy clientele, in the middle of a district, moreover, where there was a lot of building activity. The results were not long in coming. He had begun with two helpers and had worked hard himself, but soon the number of employees rose. After a few years there were twenty and thirty, and the young master had to give up working himself as a painter in his shop, on new buildings, and in private houses. Now he began to dress like a gentleman, he visited his customers, kept the books, distributed the work among his employees in the morning in his shop and spent his day inspecting the places where they worked. After a few years of rapidly rising prosperity he was able to buy the piece of land on which he lived as a tenant and to build a big new house. The number of his employees kept increasing, and the business grew so much that in the period in which painters get most of their work, in the months between Easter and mid-summer, he had one hundred and fifty or more men working for him. At that time that was an unprecedented success, and there was a lot of talk in the village and in the town, above all among the other master painters, about uncle Joachim's good luck. The latter, however, was annoyed whenever he heard such talk; he considered that he owed nothing to good luck but everything to his own industry. He said that he had not, like his envious colleagues, sat about in bars and idly waited for success. With justice but also with some self-righteousness he pointed to the fact that work was his only passion, in fact he was scarcely interested in anything else. . . . He had that passion for work which made its appearance at that time and which made something moral, almost something religious, out of hard work. 'I need no church, business is my church,' said uncle Joachim. His activity . . . acquired the features of big business and had to be conducted accordingly, and the master knew how to do this very well although he did the paper work without much help and on the basis of his modest elementary knowledge. He showed much tact in his unusual situation and found the right way to speak both to his upper-class customers and to his employees, which was not easy. His customers were mostly rich merchants who felt themselves to be patricians and wished to have the distance between themselves and the artisan observed. In his ambition to be genteel himself uncle Joachim never forgot this distance. In this he was aided by a natural respect for authority and by a willing subordination toward power and property. There were no rebellious thoughts in his heart. Intercourse with his employees was more difficult. With the oldest among them the master had worked together; a sort of intimacy bound him to those who had first entered his service. Later it became a matter of breaking away from them and to emphasise that he was the boss without wounding the suspicious sensibilities of his employees. For many years he succeeded in this, but then slowly socialism appeared, made its way into the workshops and caused disputes between masters and employees. Formerly questions of pay had been liberally handled but now there were wage demands, organisation, and threats of strikes. The master, who saw his relationship with his employees in an entirely paternalistic light, regarded it as a personal insult, as a betrayal on the part of his old employees. . . . He had been brought up at a time when authority was unchallenged and was apparently unchallengeable; he had become prosperous and happy while the German empire became united and powerful. Uncle Joachim was firmly convinced that his success was nothing but the just reward for industry and efficiency, and that the general economic prosperity of the times was also nothing but the fruit of the general industry of enterprising and socially reliable people. He was an unconditional admirer of Bismarck and saw in this statesman's successes a version, magnified into genius and greatness, of his own business successes. Therefore any socialism and any revolutionary movement seemed to him to be a crime. A Social Democrat meant for him a man with no respect for the law, and he equated him without hesitation with those assassins who had shot at the old emperor. Since workers, however, increasingly became Social Democrats and since the consequences of this were apparent in general disputes about wages, even though uncle Joachim's workshop remained for a long time free of strikes because he paid the wages demanded anyway the good old relationships between master and employees gave way to a certain tension and irritation.

But this is the way it was only in later years. In John's youth conditions in the workshop were still good. The master was respected by his employees and accommodated himself to his customers, and his successes grew greater from year to year. He was visibly the model of a self-made man and with his family maintained a high standard of living. In his house a different atmosphere prevailed from that in the houses of his petty bourgeois relations. He was the owner of a spacious house, his apartment was furnished comfortably at some expense, his workshops and sheds occupied considerable space, and the household consisted of a lot of people. . . . With an air of importance his relatives mentioned the money that it took to run the household every month, and his annual income was discussed as though the family had some share in the honour. Everyone regarded uncle Joachim as an authority. He was cited to the children as an example of how far one could get with bourgeois virtues. For his mother this eldest son was an object of pride; his reputation reflected back on her. To be sure, his old mother was always slightly embarrassed with this son; she found his presence slightly oppressive and in her heart of hearts she probably did not love him so much as her youngest son who was exactly the opposite.

The children also were not able to establish a happy human relationship with this uncle. They stared at him shyly but could talk to him as little as he could talk to them. He was always too busy with himself, too preoccupied with his work, too much of a strict representative of bourgeois virtue for the children to confide in him. . . .

Their relationship with the grandmother's youngest son was quite different. He was in all respects different from his brother; and for this reason the brothers were strangers to each other too. In latter years they never exchanged more than a brief greeting or a few words. One of them was ashamed of his happy uselessness and the other unconsciously of his excellence, although he adopted the attitude of a sentencing judge toward the younger one and did no more than tolerate him. . . . Certainly the elder brother never forgot to do what he regarded as his duty, he supported the younger one to the end of his life. . . .

This uncle Haye lived with his mother in her little house and quietly went about making cigarettes for sale in the little shop and smoked quite a lot of them himself. He had been a little good-for-nothing even as a boy. . . . He had no business ambition and had no use for any purposeful enterprise. . . . He was nothing and signified nothing; and yet in the whole large family he was the only man who in his innocence had achieved a certain pure inner harmony. . . .

The most unusual person in the family was John's father. He had come into the town and into the village from far away and remained a stranger in the district all his life. But he would have been a stranger anywhere, for he was a stranger to life itself.

He came to the town as a young painter's employee; disregarding his family he had made his way alone in the world and had wandered to and fro across Germany as a journeyman before he came to uncle Joachim, who had just founded his business, to ask for work. Soon the family of the young master were talking with astonishment about the new employee. They had never seen anyone like this. Just as he did everything that he embarked on with passion and with a certain lack of moderation, so he set about his work like a madman. He appeared first and left last at the workshop, he did everything in a great hurry and with an enormous expenditure of energy, but he worked well, thoroughly, and thoughtfully.... He was a rare find for a master who was just beginning but he was also uncomfortable, he was obstinate and sensitive and got on the nerves of the master and of his young wife. They tried to draw him into the family, but he read to them with pathetic enthusiasm all evening from *Hamlet* or the poems of Schiller and spoke so masterfully about his ideas that they timidly withdrew. This young man was profoundly restless. He was scarcely fatigued by many hours of hard work. In the evenings he would sit up until late at night with good books nourishing his restless idealism. He was either exalted or broodingly and melancholically introverted. At the same time he imposed on himself an iron discipline of work, he never mixed up the hobbies of his free time with his work. He had a high opinion of duty. It was as though he countered the dangers which might have resulted from his intellectual requirements on purpose by hard bodily effort and by a relentless self-discipline.... Whereas uncle Joachim was entirely preoccupied with his painter's business and therefore achieved great economic success, John's father was enthusiastic about the idea of work as a moral demand and for this reason never had any worldly success. He rented a house in the village near the church, built a workshed in the garden, married, and soon found work in the houses of the wealthy people from the town. When he was given a job he finished it with devotion, he was at work at sunrise and stayed until it was dark.... Almost always he worked without helpers. He worked as much as two or three ordinary men. In the few operations for which he unavoidably needed help his children had to help him if no-one else was there.... These were uncomfortable occasions. The father was impatient and flew into a violent rage at anyone who was clumsy or was not making enough effort, adding moral reflections and general home truths. The children were always happy when they could go away again and usually did so shamefacedly. The customers were satisfied with the father's work but they were not entirely happy since he was such a strange craftsman. He was too eager, too passionate about his work, and they did not know what to make of his tone of voice. He was always extremely polite to his customers but unconsciously treated them as equals; he talked freely and even inadvertently gave an impression of superiority. Often there was something about his views which unintentionally but none the less clearly corrected the views of his customers. For this reason the customers held back a little and he found it difficult to get new ones, the more so since soon competitors appeared who knew better how to make use of the conditions. When he had finished a job not infrequently there was a pause before he got a new one. With all his eagerness, with all his devotion to duty, he entirely lacked any business sense. He was too proud to go out to look for jobs, he was in no way a businessman. If he had been he would easily have been able to enlarge the business, to put his savings into land and so achieve a modest but secure standard of living. But his character was not that of a master craftsman who wants to achieve success. He moved on a higher plane, craftsmanship seemed to be something that this restless man had taken on only temporarily. He was working below his station. It was for this reason that the people among whom he moved looked at him in amazement and it was this that got in his way as a master craftsman.

In the first years of his marriage he used for cultural purposes the intervals of unemployment which, particularly in autumn and winter, were frequently long. . . . He wanted to participate in community life and had rather ambitious plans. He thought about a cultural club and theatrical performances and felt qualified to compose a prologue or a poem for such festivities himself, in which he was right. But people also went in some fear of him as a speaker. In the Masonic lodge of which he was a member he not infrequently put people off by speaking his mind and in general had an almost pathological need to tell other people home truths. He did not, however, offer his criticism either contemptuously or coldly but always enveloped in pathos, he always spoke as an advocate of idealism. . . .

He had no luck in his attempt to introduce culture into the village community. The lectures had to be stopped soon and other plans were not realised. The master craftsmen of the village lived in another world, nothing was more unpleasant for them than exaltation. John's father tried all his life to get onto a wavelength with these petty bourgeois, he played cards with them and sometimes spent the evening sitting with them at the inn and taking an interest in their activities, but he remained a stranger to them. . . .

As a matter of fact all three of them were not craftsmen, not John's father, not his uncle Joachim, and not uncle Haye either. Each one of them had left the world of craftsmanship in his own way. Uncle Joachim was not quite a craftsman any more because his business had grown too large, because he did not work with his hands any longer himself, because he ran his business like a merchant and approached the world of big business; together with a whole stratum of society he was aiming to join the bourgeoisie. Uncle Haye worked only incidentally, without real purpose and without results; his work was not much more than a way to pass the time for an idle person. He was not a craftsman and not even a real worker; socially he was lower than the bourgeoisie since he was poor and lived from his brother's generosity. John's father, finally, was striving inwardly beyond the world of craftsmanship, for him it was, as it were, only a transitional stage which, however, he never left behind; he longed to join the intellectual upper crust of society but without daring to risk the attempt to get into it for himself and his sons. None of these three men belonged to the middle class as genuine craftsmen do, they all stood at various points on the periphery. Uncle Joachim became a businessman who wanted to stand above the world of the craftsman; uncle Haye became a proletarian, he stood lower than the craftsman; John's father gave the appearance of a stranger, he stood to one side of the craftsman. Uncle Joachim embodied success and worry about it dried him up; uncle Haye embodied failure but also in addition what might be called the poetry of unsuccessful attempts; John's father embodied the conflict of idea and reality and this constant struggle devoured him. All three of them had been thrown off course; none of them lived quietly and straightforwardly. Uncle Joachim lived in the idea of the big city, uncle Haye languished in the village, and John's father was inwardly homeless and looked out into the infinite world of humanity. All of them reflected the driving, dissolving, and insecure aspects of the time.

G. Bismarck and
the liberals after 1871

53. From a speech of Bismarck in the *Reichstag*, 9 July, 1879:
from ROTHFELS, pp. 273–7.

If there were a party among us that had a natural majority and that
did not ask of me that the drop of democratic oil which, according
to a well-known phrase, is required for the anointing of the German
Emperor, should become a bucket, then I should accord to such a
party quite different rights, so far as influencing the government is
concerned, than I am prepared to accord at the moment to a party
which at its maximum and when it is united, which rarely occurs, still
constitutes barely a quarter of the whole assembly. If these gentlemen
place any value on my judgement as an expert—and I have played a
lot of politics in my time—then I can only advise them to be more
modest in the future. . . .

Since I have been a Minister I have never belonged to any party
and have not been able to belong to any party, I have been successively
hated by them all and loved by a few. . . . I have never allowed myself
to be influenced by this and have never tried to take revenge; from the
beginning of my career I have had only one guiding star: that is, by
what means and in what direction I could bring about German unity
and, in so far as it has been attained, how I can consolidate this unity,
how I can promote it and to shape it in such a manner that it will be
maintained permanently by the free will of all participants. Among
these participants I include the governments and I regard it as an
extraordinarily great advantage for Germany in comparison with other
countries that have a unitary constitution that the dynastic element
is a force outside Prussia as well. I do not require the same conviction
of everyone else, in fact, I am not seeking to persuade anyone, I am
only trying to explain how I have arrived at my present position *vis-
à-vis* the parties. When we returned from the war of 1866 it would
have been easy for me to say: now Prussia has become larger the
constitution is no longer suitable, we have to create a new one, in
other words I could have conducted a radically reactionary policy and
I could have done it successfully with the momentum of the success of
Königgrätz. As you know I did the opposite, as a result of which many
of my former political friends became alienated from me, and it was
a difficult struggle to carry out the opposite policy, namely the
indemnity and a continuation of the constitutional system. Did I do

this out of love for the constitutional system? Gentlemen, I do not wish to depict myself as better than I am; this I must categorically deny. I am not an enemy of the constitutional system, on the contrary I regard it as the only possible form of government, but if I had believed that a dictatorship in Prussia or absolutism in Prussia would have been more useful for promoting German unity then I should have unconditionally and without scruple advised the adoption of absolutism. But after much thought—in the course of which I had to combat influences that were important and that were dear and close to me—I decided that on the contrary we must continue on the constitutional road, which in any case corresponds to my own sentiments and to my convictions as to the general scope of our policy. My willingness to compromise at that time with my opponents who had once more become reconciled to me, this willingness to compromise which, perhaps owing to defects in my character, I took too far, had as its first consequence that it laid the foundations for my later break with the Conservative Party. Then, actually as a result of the connection of the ecclesiastical question with the Polish question, I was faced with the conflict on ecclesiastical matters. This conflict deprived me of the natural support of the Conservative Party on which I would have been able to count, and the direction which I had to take in order to develop and to activate the constitution of the German Empire would probably have been different if the Conservative Party had not at that time abandoned me. Added to this there was the bitter struggle occasioned by the flaring up of the thousand-year-old dispute between Church and state, between emperor and pope.... I fought this struggle with the vigour which I hope will always be characteristic of me in all matters where I am conscious that the welfare of my country and the rights of my king are at stake. But even here I must say that I may in some circumstances regard it as necessary to fight conflicts to the bitter end, though I do not regard conflicts as ever an institution to be desired in the long run, and when ways and means offer themselves to mitigate the acuteness of the divisions without affecting the principles of the dispute itself, if the parties get to know each other and get to respect each other by working in common for a common and noble purpose, in that case I have surely no right as a Minister to close or ignore these avenues.

If after 1871 I was forced into closer dependence on the Liberal Party by these events and struggles that did not originate with me than is perhaps in the long run desirable for a minister and federal chancellor, nevertheless I could not for that reason give up forever all relations with other groups in the Empire and of the population. I thought, as I said in the debate on the Socialist Law, that on the right wing we might be drawn up in three battalions which could march separately and fight together. This calculation of mine unfortunately has not been realised, and it is circumstances and not my will that have produced the situation where those gentlemen who used frequently to support me in a manner which did not exclude differences have now adopted in their press, in the most respected and acredited organs of their press, an attitude and a form of language toward me that was bound to disgust and to alienate me completely. Similar occurrences have also taken place before the assembled *Reichstag* in which particular eminent members have taken the federal chancellor to task publicly in a way which would not have been countenanced by his party in a member of a friendly party. . . .

I cannot, and the government cannot, be at the beck and call of particular parties. It must go its own way that it regards as correct; these courses are subject to the resolutions of the *Reichstag,* the government will require the support of the parties but it can never submit itself to the domination of any single party! . . .

I should like in this connection to address another warning to these gentlemen not to display the old tribal hatred in the discussion of questions that are so simple and that require such cool deliberation as customs, economic matters, and financial and budgetary affairs; tribal hatred is not relevant here, but we run the risk, in view of the sharp division among the parties, that we may substitute parties for tribes. I hope that things will never get to the point where later all connections, even family connections, between the various parties disappear and where each party develops as a separate tribe. But I would like to ask these gentlemen not to introduce into the consideration of these matters high-level politics and the fear that some political *arrière pensée* lies behind the simplest measures, and not to carry the angry party struggle so far that the interests of the Reich suffer and that if the governments were to allow themselves to be intimidated by it the first step to a financial improvement in our situation would not come about in this year either. So far as the governments are concerned I can give every assurance that they will not allow themselves to be diverted from the course on which they have embarked by these attacks which, in my opinion, are unjustified, and I for my part will continue to follow to the very end the path which I recognise as the right one in the interests of my country regardless of whether that earns me love or hatred—this is a matter of indifference to me!

54. From the diary of Ludwig Bamberger: from *Bismarcks grosses Spiel: geheime Tagebücher,* pp. 302–3, 307–8, 310–11, 322, 325. (See also Doc. 15.)

Simson, Eduard (1810–99), jurist and liberal politician, from 1869 to 1879 president of the Court of Appeal in Frankfurt on the Oder.

(*8 May, 1873.*) Yesterday I dined with Bismarck again. . . . Lately he has been repeating himself over and over again. . . . He listens only to himself, and if once in a while he hears someone else it is only something that suits his purpose; then he picks up a phrase and drops everything else. This can all be attributed to the fundamental trait of his character: concentrated energy—but this is leading to a dangerous isolation and hardening of the mental arteries. I am afraid he is losing his elasticity.

His constant theme is the power-mania of the king or rather of the Prussian monarchs who will tolerate no real prime minister (who would construct his own Cabinet), and the internecine warfare among the ministries. He talks of this incessantly. The king, he says, will give up nothing of his prerogative, he wants to have the last word about everything. There is no solution at all to differences of opinion between two ministers. 'Nobody has ever been convinced by arguments,' . . . he has said repeatedly.

The result is endless writing back and forth, finally a meeting of the Ministry where still no solution is found, and as a last resort a formal meeting of the Council of Ministers to which the ministers wear uniform. When everyone has long-windedly had his say it is up to the king alone to decide, which means that he takes aside the minister in whom he personally has the most confidence and allows himself to be influenced by him. . . .

(*19 July, 1873.*) . . . It is possible that Bismarck from the beginning in all good faith arranged things in his mind to suit his convenience, but equally possible that he arranged them afterwards. It would be consistent with his character to work himself up into a rage against someone when he is angry and needs a scapegoat, and then in his fantastical way he fashions a spectre of dark hostility or malevolence that could be personified by anybody. It is a sort of self-deception and need to react against an unpleasant impression as well as to satisfy a craving for fantastication. . . .

(*19 June, 1875.*) When on April 10 I arrived in Berlin from Paris, suddenly a rumour of war had broken out. Two semi-official articles in the 'Post' and in the 'Kölnische Zeitung' had launched it, particularly the one in the 'Post' under the headline: 'Is war in sight?' . . . What was Bismarck's purpose in this? Even today, when everything has been denied and soothed away, nobody knows. All that people seem to agree on is that Bismarck wanted the rumour and undoubtedly instigated it. . . .

(6–9 April, 1877.) It was all humbug! Sheer play-acting. This time he fooled everybody. They took it seriously even at court. The emperor left his request to resign unanswered for three days. Then he became extremely excited for fear that he might be taken at his word. When in the end it came back with the marginal comment 'No, never! ! ! !' he heaved a sigh of relief. . . .

(6 May, 1877.) . . . According to Bismarck himself, one day he was going for a walk through some empty buildings and had come to the place where the commission on justice was holding its hearings in the chancellery. Involuntarily he had heard what they were discussing there, had stayed there and listened for a while. He had heard the most extraordinary things in the world, and it was quite inconceivable to him that serious men could debate questions like this. It could make no difference at all how such things were decided. He absolutely refused to consider Simson's objection that to professionals it was not all one. . . .

55. From letters of Gustav Freytag on Bismarck: from *Gustav Freytags Briefe an Albrecht von Stosch*, pp. 93, 124–5, 137. Freytag, Gustav (1816–95), famous novelist and writer.

Stosch, Albrecht von (1818–96), commander-in-chief of the German Navy and Prussian minister, an intimate of the crown prince and of Franz von Roggenbach.

(24/25 February, 1873.) . . . It is quite in order for you to view with misgivings the great despot's tyranny and his devious ways; but I am disturbed for your sake that your relations with him are not good. . . . However much the power of the Crown may have been increased, in the long run the emperor will keep nobody that Bismarck seriously wants to get rid of. For this reason the essential question is: are you convinced that you can do more good in your ministry than anyone else, and does your activity give you the satisfaction that any self-respecting worker needs? If so, then in your place I should try to maintain my position by making peace with Bismarck. Of course I do not know whether this is possible. . . .

(10 January, 1878) . . . You are right, nothing has gone right for him for years because he has alienated all good collaborators and because in his isolation he is liable to sudden impulses; but since he has turned out this way he can be brought down only by himself and by nobody else.

Therefore, as your friend, I sincerely regret that you are in a mood to provoke a conflict with him. Dear friend, you must outlast him! . . . If the conflict comes into the open again, *which it need not do,* then the whole responsibility for it must be seen to be his. . . .

(6 November, 1881.) . . . The election results have had the expected

consequences. First of all the chancellor accused his press of being clumsy, then he invited a Jew to dinner and declared himself in public to be against the anti-Semites. But these tricks have lost much of their effectiveness; just about everyone now knows about the mixture of lion, wolf, and fox that all play a part in the soul of this dramatic character. The best outcome of the elections is the partial emancipation of people's minds from the chancellor's overwhelming influence that they indicate. Late and slowly the Germans are learning that the man to whom, after the German fashion, they have attributed everything great and good, does not possess all the qualities of a gentleman.... The life and soul of a nation should not depend for long on the mood and conscience of a single man and be led in all essentials by his autocratic domination. The people pay too high a price for such rule, however great the progress that this one man may have brought about....

56. From a letter and speech by Rudolf Haym: from ROSENBERG, pp. 303, 323–4. (See Doc. 6.)

(*To Wilhelm Schrader, 22 March, 1877.*) ... Would to God that after all this high-level politics we could get back to a little philosophy, ethics, and poetry. Elections and the Diet and the *Reichstag* do not give one much pleasure; ... I am inclined to think that we Germans are still pretty simple-minded in politics....

(*Notes for a political speech of ca. February 1881.*) ... I take as my point of departure the conviction that the policy of Prince Bismarck continues to centre on the national idea, and that anyone who is as imbued with this idea as he is can gain an influence on this policy. I am convinced that the national idea cannot and may not be separated from justified liberal demands. I am convinced that even Prince Bismarck's vigilant foreign policy is rendered more difficult if domestically he finds only enemies or only majorities casually patched together from varying elements. I am convinced that those aspects of his policy that I myself regard as errors have been only stratagems which he was forced to employ by the confusion among the parties. Some [parties] were more conservative than national, others not national at all but only clerical, yet others more liberal than national.

It is otherwise with us [National Liberals]. As the name of our party deliberately indicates, we are prompted by the idea that national and liberal interests affect each other reciprocally. For my part I have no hesitation in saying that if on any specific issues the liberal and the national interest should come into conflict I should give the latter priority before the former. Liberal institutions, in my view, are merely means to the end of attaining power for the state and the best possible

well-being for the individual. . . . We must strive for as much freedom as the national state can tolerate; we must impose on our striving
for progress whatever limits the maintenance and consolidation of
this national state demand. By and large, Prince Bismarck represents
for me the incarnation of the national state. I do not always like his
methods. Sometimes—I have in mind particularly universal and equal
suffrage—he has gone too far in the direction of liberalism for my
taste, at other times he has regrettable tendencies and sympathies towards conservatism, at yet other times he encourages interest-group
politics which appeals to egoism and therefore slights the nobler
motives in political life and must have a confusing and even corrupting
effect. But in the face of all this I remind myself that nobody else
has such a lively regard for the idea of making the young empire vital,
permanent, and resilient, and that he is untiringly and successfully at
work to realize this idea with sensible realism according to circumstances. All his twists and turns and inconsistencies can by explained
by the power of this idea. Seen in this light, all the tortuous and often
contradictory methods that he employs *vis-à-vis* the domestic factions,
even his reckless experiments, become intelligible. . . .

57. From a letter of Franz v. Roggenbach to the Empress Augusta,
10 February, 1879: from ROGGENBACH, pp. 139–40. (See
Doc. 17.)

. . . In the midst of the almost irremediable chaos into which the
internal affairs of the empire have unfortunately been plunged, we
expect . . . of the emperor that he will put a stop to this dissolution
and restore order in the empire and in its government. But I do not
call it order if the prince [Bismarck], without as prime minister having
laid his opinions before the ministry, and without as chancellor having
so much as informed His Majesty the emperor, begins purely as a
private individual to correspond with the Federal Council and to
dissolve all of Germany into hostile atoms of economic rivalry with
his senseless and reckless projects, thereby aggravating to the utmost
extreme the revolutionary disintegration of our lives. I do not call it
order if the steady influence of the regular . . . offices of state is reduced
to a nullity and if instead . . . arbitrarily composed commissions whose
views have previously been examined prepare vital decisions in order
to provide sophistical justification for the whims of an omnipotent
ruler. . . . The German people wishes to be ruled by its emperor and
his conscientious advisers.—A spectacle like that of the other day, when
the minister who is called minister of commerce but is in fact only
minister of railways is asked about the question of railway tariffs
which the chancellor has personally raised, and is obliged to reply that

he knows nothing about it, constitutes an utterly damaging confirmation of the dangerous chaos prevailing in the highest government circles. It is only too true that because of the silly whims of one man a large part of the moral esteem that Germany has won among educated world opinion has already been lost, and there is no knowing into what abyss of internal insecurity, moral depravity, and economic misery we shall sink if an end is not put quickly to this constant undermining of all existing relationships. . . . In my opinion the plans for customs and railway tariffs, introduced as a personal measure without consultation with colleagues either in the Federal Council or in the ministry, are the last straw in the almost uninterrupted series of mistakes in the internal administration of the empire, and it can only be a question of time until His Majesty the emperor finds himself obliged to transfer the government of the empire to sober persons who are less extravagant in their conduct of affairs. . . .

H. Bismarck's fall

58. From the minutes of the meeting of the Crown Council (24 January, 1890): from HOHLFELD, pp. 457–61.

... (1). His Majesty was pleased to inform the Ministers that he had called the meeting to discuss the domestic situation, particularly the problem of the workers. ... The present situation was a disagreeable one of which it was necessary to take account. It had arisen because of the rapid development of our industry. ... The demand for workers had brought great masses of them into the centres of industry and these had turned into a proletariat. The industrialists had paid no attention to the workers but had merely exploited them, and those whose strength had been exhausted had been allowed to perish. In this way the idea had come into the minds of the workers that they need not allow themselves to be exploited like machines but that since it was their work that provided their employers with their profits they had a right to convert their relationship to them into one of partnership. ...

The uneducated worker left to his own resources had in consequence fallen prey to the teachings of the Social Democrats. ... Although in earlier times the mine workers had behaved in exemplary fashion, in the end these mistakes had gained ground among them as well, and this could have been prevented if the industrialists had maintained touch with them, if they had concerned themselves with them personally like a good company commander with his men. Even though after last year's strikes peace had been restored, nevertheless the problem of the lock-out which had arisen subsequently showed that the promises given to the workers had not been kept strictly enough. The administrative authorities had done their best by means of the inquiry that had been undertaken. But in the meantime things had gone further, justified demands had been followed by unjustified ones and finally by totally impossible ones (a fifty per cent rise in wages and a reduction of working hours below eight). It was no use yielding further on these points since this would lead only to even higher demands. If there were renewed strikes then the workers would be better organized and more inflamed by Social Democratic agitators than last year. This would inevitably lead to intervention by the armed forces in the interests of maintenance of public order and security. Such a development must be prevented as much as possible in the light of the fact that almost all revolutions had their origins in a failure to institute reforms in good time. His Majesty, therefore, wished to issue a decree to the Ministry with a view to immediate consultations on suitable measures. In this connection it ought to be stated that His Majesty had the welfare of the workers at heart and was willing to help them, but was at the same time determined to require them to obey the law and to punish any act of violence. . . . Much could be done to improve the situation of the workers by limiting Sunday work to the unavoidable minimum, by limiting night work and work by women and children. . . . His Majesty was pleased to cause a programme to be read out in which the relevant points of view were expressed.

Upon His Majesty's request to make observations on his intentions the prime minister declared to begin with that His Majesty presumably did not expect a decision by the Ministry on this programme today. It was not possible to express a considered opinion on all these questions immediately since they were too comprehensive and were of too far-reaching a political, economic, and financial importance.

Whenever the now so popular phrase 'protection of the workers' was used the question arose against whom the worker was to be protected, against his employer or against his own desire to make money which caused him to work on Sundays and at night and to get his wife and children to work as well. It was very doubtful whether one would earn the gratitude of the working population by restricting opportunities for making money. In the strike movements that had occurred it was not the questions of Sunday work or work by women and children that had been prominent but the problem of higher wages and limitation of working hours. Any such prohibitions on work would therefore involve the risk of arousing discontent among the workers and of placing domestic industry at a disadvantage compared to foreign industry. It was not without its dangers to raise such far-reaching and contentious questions at election time. If such an announcement were made by the Emperor himself legislative measures would inevitably follow, and such an announcement therefore required as thorough deliberations as legislative measures themselves. He therefore urged that His Majesty should today merely require a report of the Ministry on all the matters that had been raised.

The deputy prime minister added that the programme went further than any proposals that had yet been made in this field but that on the other hand the *Reichstag* had already given detailed consideration to several of the questions that were contained in it and that much preliminary work had already been done on them, for example on the question of Sunday work, and a draft law on arbitration tribunals . . . was before the Federal Council. Although it was for the moment only a question of drafting the decree which His Majesty proposed to issue, nevertheless if this decree were to put any particular measures in prospect then, to be sure, it required detailed deliberation.

o

His Majesty was pleased to reply that the programme was in the first place nothing more than a collection of materials and that he did not require a definitive expression of opinion today but that he did expect an early submission of the decree. Another strike was perhaps not far away. The people should therefore know soon that the Crown was seriously concerned with their welfare, that measures to relieve existing need were in prospect, and that this relief could be obtained more surely by legal means than by violence. If there were a riot it would certainly need to be suppressed, but no means of preventing it should be left untried. No time was therefore to be lost, otherwise the Social Democratic leaders would take the opportunity to pre-empt the situation and to represent themselves as truer benefactors of the people than the Crown.

... (2). His Majesty was pleased to accede to the proposal of the secretary of state for the interior ... that the *Reichstag* should be dissolved after tomorrow's debate on the third reading of the Socialist Law and to declare his intention of performing the dissolution himself. With respect to the decision of the *Reichstag* on this bill His Majesty was pleased to remark that the power of deportation was scarcely of so far-reaching an importance as to jeopardize the passage of the bill in case of its rejection. It was undesirable to close this *Reichstag* which had performed much useful work in disharmony which might, moreover, have an unfavourable effect on the elections and on the maintenance of the *Kartell*. Perhaps it was possible to postpone a consideration of this question for the future.

The ministers having been asked for their individual views, the prime minister declared to begin with that it was scarcely possible any longer to secure the agreement of the federated governments to forgoing a part of the bill laid before the *Reichstag* and that moreover he would emphatically advise against taking any such step which would be the first step down the road of concessions. Such a step would be calculated to damage the prestige of the governments and to weaken their position. The Socialist Law contained the minimum that the governments required in the way of the use of force. Probably more would have to be asked for later. This possibility was precluded if it was now conceded that one could do with less. Even in the expected new strikes in the coal districts the power of deporting the agitators out of this area would be very useful. According to his political experience he assumed that it would have an undesirable effect on the elections if the law was defective owing to faults *committed by the governments*. The maintenance of the *Kartell* would not be endangered if the law was rejected.

The deputy prime minister said that the question was predominantly a police matter. The National Liberals objected to the deportations mainly on the ground that this led to the activity of the agitators being transferred to another place. On the other hand, however, the fear of being deported was an even more effective barrier against agitation than deportation itself.

The minister of the interior said that of the measures which the Socialist Law made available to the governments those against clubs, assemblies, and pamphlets applied to the whole Empire, whereas the power of deportation applied only to a small part. . . . In these places it would be possible to maintain law and order even without deportations by means of a strong and well-organized police force. But this was not true in several localities where those who were deported might go instead. . . . Nevertheless the possibility of deportation was a strong deterrent and in areas of strikes, for example, it would be very valuable. . . .

The minister of justice said that deportation was the only measure which was directed against the agitators personally. All the other measures were directed only against the means employed by them (press, clubs, and assemblies). By using their good international organization and plentiful financial resources the Social Democrats could easily get around the prohibition of a newspaper or a club by founding new newspapers and clubs. In his opinion it was not advisable to forgo deportation which had an immediate and dramatic impact.

The minister of cultural affairs said that what was under discussion was not a new law but the question whether an existing law should be repealed in an essential respect, and he saw no sufficient reason for doing so. If they did so they would preclude themselves from submitting a harsher law which might soon be necessary. He did not fear the disintegration of the *Kartell*. The National Liberals had fallen out too badly with both the Progressives and the Centre Party to be able to turn in either of these directions.

The minister of war said that the masses were easily liable to be dominated by agitators against whom all existing measures were necessary and perhaps even more rigorous ones. He was unable to advise forgoing an effective means of intervention.

Thereupon His Majesty was pleased to approve that action should be taken in the sense of the opinions expressed and closed the meeting.

59. The Cabinet Order of 8 September, 1852: from HOHLFELD, pp. 467–8.

I find it necessary to assure to the prime minister a greater degree of general supervision over the various branches of the internal administration, and with it the possibility, commensurate with his position, of maintaining the necessary unity within it and to give me information, upon request, concerning all important administrative measures. To this end I decree as follows:

(1). The head of department concerned must secure the prior agreement, oral or written, of the prime minister on all administrative measures of any importance which do not require a prior decision by the Cabinet under existing regulations. The prime minister is free, at his discretion, to initiate a discussion of the matter in the Cabinet or to report on it to me.

(2). If, according to established principles, administrative measures of the kind described require my consent, the necessary report must be communicated in advance to the prime minister, who shall submit it to me with any comments.

(3). If an administrative head is moved to report directly to me in matters concerning his department he must inform the prime minister of this in good time in advance, so that the latter may attend such audiences if he finds it necessary.—The regular direct reports of the minister of war are excluded from this decree.

(signed) Frederick William
Manteuffel

60. Bismarck's memorandum of 4 March, 1890: from HOHLFELD, p. 468.

At the last meeting of the Cabinet it became apparent that the royal Order of September 8, 1852 . . . was not known to certain ministers. I therefore take the liberty of sending herewith a copy of it for information. I combine with this transmission, not a claim to participate in the exchanges of ministers with the king on current and well-known matters, but the desire to be informed by them in good time of any audiences intended to initiate a change in legislation and in legal conditions.

61. From Bismarck's letter of resignation (18 March, 1890): from HOHLFELD, pp. 469–72.

On the occasion of my respectful audience of the 15th of this month Your Majesty commanded me to submit the draft of an Order designed to repeal the royal Order of 8 September, 1852 which has since that time governed the relations of the prime minister with his colleagues. . . .

This Order . . . alone has given the prime minister the authority which enabled him to assume that degree of responsibility for the whole policy of the Cabinet which is imputed to him in the Diet and by public opinion. If every individual minister can obtain decrees from the king without prior agreement with his colleagues a unified policy for which someone can be responsible is not possible. The possibility is precluded that any minister, specifically the prime minister, can bear constitutional responsibility for the entire policy of the Cabinet. In the days of absolute monarchy a regulation such as the one contained in the Order of 1852 was not necessary and would still not be necessary today if we were to return to absolutism without ministerial responsibility. According to the legally established constitutional arrangements, however, a presiding leadership of the body of ministers on the basis of the Order of 1852 is indispensable. On this point, as was established at yesterday's meeting of ministers, all my colleagues are in agreement with me and they are also agreed that any successor of mine in the office of prime minister would not be able to carry this responsibility if he lacked the authority that the Order of 1852 provides. Any successor of mine will feel this need even more strongly than I do for he will not have the authority that I have enjoyed as a result of my many years of presiding over the ministry and the confidence of the two late emperors. I have never before felt the need to refer specifically to the Order of 1852 with my colleagues, its existence and the certainty that I possessed the confidence of the two late emperors William and Frederick sufficed to secure my authority among the ministers. This certainty, however, is no longer present today either for my colleagues or for myself. I have therefore had to refer to the Order of 1852 in order to secure the necessary unity in Your Majesty's service.

For the preceding reasons I am unable to carry out Your Majesty's command according to which I was myself to initiate and to countersign the repeal of the Order of 1852 to which I recently referred but was nevertheless to continue in the office of prime minister.

According to the reports made to me yesterday by Lieutenant-General v. Hahnke and Privy Councillor v. Lucanus I can be in no doubt that Your Majesty knows and believes that it is not possible for me at the same time to repeal the Order and to remain a minister. Nevertheless Your Majesty has maintained the command issued to me on the 15th and has opened the prospect of granting my request to resign which it makes necessary. After the earlier conversations that I had with Your Majesty on the question of whether my remaining in office would be undesirable to Your Majesty I could assume that Your Majesty would consent to my resigning from my position in His Majesty's Prussian service while retaining my position in the imperial service. On closer examination on this question I took the liberty respectfully to draw attention to several dubious consequences of such a separation of my offices, particularly the future appearance of the chancellor in the *Reichstag,* and I refrain from repeating here all the

O*

consequences which would flow from such a division between Prussia and the imperial chancellor. Your Majesty was thereupon pleased to permit that for the time being things should remain unchanged.

But, as I have had the honour to explain, it is not possible for me to retain the office of prime minister after Your Majesty has repeatedly ordered the *capitis diminutio* which would be implied in the repeal of the Order of 1852.

Your Majesty was, moreover, pleased on the occasion of my respectful audience of the 15th of this month to impose limits on me with respect to the extension of my official prerogatives which do not assure me of that degree of participation in official business, of supervision over it, and of freedom of movement in my ministerial decisions and in my relations with the *Reichstag* and with its members which I require if I am to take the constitutional responsibility for my official activity.

But even if it were feasible to conduct our foreign policy independently of our domestic policy and therefore the foreign policy of the Empire independently of that of Prussia, as would be the case if the imperial chancellor took no more part in Prussian politics than he did in Bavarian or Saxon and played no role in formulating the Prussian vote in the Federal Council *vis-à-vis* the *Reichstag*, I would still find it impossible after Your Majesty's most recent decisions on the direction of our foreign policy as they are summarized in Your Majesty's own manuscript . . . to carry out the orders contained in it concerning our foreign policy. If I did so I would jeopardize for the German Empire all the important successes that our foreign policy has for decades achieved in our relations with Russia, in unfavourable conditions, in accordance with the views of both of Your Majesty's late predecessors. . . .

According to my impressions during the last weeks and after the disclosures that I gathered yesterday from the reports from Your Majesty's civil and military Cabinet I may respectfully assume that this my request to be allowed to resign is in accordance with Your Majesty's wishes. . . . I would have submitted this request to be relieved of my offices to Your Majesty long ago if I had not had the impression that Your Majesty wished to make use of the experiences and abilities of a faithful servant of your ancestors. Since I am now certain that Your Majesty does not require them I may retire from political life without having to fear that my decision may be condemned as untimely by public opinion.

62. Bismarck's revenge in his Memoirs: from *Bismarck, the Man and the Statesman: Being the Reflections and Reminiscences of Otto Prince von Bismarck Written and Dictated by Himself after*

His Retirement from Office, I, 316–8, II, 66–7, 75, 92–6, 99–101, 136, 138–9, 141–4, 147–9, 267, 270, 280–1, 288–91.

In order that German patriotism should be active and effective, it needs as a rule to hang on the peg of dependence upon a dynasty; independent of dynasty it rarely comes to the rising point, though in theory it daily does so, in parliament, in the press, in public meeting; in practice the German needs either attachment to a dynasty or the goad of anger, hurrying him into action: the latter phenomenon, however, by its own nature is not permanent.... The German's love of Fatherland has need of a prince on whom it can concentrate its attachment. Suppose that all the German dynasties were suddenly deposed; there would then be no likelihood that German national sentiment would suffice to hold all Germans together from the point of view of international law amid the friction of European politics, even in the form of federated Hanse towns and imperial village communes. The Germans would fall a prey to more closely welded nations if they once lost the tie which resides in the princes' sense of community of rank. . . .

Dynastic interests are justified in Germany so far as they fit in with the common national imperial interests: the two may very well go hand in hand; and a duke loyal to the Empire in the old sense is in certain circumstances more serviceable to the community than would be direct relations between the Emperor and the duke's vassals. So far, however, as dynastic interests threaten us once more with national disintegration and impotence, they must be reduced to their proper measure.

The German people and its national life cannot be portioned out as private possessions of princely houses. It has always been clear to me that this reflection applies to the electoral house of Brandenburg as well as to the Bavarian, the Guelf, or other houses; I should have been weaponless against the Brandenburg princely house, if in dealing with it I had needed to reinforce my German national feeling by rupture and resistance; in the predestination of history, however, it so fell out that my courtier-talents sufficed to gain the King, and with him by consequence his army, for the national cause. I have had perhaps harder battles to fight against Prussian particularism than against the particularism of the other German states and dynasties, and my relation to the Emperor William I as his born subject made these battles all the harder for me. Yet in the end, despite the strongly dynastic policy of the Emperor, but thanks to his national policy which, dynastically justified, became ever stronger in critical moments, I always succeeded in gaining his countenance for the German side of our development, and that too when a more dynastic and particular-ist policy prevailed on all other hands. . . .

Absolutism would be the ideal form of government for an European political structure were not the King and his officials ever as other men are to whom it is not given to reign with superhuman wisdom, insight and justice. The most experienced and well-meaning absolute rulers are subject to human imperfections, such as overestimation of their own wisdom, the influence and eloquence of favourites, not to mention petticoat influence, legitimate and illegitimate. Monarchy and the most ideal monarch, if in his idealism he is not to be a common danger, stand in need of criticism; the thorns of criticism set him right when he runs the risk of losing his way. Joseph II is a warning example of this.

Criticism can only be exercised through the medium of a free press and parliaments in the modern sense of the term. Both correctives may easily weaken and finally lose their efficacy if they abuse their powers. To avert this is one of the tasks of a conservative policy, which cannot be accomplished without a struggle with parliament and press. The measurement of the limits within which such a struggle must be con-fined, if the control of the government, which is indispensable to the country, is neither to be checked nor allowed to gain a complete power, is a question of political tact and judgement.

It is a piece of good fortune for his country if a monarch possess the judgement requisite for this—a good fortune that is temporary, it is true, like all human fortune. The possibility of establishing ministers in power who possess adequate qualifications must always be granted in the constitutional organism; but also the possiblity of maintaining in office ministers who satisfy these requirements in face of occasional votes of an adverse majority and of the influence of courts and camar-illas. This aim, so far as human imperfections in general allow its attainment, was approximately reached under the government of William I. . . .

I do not consider absolutism by any means a form of government that is desirable or successful in Germany in the long run. The Prussian Constitution, disregarding a few meaningless articles trans-lated from that of Belgium, is in the main reasonable. It has three factors, the King and two Chambers, each of which by its vote can prevent arbitrary alterations of the legal *status quo*. This is a just apportionment of legislative power, but if the latter is emancipated from the public criticism of the press and from parliamentary control, there is increased danger of its going astray. The absolutism of the Crown is just as little tenable as the absolutism of parliamentary majorities. . . .

On July 12 I decided to hurry off from Varzin to Ems to discuss with his Majesty about summoning the Reichstag for the purpose of the mobilisation. . . . As I entered the courtyard of my house at Berlin, and before leaving the carriage, I received telegrams from which it appeared that the King was continuing to treat with Benedetti, even after the French threats and outrages in parliament and in the press, and not referring him with calm reserve to his ministers. During dinner, at which Moltke and Roon were present, the announcement arrived from the embassy in Paris that the Prince of Hohenzollern had renounced his candidature in order to prevent the war with which France threatened us. My first idea was to retire from the service, because, after all the insolent challenges which had gone before, I perceived in this extorted submission a humiliation of Germany for which I did not desire to be responsible. This impression of a wound to our sense of national honour by the compulsory withdrawal so dominated me that I had already decided to announce my retirement at Ems. I considered this humiliation before France and her swaggering demonstrations as worse than that of Olmütz, for which the previous history on both sides, and our want of preparation for war at the time, will always be a valid excuse. I took it for granted that France would lay the Prince's renunciation to her account as a satisfactory success, with the feeling that a threat of war, even though it had taken the form of international insult and mockery, and though the pretext for war against Prussia had been dragged in by the head and shoulders, was enough to compel her to draw back, even in a just cause; and that even the North German Confederation did not feel strong enough to protect the national honour and independence against French arrogance. I was very much depressed, for I saw no means of repairing the corroding injury I dreaded to our national position from a timorous policy, unless by picking quarrels clumsily and seeking them artificially. I saw by that time that war was a necessity, which we could no longer avoid with honour. I telegraphed to my people at Varzin not to pack up or start, for I should be back again in a few days. I now believed in peace; but as I would not represent the attitude by which this peace had been purchased, I gave up the journey to Ems and asked Count Eulenburg to go thither and represent my opinion to his Majesty. In the same sense I conversed with the Minister of War, von Roon: we had got our slap in the face from France, and had been reduced, by our complaisance, to look like seekers of a quarrel if we entered upon war, the only way in which we could wipe away the stain. My position was now untenable, solely because, during his course at the baths, the King, under pressure of threats, had given audience to the French ambassador for four consecutive days, and had exposed his royal person to insolent treatment from this foreign agent without ministerial assistance. . . .

Having decided to resign, in spite of the remonstrances which Roon made against it, I invited him and Moltke to dine with me alone on the 13th, and communicated to them at table my views and projects for doing so. Both were greatly depressed, and reproached me indirectly with selfishly availing myself of my greater facility for withdrawing from service. I maintained the position that I could not offer up my sense of honour to politics, that both of them, being professional soldiers and consequently without freedom of choice, need not take the same point of view as a responsible Foreign Minister. During our conversation I was informed that a telegram from Ems, in cipher, if I recollect rightly, of about 200 'groups,' was being deciphered. When the copy was handed to me it showed that Abeken had drawn up and signed the telegram at his Majesty's command, and I read it out to my guests, whose dejection was so great that they turned away from food and drink. On a repeated examination of the document I lingered upon the authorisation of his Majesty, which included a command, immediately to communicate Benedetti's fresh demand and its rejection both to our ambassadors and to the press. I put a few questions to Moltke as to the extent of his confidence in the state of our preparations, especially as to the time they would still require in order to meet this sudden risk of war. He answered that if there was to be war he expected no advantage to us by deferring its outbreak. . . .

Under this conviction I made use of the royal authorisation communicated to me through Abeken, to publish the contents of the telegram; and in the presence of my two guests I reduced the telegram by striking out words, but without adding or altering, to the following form: 'After the news of the renunciation of the hereditary Prince of Hohenzollern had been officially communicated to the imperial government of France by the royal government of Spain, the French ambassador at Ems further demanded of his Majesty the King that he would authorise him to telegraph to Paris that his Majesty the King bound himself for all future time never again to give his consent if the Hohenzollerns should renew their candidature. His Majesty the King thereupon decided not to receive the French ambassador again, and sent to tell him through the aide-de-camp on duty that his Majesty had nothing further to communicate to the ambassador.' The difference in the effect of the abbreviated text of the Ems telegram as compared with that produced by the original was not the result of stronger words but of the form, which made this announcement appear decisive, while Abeken's version would only have been regarded as a fragment of a negotiation still pending, and to be continued at Berlin.

After I had read out the concentrated edition to my two guests, Moltke remarked: 'Now it has a different ring; it sounded before like a parley; now it is like a flourish in answer to a challenge.' I went on to explain: 'If in execution of his Majesty's order I at once communicate this text, which contains no alteration in or addition to the telegram, not only to the newspapers, but also by telegraph to all our embassies, it will be known in Paris before midnight, and not only on account of its contents, but also on account of the manner of its distribution, will have the effect of a red rag upon the Gallic bull. Fight we must if we do not want to act the part of the vanquished without a battle. Success, however, essentially depends upon the impression which the origination of the war makes upon us and others; it is important that we should be the party attacked, and this Gallic overweening and touchiness will make us if we announce in the face of Europe, so far as we can without the speaking-trumpet of the Reichstag, that we fearlessly meet the public threats of France.'

This explanation brought about in the two generals a revulsion to a more joyous mood, the liveliness of which surprised me. They had suddenly recovered their pleasure in eating and drinking and spoke in a more cheerful vein. Roon said: 'Our God of old lives still and will not let us perish in disgrace.' Moltke so far relinquished his passive equanimity that, glancing up joyously towards the ceiling and abandoning his usual punctiliousness of speech, he smote his hand upon his breast and said: 'If I may but live to lead our armies in such a war, then the devil may come directly afterwards and fetch away the "old carcass".' He was less robust at that time than afterwards, and doubted whether he would survive the hardships of the campaign. . . .

In religious matters, my toleration has at all times been restricted only by the boundaries which the necessity of various denominations co-existing in the same body politic imposes on the claims of each particular creed. The therapeutic treatment of the Catholic Church in a temporal state is, however, rendered difficult by the fact that the Catholic clergy, if they desire properly to discharge what is theoretically their duty, must claim a share in the secular government extending beyond the ecclesiastical domain; they constitute a political institution under clerical forms, and transmit to their collaborators their own conviction that for them *freedom* lies in *dominion,* and that the Church, wherever she does not rule, is justified in complaining of Diocletian-like persecution. . . .

The beginning of the *Culturkampf* was decided for me preponderantly by its Polish side. . . . According to official reports, there were whole villages in Posen and West Prussia containing thousands of Germans who through the influence of the Catholic section had been educated according to Polish ideas, and were officially described as 'Poles,' although in the previous generation they were officially Germans. . . .

I should never have thought of occupying myself with the legal details of the May Laws; they were outside my department, and I had neither the intention nor the qualifications to control or to correct Falk as a jurist. I could not, as Minister-President, fulfil the duties of the Minister of Public Worship at the same time, even if I had been in perfect health. It was only by seeing them in practice that I became convinced that the legal details had not been properly conceived for the effect they were wanted to produce.... Whoever supposes that such critical considerations surging up in me would immediately have been embodied in the form of a cabinet crisis between Falk and myself has not the correct judgement, which can only be gained by experience, of the manner in which the state machine has to be driven, both as regards itself and its connexion with the monarch and the parliamentary elections. That machine is unable to perform sudden evolutions, and ministers of Falk's talents do not grow wild with us. It was better to have a fellow combatant of such ability and courage in the ministry than to make myself responsible for the administration of the Department of Public Worship, or for a new appointment to it, by encroaching upon the constitutional independence of his office. I adhered to this view as long as I could prevail upon Falk to stay. Only when, contrary to my wishes, he had been so put out by feminine Court influence and ungracious letters from the royal hand that it became impossible to keep him, did I proceed to a revision of what he had left behind—a thing I was unwilling to do so long as that was only possible by a rupture with him....

I repeatedly dissuaded Falk from plans of resignation in connexion either with letters of displeasure from the Emperor, which were probably not due to the initiative of the august ruler himself, or with slights offered to his wife at court. I recommended him to maintain a passive attitude towards the ungracious communications of his Majesty.... Finally, however, being exposed to mortifications that wounded his sense of honour, he decided to resign. All the accounts which state that I ousted him from the ministry rest upon invention....

After his departure I found myself face to face with the question whether, and how far, in choosing a new Minister of Public Worship, I was to keep in sight Falk's rather juristic than political leanings, or follow exclusively my own views, tending more towards Polonism than Catholicism. In the *Culturkampf*, the parliamentary policy of the government had been crippled by the defection of the Progressive party and its transition to the Centrum. Meantime in the Reichstag, without getting any support from the Conservatives, it was opposed by a majority of Democrats of all shades, bound together by a common enmity, and in league with Poles, Guelfs, friends of France, and Ultramontanes. The consolidation of new imperial unity was retarded by these circumstances, and would be imperilled were they to continue or to become aggravated. The mischief to the nation might be rendered more serious in this way than by an abandonment of what was in my opinion the superfluous part of the Falk legislation. . . .

It is impossible to confine within stated limits the claims of Rome upon countries that have religious equality and a Protestant dynasty. It cannot be done even in purely Catholic states. The conflict that has been waged from time immemorial between priests and kings cannot be brought to a conclusion at the present day, and of all places not in Germany. . . . In any *modus vivendi* Rome will regard a Protestant dynasty and Church as an irregularity and a disease which it is the duty of its Church to cure. The conviction that this is the case is no reason for the state itself to commence the conflict and to abandon its defensive attitude with regard to the Church of Rome, for all treaties of peace in this world are provisional, and only hold good for a time. The political relations between independent powers are the outcome of an unbroken series of events arising either from conflict or from the objection of one or other of the parties to renew the conflict. . . . Eternal peace with the Roman Curia is in the existing state of affairs as impossible as is peace between France and her neighbours. If human life is nothing but a series of struggles, this is especially so in the mutual relations of independent political bodies, for the adjustment of which no properly-constituted court exists with power to enforce its decrees. The Roman Curia, however, is an independent political body, possessing among its unalterable qualities the same propensity to grab all round as is innate in our French neighbours. In its struggles against Protestantism, which no concordat can quiet, it has always the aggressive weapons of proselytism and ambition at its disposal; it tolerates the presence of no other gods. . . .

Even in the last century it was perilous to reckon on the constraining force of the text of a treaty of alliance when the conditions under which it had been written were changed; to-day it is hardly possible for the government of a great Power to place its resources unreservedly at the disposal of a friendly state when the sentiment of the people disapproves it. No longer, therefore, does the text of a treaty afford the same securities as in the days of the 'cabinet wars,' which were waged with armies of from 30,000 to 60,000 men; a family war, such as Frederick William II waged on behalf of his brother-in-law in Holland, could hardly to-day be put upon the European stage, nor could the conditions preliminary to such a war as Nicholas waged on Hungary be readily again found. Nevertheless the plain and searching words of a treaty are not without influence on diplomacy when it is concerned with precipitating or averting a war; nor are even treacherous and violent governments usually inclined to an open breach of faith, so long as the *force majeure* of imperative interests does not intervene. . . .

All contracts between great states cease to be unconditionally binding as soon as they are tested by 'the struggle for existence.' No great nation will ever be induced to sacrifice its existence on the altar of fidelity to contract when it is compelled to choose between the two. The maxim 'ultra posse nemo obligatur' holds good in spite of all treaty formulas whatsoever, nor can any treaty guarantee the degree of zeal and the amount of force that will be devoted to the discharge of obligations when the private interest of those who lie under them no longer reinforces the text and its earliest interpretation. . . .

International policy is a fluid element which under certain conditions will solidify, but on a change of atmosphere reverts to its original diffuse condition. The clause *rebus sic stantibus* is tacitly understood in all treaties that involve performance. The Triple Alliance is a strategic position, which in the face of the perils that were imminent at the time when it was concluded was politic, and, under the prevailing conditions, feasible. It has been from time to time prolonged, and may be yet further prolonged, but eternal duration is assured to no treaty between Great Powers; and it would be unwise to regard it as affording a permanently stable guarantee against all the possible contingencies which in the future may modify the political, material, and moral conditions under which it was brought into being. It has the significance of a strategic position adopted after strict scrutiny of the political situation of Europe at the time when it was concluded, but it no more constitutes a foundation capable of offering perennial resistance to time and change than did many another alliance (triple or quadruple) of recent centuries, and in particular the Holy Alliance and the German Confederation. It does not dispense us from the attitude of *toujours en vedette*. . . .

If Germany has the advantage that her policy is free from direct interests in the East, on the other side is the disadvantage of the central and exposed position of the German Empire, with its extended frontier which has to be defended on every side, and the ease with which anti-German coalitions are made. At the same time Germany is perhaps the single Great Power in Europe which is not tempted by any objects which can only be attained by a successful war. It is our interest to maintain peace, while without exception our continental neighbours have wishes, either secret or officially avowed, which cannot be fulfilled except by war. We must direct our policy in accordance with these facts—that is, we must do our best to prevent war or limit it. We must reserve our hand, and not allow ourselves before the proper time to be pushed out of a waiting into an active attitude by

any impatience, by the desire to oblige others at the expense of the country, by vanity or other provocation of this kind. . . .
During the time that I was in office I advised three wars, the Danish, the Bohemian, and the French; but every time I first made myself clear whether the war, if it were successful, would bring a prize of victory worth the sacrifices which every war requires, and which now are so much greater than in the last century. Had I had to say to myself that after one of these wars we should find some difficulty in discovering conditions of peace which were desirable, I should scarcely have convinced myself of the necessity for these sacrifices as long as we were not actually attacked. I have never looked at international quarrels which can only be settled by a national war, from the point of view of the Göttingen student code or the honour which governs a private duel, but I have always considered simply their reaction on the claim of the German people, in equality with the other great states and Powers of Europe, to lead an autonomous political life, so far as is possible on the basis of our peculiar national capacity. . . .

A NOTE ON FURTHER READING

There is as yet no entirely satisfactory treatment of Bismarck or of the period in English. Erick Eyck's three-volume biography was not well served by its condensation and translation into English under the title *Bismarck and the German Empire*. The best books in the field are therefore A. J. P. Taylor's *Bismarck: the Man and the Statesman* and W. N. Medlicott's *Bismarck and Modern Germany*, both relatively short. Arthur Rosenberg's pre-war *Birth of the German Republic*, more recently issued in paperback under the less misleading title *Imperial Germany*, is still very much worth reading. Probably all these will be rendered more or less obsolete when Otto Pflanze completes his *Bismarck and the Development of Germany*.

Some of the monographic literature in English is referred to in the footnotes in the Introduction and at the end of my *Germany*. More comprehensive bibliographies are provided in the American Historical Association's *Guide to Historical Literature*, K. S. Pinson's *Modern Germany*, and the historical journals. Any thorough research will require work in both sources and secondary materials in German. Many collections and selections of primary sources are being published in Germany; most of the relevant ones have been drawn on for translation for the present volume.

Table of Sources of Documents
and abbreviations used

Abbrev.	*Sources*
ADELMANN	Adelmann, Gerhard, ed. *Quellensammlung zur Geschichte der sozialen Betriebsverfassung: Ruhrindustrie unter besonderer Berücksichtigung des Industrie- und Handelskammerbezirks Essen.* Vol. I: *Überbetriebliche Einwirkungen auf die soziale Betriebsverfassung der Ruhrindustrie.* Bonn, 1960.

Bamberger, Ludwig. *Bismarcks grosses Spiel: geheime Tagebücher* (ed. Ernst Feder). Frankfurt, 1932.

Bamberger, Ludwig. *Herr von Bismarck* (tr. from the French by K. A., revised and with an Introduction ('Deutschland, Frankreich und die Revolution') and an Epilogue by the author). Breslau, 1868.

Baumgarten, Hermann. 'Der deutsche Liberalismus: eine Selbstkritik,' in his *Historische und politische Aufsätze und Reden.* Strassburg, 1894.

Bismarck, the Man and the Statesman: Being the Reflections and Reminiscences of Otto Prince von Bismarck Written and Dictated by Himself after His Retirement from Office (tr. A. J. Butler and others). 2 vols., London, 1898.

BONNIN — Bonnin, Georges, ed. *Bismarck and the Hohenzollern Candidature for the Spanish Throne: The Documents in the German Diplomatic Archives* (tr. Isabella M. Massey). London, 1957.

Bronsart von Schellendorff, Paul. *Geheimes Kriegstagebuch 1870–1871* (ed. Peter Rassow). Bonn, 1954.

CONSTABEL — Constabel, Adelheid, ed. *Die Vorgeschichte des Kulturkampfes: Veröffentlichung aus dem Deutschen Zentralarchiv.* Berlin, 1956.

Cornicelius, Max von, ed. *Heinrich von Treitschkes Briefe.* 3 vols., Leipzig, 1912–20.

Droysen, Johann Gustav. *Briefwechsel* (ed. Rudolf Hübner). 2 vols., Berlin and Leipzig, 1929.

Fischer, Wolfram, ed. *Quellen zur Geschichte des deutschen Handwerks.* Göttingen, 1957.

Gerlach, Ernst Ludwig von. *Die Annexionen und der Norddeutsche Bund.* 6th ed., Berlin, 1866. (Published anonymously.)

Gierke, Otto. *Natural Law and the Theory of Society, 1500 to 1800* (tr. Ernest Barker). Boston, 1960.

Gustav Freytags Briefe an Albrecht von Stosch (ed. Hans. F. Helmolt). Stuttgart and Berlin, 1913.

HEYDERHOFF   Heyderhoff, Julius and Paul Wentzcke, ed. *Deutscher Liberalismus im Zeitalter Bismarcks: eine politische Briefsammlung,* Vol. 1. Osnabrück, 1967.

ROGGENBACH   Heyderhoff, Julius, ed. *Im Ring der Gegner Bismarcks: Denkschriften und politischer Briefwechsel Franz v. Roggenbachs mit Kaiserin Augusta und Albrecht v. Stosch, 1865–1896* (Leipzig, 1943).

HOHLFELD   Hohlfeld, Johannes, ed. *Dokumente der deutschen Politik und Geschichte von 1848 bis zur Gegenwart,* Vol. I. Berlin, 1952.

Huber, Ernst Rudolf, ed. *Dokumente zur deutschen Verfassungsgeschichte,* Vol. II. Stuttgart, 1964.

Nietzsche, Friedrich. 'David Strauss, der Bekenner und der Schriftsteller' (1873), in his *Werke* (Klassiker-Ausgabe), Vol. II. Stuttgart, 1921.

PUTTKAMER   Puttkamer, Ellinor von, ed. *Föderative Elemente im deutschen Staatsrecht seit 1648.* Göttingen, 1955.

Rochau, A. L. von. *Grundsätze der Realpolitik, angewendet auf die staatlichen Zustände Deutschlands,* Vol. II. Heidelberg, 1869. (Published anonymously.)

Rochau, A. L. von. 'Recht und Macht,' *Wochen-Blatt des National-Vereins,* No. 72 (Oct. 4, 1866), pp. 564-565. (Published anonymously.)

ROSENBERG   Rosenberg, Hans, ed. *Ausgewählter Briefwechsel Rudolf Hayms.* Osnabrück, 1967.

ROTHFELS   Rothfels, Hans, ed. *Bismarck und der Staat: ausgewählte Dokumente.* Stuttgart, 1953.

R. v. Ihering in Briefen an seine Freunde. Leipzig, 1913.

Schmidt, Adolf. *Preussens deutsche Politik: 1785, 1806, 1849, 1866.* 3rd revised ed., Leipzig, 1867.

SCHRAEPLER

Schraepler, Ernst, ed. *Quellen zur Geschichte der sozialen Frage in Deutschland.* 2 vols., Berlin and Frankfurt, 1964.

Sybel, Heinrich von. 'Klerikale Politik im 19. Jahrhundert,' in his *Kleine historische Schriften*, Vol. III. Stuttgart, 1880.

Treitschke, Heinrich von. *Zehn Jahre deutscher Kämpfe: Schriften zur Tagespolitik.* 2nd ed., Berlin, 1879.

Venedey, J. *An Prof. Heinrich v. Treitschke.* Mannheim, 1866.

INDEX TO THE INTRODUCTION